Perspectives on Impact

T0293050

Perspectives on Impact and its sister book, *Perspectives on Purpose*, bring together leading voices from across sectors to discuss how we must adapt our organizations for the twenty-first century world. *Perspectives on Impact* focuses on the recalibration of social impact approaches to tackle complex humanitarian, social, and environmental challenges; *Perspectives on Purpose* looks at the shifting role of the corporation in society through the lens of purpose.

Margarita ('Nina') S. Montgomery is an archaeologist-turned-strategist currently working at IDEO. A PhD candidate at Oxford, she holds a fellowship at TRIPTK and has spoken on organizations and society at Harvard Business School and Oxford's Saïd Business School, among others. Nina received a BA in Classics from Dartmouth and a master's in Classical Archaeology from Oxford as a Reynolds Scholar.

"We are witnessing a moment of revolution when it comes to how we think about and address inequality. This timely book documents how social impact leaders are challenging institutional norms and developing new approaches that acknowledge all people's capacity to solve the human problems we face as a civilization."

—Professor Muhammad Yunus, 2006 Nobel Peace Laureate
and Founder at Grameen Bank

"Over the last decade it has become clear that the only way to solve the world's most pressing problems is to understand and then change the systems that are the source of the problems. Good intentions are not good enough. *Perspectives on Impact* brings together insightful essays from people across all sectors of society who have been at the forefront of devising better ways to create social impact."

—Eric Nee, Editor-in-Chief, *Stanford Social Innovation Review*

"An excellent compilation of diverse and insightful perspectives from top leaders in the field on how to magnify our social impact. This book will be valuable to anyone who seeks to move beyond bandaids to drive lasting systemic change."

—Ann Mei Chang, former Chief Innovation Officer
at USAID and author of *Lean Impact*

"The problems of today and tomorrow demand collective action and creative solutions. The first step in developing the necessary culture of community-based problem-solving is to convene diverse leaders from industry and academia whose imagination and experience help us see with new, more inclusive eyes. The Perspectives book series, and especially the volumes on Impact and Purpose, does just that by amplifying the voices of underrepresented thought innovators whose perspective is vital to the future success, stability, and security of our society."

—Dan Porterfield, President and CEO at the Aspen Institute

"The humanitarian, environmental, and social challenges we face today cut across the boundaries of traditional organizations. No one organization, or even sector, can solve these challenges alone. From Sesame Workshops' work with refugees in Syria to Women's March Global's advancement of equality around the world, this book's diverse case studies show how cross-sectoral leaders are thinking more systemically and working more collaboratively to create a more open, just, and habitable world."

—Jeremy Heimans, Co-Founder and CEO at Purpose and author of *New Power*

"At a time when the world is creating endless societal challenges, *Perspectives on Impact* provides critical real world context on how a number of leaders and their organizations have accelerated systems change and created lasting impact. With clear examples and lessons learned, it is a timely compendium of the 'road maps' others have taken to make a difference in the world."

—Jim Bildner, CEO at Draper, Richards, Kaplan Foundation

"We are all born systems thinkers, but many of us have had this way of seeing trained out of us during the course of our educational and professional lives. Thank goodness books like *Perspectives on Impact* are successfully reintroducing a systems orientation – the most viable path for mankind in collectively overcoming today's most daunting social and environmental problems."

—John Kania, Managing Director at FSG, Executive in Residence
at New Profit, and co-author of recent *Stanford Social Innovation
Review* articles: *Collective Impact* and *The Dawn of System Leadership*

"We live in a time when the smartest investments we can make are in saving nature and in building our human capacities to act together. *Perspectives on Impact* synthesizes critical lessons on how to change systems for the better, and shares case studies that break new ground. The chapters in this collection each illustrate important aspects of how we can preserve our heritage and shape our future."

—Mark Tercek, CEO at The Nature Conservatory

Perspectives on Impact

Leading Voices on Making Systemic
Change in the Twenty-First Century

Edited by Nina Montgomery

Routledge
Taylor & Francis Group

LONDON AND NEW YORK

First published 2019
by Routledge
2 Park Square, Milton Park, Abingdon, Oxon OX14 4RN

and by Routledge
52 Vanderbilt Avenue, New York, NY 10017

Routledge is an imprint of the Taylor & Francis Group, an informa business

British Library Cataloguing-in-Publication Data
A catalogue record for this book is available from the British Library

Library of Congress Cataloging-in-Publication Data
A catalog record for this book has been requested

ISBN: 978-1-138-32119-9 (hbk)
ISBN: 978-0-367-11247-9 (pbk)
ISBN: 978-0-429-45279-6 (ebk)

Typeset in Bembo
by Apex CoVantage, LLC

cui dono lepidum novum libellum?

**To my Yaya and Poppop, Margarita and Thomas Halikias
And to my Grammie and Granddad, Pauline and Robert
Montgomery**

Contents

Conclusion   213

Acknowledgements

This book has grown far beyond any scope I ever imagined for it. It was made possible by a number of people to whom I'm very grateful and forever indebted.

First, to the wonderful contributors, especially those who agreed to participate early on in the process, I am honored and grateful that you took a chance on a young, excitable editor. Any value this book offers is derived entirely from you and your willingness to share your perspectives with the world.

Beyond written contributions, this project and its overall framing has benefited greatly from an early conversation with Banny Banerjee, and from continued conversations with Jane Nelson, Cynthia Warner, and Amirah Jiwa. There were also many, many other mentors and friends who offered advice over coffees and phone calls along the way; you know who you are, and I'm very appreciative of your endless support.

As this project grew, it became clear that to deliver on the potential of the book I needed support, and I'm also grateful for the amazing army of assistant editors who were up for the task. The word-smithing genius and editorial advice of Caela Murphy, Deirdre Dlugoleski, Summer Modelfino, Lulu Chang, Natalie Shell, and Allison McKeon were invaluable, and these volunteers are responsible for making many of these chapters sing. A special shout out to Caela and Deidre whose fingerprints can be found across a number of these chapters. Thank you!

I'm also incredibly thankful for my brilliant publishers – Amy Laurens and Alex Atkinson. You two were the dream team for a first-time editor/author, from first proposal through to final proofs.

To Pramit Chaudhuri – who would have thought I'd edit not just one, but two books back during my Latin love affair with young Horace and Virgil. You are the ultimate educator, and my path would be entirely different today without the confidence and education you gave me. To Niko Canner, who has been a friend and mentor to many of the authors in this book – thank you for modeling the philosopher-practitioner role and encouraging us all to think differently about professional and personal purpose.

And finally, to my family. From Poppop's ancient history lessons and Yaya's Spanish charm to G-dad's emphatic, sociological curiosity and Grammie's principled devotion – you have all left such a significant impression on my sense of self and modes of thinking. I'm so proud of this personal heritage. To my parents, who encouraged me to study Latin and wander a bit before finding my way, you both are such incredible listeners, cheerleaders, educators, and nurturers. I hope to be half the parent and person you each are. And to my siblings – Cece, Will, Sophie, and Tommy. I love and am so proud of all four of you. You're my favorite people and best friends.

Figures, boxes, and tables

Figures

Boxes

Tables

The perspectives shared in this book belong to individual contributors. They do not reflect the official beliefs of any employer or organization.

Introduction

Nina Montgomery

In any field of endeavor, impact is generally synonymous with a particularly far-reaching kind of success.[1] Certain products don't just win companies new markets, they also change the very way we live. For some athletes, the measure of success isn't winning but revolutionizing the nature of the game itself. In the social sector, however, impact represents an especially daunting goal. How on earth do we mitigate, let alone solve, perennial, global problems affecting education, health, equality, and other crucial aspects of human welfare? In such contexts, genuine impact – change that is positive, profound, and enduring – can seem to be an impossibly distant goal.[2]

This book surveys recent developments in the field to offer a more optimistic response: we are now in a position to sketch a general framework for impact across a range of social issues, and we can already see path-breaking initiatives exploiting this framework to great success.

Before we turn to the contents of this book, however, it's important to acknowledge a major shift that has taken place in the social sector over the past few decades. It's increasingly been recognized that the most intractable social, humanitarian, and environmental problems facing the world cannot be understood as independent issues reducible to a single or even handful of factors. Whether homelessness in San Francisco, an HIV epidemic in Malawi, or – at the extreme end of the scale – global climate change, these complex challenges are produced by a deeply interconnected set of elements.[3] They are made up of many systems – including social strata, data systems, economic structures, government policies, hard and soft infrastructures, cultural norms, and socio-historical contexts, among others – encompassing numerous agents and subject to diverse influences.[4]

And yet this realization runs counter to core practices in the social sector that have prevailed for decades. A primary focus of social impact work has been optimizing individual interventions to produce maximum change.[5] The underlying logic was that more efficient interventions could stretch funding dollars across more projects; more projects meant more positive change; and more positive change meant the well-being of more people improved. High-efficiency impact efforts, on this view, allow for change at scale.

Alongside this conceptual framework for change-making arose the dominant grant-based funding model designed to invest in high-efficacy solutions – ones that followed best practices learned from 'successful' past projects, that isolate interventions for isolated problems, and that can attribute, in the near-term, change produced to a specific action. Overall, this approach has resulted in a highly atomized field of practitioners working in their various silos across sectors, organizations, and disciplines.

Though an oversimplified picture of the social impact landscape, it illustrates a general tendency: the institutions – both intellectual and organizational – underpinning our approach to social impact share a priority of maximizing individual, isolated interventions. This work has not produced the scale and speed of change needed to address the systemic problems at hand. At best, our isolated efforts offer only local or temporary improvements. At worst, they produce negative, unintended consequences.

A first step in moving away from this model is recognizing the variety of cross-sectoral participants in the 'field' of social impact, each with different training and experience even if they share a common goal. From government officials and foundation philanthropists to corporate employees and social entrepreneurs, these practitioners are characterized by occupational diversity: their roles span research, innovation, implementation, measurement, strategy, fundraising, and communications, and much else besides. Any successful approach to problem-solving must leverage this broad and manifold expertise to ensure that any actions are informed by a wealth of evidence and are executed in close coordination with all stakeholders.

In order to solve, or at least mitigate, complex, integrated challenges, we need integrated solutions. The basic premise of this evolved approach is as simple as it is radical: put the problem at the center and orient networks of partners and stakeholders around it; first, to see the problem holistically, and, second, to design and implement interventions collaboratively.

In practice, this means updating our own intellectual and organizational structures to enable such an approach to change-making: one that encourages practitioners to learn what has been called the 'dance of systems' – compiling the most complete map of the problem at hand to see how overlapping dynamics balance, amplify, or limit particular outcomes. Having identified leverage points where focused, concerted action can have the biggest influence on systems behavior, we can begin to re-choreograph the systems dance through interventions. This means changing "policies, processes, relationships, knowledge, power structures, values, or norms of participants within a system that affects a social issue."[6] From this work, we can fundamentally alter the components and structures that cause the system to behave in a certain way, designing them to produce new behaviors, new relationships, and new paradigms.

Excitingly, never before has there been so much collective energy focused on such innovation – there are countless projects experimenting with how to climb out of our silos and engage in new ways of making change in the twenty-first century. This book joins many valuable initiatives within and beyond the social sector seeking to capture our thinking and practice in this moment. It brings together leading voices from various corners of the impact field to offer perspectives on how we are adapting our approaches to maximize the change we can – and indeed must – accomplish as a larger collective.

The book's first section overviews what a more synergistic approach to systems change might look like. It begins with Duncan Green's (Oxfam) overview of the systems thinking mindset. He demonstrates the value of this systems lens for orienting various stakeholders around the same problem, while better embracing the complexity, scale, and ambiguity inherent in the problems we face. Niko Canner, Shanti Nayak, and Cynthia Warner (Incandescent) then ask what applying strategy to systems change might look like. They consider the need for explicit, imaginative thinking in the face of scale and complexity – thinking that neither over-determines a plan nor simply assumes progress will emerge on its own. Next, Jane Nelson (Harvard Kennedy School) outlines the models of leadership required to align actors, and sets an agenda for collective action partnerships moving forward. We then move to Fay Twersky's (William and Flora Hewlett Foundation) discussion on how we need to evolve our measurement methods. She argues for a more adaptive approach, incorporating ongoing feedback from the people whom interventions or programs are meant to benefit. The final chapter of this section is Joi Ito's on the need to rethink how we generate solutions to our biggest challenges. Taking the Massachusetts Institute of Technology's Media Lab as an example, he discusses how this home for diverse and anti-disciplinary thinking allows us to better configure novel solutions to real-world problems.

With this frame set, the bulk of the book, its second part, brings different disciplinary approaches to impact around a shared table for comparative study. By discipline I mean the actual methods to our madness: the perceptual lenses and tool kits we use to diagnose and design impact efforts. The ones discussed in this book are design, product development and engineering, behavioral science, open innovation, technology, grassroots activism, brands, media, advertising, public policy, investment, and social entrepreneurship – but there are many more deployed in the daily work of change-making.

We'll see how these practitioners are thinking about social challenges of different shapes and sizes – from climate change, global poverty, and crisis response to Liberian education reform, American unemployment, and the Syrian refugee crisis. And we'll see how different disciplines address similar problems: the chapters on design, media, brands, grassroots activism, and social entrepreneurship, for example, all focus on the complex challenge of gender inequality. By placing these perspectives side by side, the hope is to continue building bridges across our silos by raising awareness for others' work – of our respective innovations, languages, blind spots, and super powers. To this end, each chapter is designed to give a short introduction of its subject matter to the unfamiliar, overviewing current discourses and future directions.

As the convener of these perspectives, I've grappled with how best to present contributors' varying starting points in a coherent and informative way. I've encouraged a somewhat uniform structure across chapters, while also allowing contributors to organically reflect the way they think about impact given their respective areas of expertise – the various conceptual models they employ are themselves telling. The result of this editorial choice is that there are noticeable disparities between some chapters. I've chosen not to iron out these seams, with the intent that the reader will identify any incongruities as opportunities for cross-pollination, as well as potential areas for evolution of thought or practice.

But I hope these disparities don't distract from the many synergies across these chapters. They emphasize the need for a systems mindset, for audacious, moon-shot goals, for inclusive co-creation with local stakeholders, for consideration of entrenched systems of power, for experimental and iterative approaches, for obses-sion with scale, and for new definitions and metrics of success.

A subtler theme of the book – one that has left the biggest impression on me as I got to know the contributors featured here – reflects on the quality and caliber of leadership that our complex problems demand. In her concluding note to future change-makers, Jacqueline Novogratz calls this 'moral leadership,' and advocates for building this character muscle in the next generation. Following her letter is a series of notes by young change-makers, all leaders in their own right. They share stories about their inspiring work and how they are redefining success, boldly imagining the world as it should be, and building partnerships across boundaries to realize new visions.

As a collective, we offer what we've learned with humility and invite others to join us in reflecting on our approaches to solving today's most complex chal-lenges. We hope these perspectives, and a raised awareness of others' points of view, can contribute to readers' work and thinking, and encourage new ways of collaborating.

I

Framing thoughts on systemic change

1

Thinking in systems changes everything

Duncan Green

Dr Duncan Green is Senior Strategic Advisor at Oxfam Great Britain and a Professor in Practice at the London School of Economics. Duncan was previously Oxfam GB's Head of Research, a Visiting Fellow at Notre Dame University, a Senior Policy Adviser on Trade and Development at the Department for International Development (DFID), a Policy Analyst on trade and globalization at CAFOD, the Catholic aid agency in England and Wales and Head of Research and Engagement at the Just Pensions project on socially responsible investment. He is the author of How Change Happens *and* From Poverty to Power: How Active Citizens and Effective States Can Change the World. *He also authors the* From Poverty to Power *blog.*

★ ★ ★

I was first moved to write on how change happens and systems thinking by a combination of excitement, fascination, and frustration: excitement at the speed and grandeur of many of the social changes occurring today – continents rising from poverty, multitudes becoming literate and gaining access to decent healthcare for the first time, and women in dozens of countries winning rights, respect, and power.[1] Working at Oxfam gives me an extraordinary and privileged ringside seat from which to appreciate both the bigger picture and the individual stories of inspiring activists across the globe.

This daily excitement is laced with frustration when I see activists take steps that seem destined to fail. Within months of joining Oxfam in 2004, I witnessed two examples, one big and one small. On a field visit to Vietnam, I was taken to see Oxfam's work with Hmong villagers in the north. As we drove to the remote home of this impoverished ethnic minority, we passed the first, more intrepid backpackers starting to arrive in the area. The Hmong produce wonderful textiles, and it was obvious that a tourist boom was in the offing. Yet our project consisted of training villagers to keep their prized water buffalo warm and well during the winter (involving rubbing them regularly with alcohol, among other things). There is nothing wrong with working on livestock, but what were we doing to help them prepare for the coming influx of tourists? When challenged, our local (non-Hmong, middle-class Vietnamese) staff replied that they wanted to 'protect' the villagers' traditional ways against the invasion of the outside world.

On a grander scale, I had growing misgivings about an enormous, global campaign Oxfam was then leading that implied global activism around trade, debt, aid, and climate change could somehow 'Make Poverty History.' The campaign seemed to gravely downplay the primacy of national politics. I developed my argument a couple of years later in a book, *From Poverty to Power: How Active Citizens and Effective States Can Change the World.* One of the inputs to that book was a paper we commissioned on the theories of change used by different academic disciplines.[2] It turns out they each operate with separate and often conflicting theories of change, and there is no 'department of change studies' to sort it out. I was intrigued, and set out some rather rudimentary ideas about 'how change happens' in an annex to the book, marking the starting point for the prolonged conversation that led eventually to yet another book, *How Change Happens.*

I believe that activists can change the world, but first let's define what we mean by the word 'activist.' A narrow interpretation would say that it means people engaged in protest movements and campaigns around topics as disparate as climate change and disabled peoples' rights, usually on the margins of 'the system,' people who from the days of the abolitionists have been making change happen. But the list of 'change agents' (English is sadly devoid of non-clunky descriptors in this field) is much wider. I include reformers inside the system, such as politicians (both elected and unelected), public officials, and enlightened business people. And the civic world beyond formal institutions is far too rich to narrow down to a single category of 'campaigners.' Faith groups, community leaders, and the many self-help organizations that women form are all often influential players. Even within aid organizations, those engaged in what we call 'programs' – funding or running projects to create jobs or improve health and education services, or responding to emergencies such as wars or earthquakes – are just as involved in seeking change as campaigners. When I use the word 'activists' I mean all of the above.

This chapter argues that systems thinking – embracing the complexity of the world, rather than trying to reduce it to simple (and simplistic) chains of cause and effect – can transform the ability of activists to bring about the changes they seek, whether in society, politics, or business. It sets out the practical implications of learning to 'dance with the system,' in terms of the kinds of people we need to be, and the kinds of questions we need to ask (and keep asking), as we seek to change the world.

How change happens: Systems thinking changes everything

Political and economic earthquakes are often sudden and unforeseeable, despite the false pundits who pop up later to claim they predicted them all along – take the fall of the Berlin Wall, the 2008 global financial crisis, the Arab Spring (and ensuing winter), Brexit, or the rise of populism. Even at a personal level, change is largely unpredictable: how many of us can say our lives have gone according to the plans we had as 16-year-olds?

The essential mystery of the future poses a huge challenge to activists. If change is only explicable in the rear-view mirror, how can we accurately envision the future changes we seek, let alone achieve them? How can we be sure our proposals will make things better, and not fall victim to unintended consequences? People employ many concepts to grapple with such questions. I find 'systems' and 'complexity' two of the most helpful.

A 'system' is an interconnected set of elements coherently organized in a way that achieves something. It is more than the sum of its parts: a body is more than an aggregate of individual cells; a university is not merely an agglomeration of individual students, professors, and buildings; an ecosystem is not just a set of individual plants and animals.

A defining property of human systems is complexity: because of the sheer number of relationships and feedback loops among their many elements, they cannot be reduced to simple chains of cause and effect. Think of a crowd on a city street, or a flock of starlings wheeling in the sky at dusk. Even with super-computers, it is impossible to predict the movement of any given person or starling, but there is order; amazingly few collisions occur even on the most crowded streets.

In complex systems, change results from the interplay of many diverse and apparently unrelated factors. Those of us engaged in seeking change need to identify which elements are important and understand how they interact.

My interest in systems thinking began when collecting stories for my book *From Poverty to Power*.[3] The light bulb moment came on a visit to India's Bundelkhand region, where the poor fishing communities of Tikamgarh had won rights to more than 150 large ponds. In that struggle numerous factors interacted to create change. First, a technological shift triggered changes in behavior: the introduction of new varieties of fish, which made the ponds more profitable, induced landlords to seize ponds that had been communal. Conflict then built pressure for government action: a group of 12 brave young fishers in one village fought back, prompting a series of violent clashes that radicalized and inspired other communities; women's groups were organized for the first time, taking control of nine ponds. Enlightened politicians and nongovernmental organizations (NGOs) helped pass new laws and the police amazed everyone by enforcing them.

The fishing communities were the real heroes of the story. They tenaciously faced down a violent campaign of intimidation, moved from direct action to advocacy, and ended up winning not only access to the ponds but a series of legal and policy changes that benefited all fishing families.

The neat narrative sequence of cause and effect I've just written, of course, is only possible in hindsight. In the thick of the action, no one could have said why the various actors acted as they did, or what transformed the relative power of each. Tikamgarh's experience highlights how unpredictable is the interaction between structures (such as state institutions), agency (by communities and individuals), and the broader context (shifts in technology, environment, demography, or norms).

Unfortunately, the way we commonly think about change projects onto the future the neat narratives we draw from the past. Many of the mental models we use are linear plans – 'if A, then B' – with profound consequences in terms of failure, frustration, and missed opportunities. As Mike Tyson memorably said, "Everyone has a plan 'til they get punched in the mouth."

Let me illustrate with a metaphor. Baking a cake is a linear 'simple' system. All I need do is find a recipe, buy the ingredients, make sure the oven is working, mix, bake, *et* voila! Some cakes are better than others (mine wouldn't win any prizes), but the basic approach is fixed, replicable, and reasonably reliable. However bad your cake, you'll probably be able to eat it.

The trouble is that real life rarely bakes like a cake. Engaging a complex system is more like raising a child. What fate would await your new baby if you decided to go linear and design a project plan setting out activities, assumptions, outputs, and outcomes for the next 20 years and then blindly followed it? Nothing good, probably.

Instead, parents make it up as they go along. And so they should. Raising a child is iterative, an endless testing of assumptions about right and wrong, a constant adaptation to the evolving nature of the child and his or her relationship with their parents and others. Despite all the 'best practice' guides preying on the insecurity of new parents, child-rearing is devoid of any 'right way' of doing things. What really helps parents is experience (the second kid is usually easier), and the advice and reassurance of people who've been through it themselves – 'mentoring' in management speak. Working in complex systems requires the same kind of iterative, collaborative, and flexible approach. Deng Xiaoping's recipe for China's takeoff epitomizes this approach: "We will cross the river by feeling the stones under our feet, one by one."[4]

Systems are in a state of constant change. Jean Boulton, one of the authors of *Embracing Complexity*, likes to use the metaphor of the forest, which typically goes through cycles of growth, collapse, regeneration, and new growth.[5] In the early part of the cycle's growth phase, the number of species and of individual plants and animals increases quickly, as organisms arrive to exploit all available ecological niches. The forest's components become more linked to one another, enhancing the ecosystem's 'connectedness' and multiplying the ways the forest regulates itself and maintains its stability. However, the forest's very connectedness and efficiency eventually reduce its capacity to cope with severe outside shocks, paving the way for a collapse and eventual regeneration. Jean argues that activists need to adapt their analysis and strategy according to the stage that their political surroundings most closely resemble: growth, maturity, locked-in but fragile, or collapsing.

I was not a quick or easy convert to systems thinking, despite the fact that my neural pathways were shaped by my undergraduate degree in physics, where linear Newtonian mechanics quickly gave way to the more mind-bending world of quantum mechanics, wave particle duality, relativity, and Heisenberg's uncertainty principle. Similarly, my experience of activism has obliged me to question linear approaches to campaigning, for example, as I hesitantly embraced the realization that change doesn't happen like that.

Once I began thinking about systems, I started to see complexity and unpredictable 'emergent change' everywhere – in politics, economics, at work, and even in the lives of those around me.

When change happens: Crises at critical junctures

Change in complex systems occurs in slow, steady processes such as demographic shifts and in sudden, unforeseeable jumps. Nothing seems to change until suddenly it does, a stop – start rhythm that can confound activists. When British Prime Minister Harold Macmillan was asked what he most feared in politics, he reportedly replied in his wonderfully patrician style, "Events, dear boy." Such 'events' that disrupt social, political, or economic relations are not just a prime ministerial headache. They can open the door to previously unthinkable reforms.

Such 'critical junctures,' as the economists Daron Acemoglu and James A. Robinson call them, force political leaders to question their long-held assumptions about what constitutes 'sound' policies, and make them more willing to take the risks associated with innovation, as the status quo suddenly appears less worth defending.[6]

Much of the institutional framework we take for granted today was born of the trauma of the Great Depression and the Second World War. The disastrous failures of policy that led to these twin catastrophes profoundly affected the thinking of political and economic leaders across the world, triggering a vastly expanded role for government in managing the economy and addressing social ills, as well as precipitating the decolonization of large parts of the globe.

Similarly, in the 1970s the sharp rise in oil prices (and consequent economic stagnation and runaway inflation) marked the end of the post-war 'Golden Age' and gave rise to a turn away from government regulation and to the idealization of the 'free market.' In communist systems, at different moments, political and economic upheaval paved the way for radical economic shifts in China and Vietnam.

Milton Friedman, the father of monetarist economics, wrote:

> Only a crisis – actual or perceived – produces real change. When that crisis occurs, the actions that are taken depend on the ideas that are lying around. That, I believe, is our basic function: to develop alternatives to existing policies, to keep them alive and available until the politically impossible becomes politically inevitable.[7]

Naomi Klein, in her 2007 book *The Shock Doctrine*, argues that the Right has used shocks much better than the Left, especially in recent decades.[8] Klein cites the example of how proponents of private education in the U.S. managed to turn Hurricane Katrina to their advantage: "Within 19 months, New Orleans' public school system had been almost completely replaced by privately-run charter schools."

According to the American Enterprise Institute, "Katrina accomplished in a day what Louisiana school reformers couldn't do after years of trying."[9]

NGOs are not always so nimble in spotting and seizing such opportunities. Three months into the 2011 Egyptian revolution, I attended a meeting of Oxfam International's chief executive officers (CEOs), at which they spent hours debating whether the uprising in Tahrir Square was likely to lead to a humanitarian crisis. Only then did the penny drop that the protests, upheaval, and overthrow of an oppressive regime were also a huge potential opportunity, at which point the assembled bosses showed admirable speed in allocating budgets for supporting civil society activists in Egypt, and backing it up with advocacy at the Arab League and elsewhere. But by then valuable time had passed; soon the optimism of revolution gave way to the violence and misery of repression.

Some progressive activists engaged in policy advocacy are better attuned to Friedman's lesson. Within weeks of the appalling Rana Plaza factory collapse in Bangladesh that killed more than 1,100 people in April 2013 an international 'Accord on Fire and Building Safety in Bangladesh' was signed and delivered.[10] A five-year legally binding agreement between global companies, retailers, and trade unions, the accord mandates some astounding breakthroughs: an independent inspection program supported by the brand-name companies and involving workers and trade unions; the public disclosure of all factories, inspection reports, and corrective action plans; a commitment by signatory brands to fund improvements and maintain sourcing relationships; democratically elected health and safety committees in all factories; and worker empowerment through an extensive training program, complaints mechanism, and the right to refuse unsafe work.

In hindsight, we can point to several factors to explain how this grisly 'shock as opportunity' drove rapid movement toward better regulation:

- A forum on labor rights in Bangladesh (the Ethical Trading Initiative) had already built a high degree of trust between traditional antagonists (companies, unions, and NGOs). Trust allowed people to get on the phone to each other right away.
- Prior work, underway since 2011, had sketched the outline of a potential accord; the Rana Plaza disaster massively escalated the pressure to act on it.
- A nascent national process (the National Action Plan for Fire Safety) gave outsiders something to support and build on.

Energetic leadership from two new international trade unions (IndustriALL and UNI Global Union) helped get the right people in the room. Perhaps we should add to Friedman's instruction "to keep alternatives alive and available": progressive activists also need to build trust and connections among the key individuals who could implement the desired change. I am not suggesting that activists become ambulance chasers, jumping on every crisis to make their point. Rather, we must understand the windows of opportunity provided by "events, dear boy" as critical junctures when our long-term work creating constituencies for change, transforming attitudes and norms, and so on can suddenly come to fruition.

The world is complex – so what?

Many activists are, above all, doers, keen to change the world, starting today. They instinctively reject the first lesson of systems thinking: look hard before you leap. They get itchy with anything that smacks of ivory tower 'beard stroking' and worry about 'analysis paralysis.' In the development arena, donors often accentuate the penchant for short-termism by demanding tangible results within the timescales of project funding cycles.

My advice would be to take a deep breath, put your sense of urgency to one side for a moment, and become a 'reflectivist' who, in the words of Ben Ramalingam, should "map, observe, and listen to the system to identify the spaces where change is already happening and try to encourage and nurture them."[11]

That said, another lesson of systems thinking is that you cannot understand and plan everything in advance. If each situation is different, so must be the response. One of the founders of systems thinking, Donella Meadows, talks of the need to learn to 'dance with systems.'[12] But even that may be too choreographed. Perhaps a better analogy is that activists should switch from being architects and engineers to becoming 'ecosystem gardeners.'

Combining these two lessons makes for some surprising principles for how to bring about change:

> *Be flexible:* You should be willing to shelve the current plan in response to emerging events and your organization's culture should thank the staff who alert it to signals of change. In the world of humanitarian response, this approach is standard, whereas in long-term aid programs or campaigns people are often reluctant to shift gears, or simply fail to notice that new opportunities have opened up.

> *Seek fast and ongoing feedback:* If you don't know what is going to happen, you have to detect changes in real time, especially when the windows of opportunity around such changes are short-lived. That means having (or developing) acute antennae and embedding them in multiple networks to pick up signals of change and transmit them to your organization.

> *Success is often accidental:* "Fortune favors the prepared mind," according to Louis Pasteur, pioneer of the germ theory of disease.[13] Surprising breakthroughs (often subsequently rewritten as triumphs of planning!) are a recurring feature of innovation and change. One reason you need fast feedback is to spot and respond to accidental successes as early as possible.

> *Undertake multiple parallel experiments:* Activists hate failure. No one wants to think they've wasted their time, or wake up to newspaper headlines about money lost or 'wasted' on failed projects. Compare this risk aversion to a venture capitalist who backs ten projects knowing that nine will fail, but he or she will make enough money on the tenth to more than

compensate for the rest. With a venture approach you would spend less time and money designing the perfect plan, and instead pursue a 'lean start-up' based on best guesses about what will work, followed by a fast and frugal cycle of experimentation and adaptation until you find something that really does.[14]

Learn by doing (and failing): In a complex system, it is highly unlikely you will get things right from the outset, or that they will stay right. You and your colleagues have to be ready to discuss and learn from failure, rather than sweep it under the carpet. Fast feedback on your own impact is thus just as important as feedback on the outside world, not least to detect unintended consequences. If people are keeping chickens in the latrines you are building, you probably need to go back to the drawing board.[15] Alas, my experience is that colleagues are reluctant to admit, let alone discuss, failure. A better way may be to ask "What have you learned?" during the course of any given effort, which covers the same ground in a less embarrassing fashion.

Identify and discuss your rules of thumb: When the U.S. Marines go into combat (an archetypal complex system), they use rules of thumb (stay in contact, take the high ground, keep moving) rather than detailed 'best-practice guidelines.' Activists do too (Have we thought about gender? What is the government doing?), but these often remain tacit, and so are not questioned, tested, or improved upon. Make them explicit and review them regularly.

Convene and broker relationships: Bringing dissimilar local players together to find their own solutions can be a particularly useful role for foreign aid organizations and other activists from outside the community in question. Effective convening and brokering requires understanding who should be invited to the table. Which players have, or could have, their hands on the levers of change? Providing them with a space for dialogue outside of their home institutions can encourage them to think in new ways.

Box 1.1 Working in systems

How we think/feel/work:

- Curiosity – study the history; 'learn to dance with the system.'
- Humility – embrace uncertainty/ambiguity.
- Reflexivity – be conscious of your own role, prejudices, and power.
- Include multiple perspectives, unusual suspects; be open to different ways of seeing the world.

The questions to ask (and keep asking):

- What kind of change is involved (individual attitudes, social norms, laws and policies, access to resources)?
- What precedents are there that we can learn from (positive deviance, history, current political and social tides)?
- Power analysis: who are the stakeholders and what kind of power is involved (look again – who have we forgotten?)
- What kind of approach makes sense for this change (traditional project, advocacy, multiple parallel experiments, fast feedback and rapid response)?
- What strategies are we going to try (delivering services, building the broader enabling environment, demonstration projects, convening and brokering, supporting local grassroots organizations, advocacy)?
- Learning and course correction: how will we learn about the impact of our actions or changes in context (e.g. critical junctures)? Schedule regular time-outs to take stock and adapt accordingly.

Conclusion: Thinking in systems should change everything

In the first film in the *Matrix* series (the only one worth watching), the hero, Neo, suddenly starts to see the matrix of ones and zeroes that lies beneath the surface of his world, at which point he becomes invincible. I have the same feeling about systems (aside from the invincibility part). Thinking in systems should change everything, including the way we look at politics, economics, society, and even ourselves, in new and exciting ways.

It also poses a devastating challenge to traditional linear planning approaches and to our ways of working. We activists need to become better 'reflectivists,' taking the time to understand the system before (and while) engaging with it. We need to better understand the stop – start rhythm of change exhibited by complex systems and adapt our efforts accordingly. And we need to become less arrogant, more willing to learn from accidents, from failures, and from other people and disciplines. Finally, we have to make friends with ambiguity and uncertainty, while maintaining the energy and determination so essential to changing the world.

In *How Change Happens*, I summarized what I saw as the implications of systems thinking for activists (see Box 1.1), broadly defined as anyone trying to intentionally change the world around them. I called this a 'power and systems approach,' which fell short of a new checklist or blueprint, but concentrated instead on how activists should think, feel, and work, and the kinds of questions they should ask themselves and others.

This way of driving change isn't easy, but it is entirely possible, as I hope I have shown. Once we learn to 'dance with the system,' no other partner will do.

2 Shaping strategy to change systems

Niko Canner, Shanti Nayak, and Cynthia Warner

Niko Canner is the founder of Incandescent, a boutique firm that advises clients in the private and social sectors on questions relating to strategy, organization and change. In addition to its advisory work, Incandescent pursues its own research and develops ventures.

Shanti Nayak is a principal at Incandescent leading the development of the firm's practice focused on philanthropy and systems change.

Cynthia Warner leads research for Incandescent. Incandescent participated as an advisor in the main cases shared in this chapter, which the authors have chosen in part because the work in each case remains unfinished. In each case, it is too soon to say whether the system will change or whether change will be lasting, which brings to life the fundamental uncertainties involved in work of this kind.

★ ★ ★

Mark Pollock simply wanted to walk again.

After going blind at 22, Mark had renewed his commitment to being an athlete, winning medals at the Commonwealth Rowing Championships and successfully completing an expedition race to the South Pole – trekking for 43 days, without sight, to reach one of the world's most difficult destinations. The next year, Mark fell out of a third-story window. He fractured his skull and broke his back, rendering him paralyzed from the stomach down.

Amidst his disbelief and shock at what had happened, one thing stood out as absolutely clear. The work that remained for him to do in life was somehow to make it possible for people injured like him to regain function and movement.

Mark faced the question of how to change a system. Treatments were advancing, but nowhere near fast enough. He was determined to *bend upwards the curve of improvement* of the field, becoming a catalyst for treatments to improve more rapidly and reach patients in need sooner than they otherwise would. But he needed a strategy. We often think of strategy through the lens of business, or at the very least through the lens of an organization. Mark didn't have an organization – he simply wanted to change the world. What does strategy mean in a context like his?

Strategic clarity begins with commitment to a destination. Mark's destination was crystal clear: cure paralysis, by making it possible for injury victims like him to meaningfully regain function and movement. His commitment was absolute. But there in his hospital bed, Mark was at a loss to say what choices he could make that would advance him toward his goal. He needed a picture of how to change the world: guiding ideas that together could orient him and those working with him to what could advance science, bring solutions to market, and enable men and women like him to change their condition.

What does it mean to have a strategy for systems change?

The nature of Mark's goal required more than what he could conceivably achieve himself or even build a single organization to achieve. Realizing Mark's goal would only be possible through the interplay of a broader system: different actors functioning as a 'we' conducting research, developing treatments, navigating regulatory approval, obtaining capital, educating doctors, and doing all the other work needed to find a cure (on the differences between strategy for an institution and strategy for systems change, see Table 2.1).

Many people equate strategy with planning, which is a mistake in any context, and a particularly pernicious mistake in the context of systems change. Duncan Green, in the opening chapter to this volume, points out the danger of approaching systems change simplistically – like baking a cake, in his metaphor – or deterministically, marching through a grand plan even as the world shifts under the marching feet. Just as common a trap is for a changemaker like Mark simply to do what

Table 2.1 How is strategy for systems change different?

	Strategy for an institution	Strategy for systems change
Core question	How can a particular institution create and realize the most value (institution in foreground)?	What will cause a system in the world to evolve in the desired way (large goal in foreground)?
Actors	Clearly defined organization, shaping strategy to achieve explicitly defined objectives	Strategy provides a framework for shaping a new 'we,' made up of different actors who have diverse goals and commitments
Resources	Strategy drives allocation of the organization's resources to achieve a direct outcome	Strategy seeks to unlock resources and energy in multiple parts of a system, so that the direct actions of a core group have larger, cascading effects

comes naturally, guided by faith that if he is pure in his commitment to the cause, opportunistic and resourceful, achievement of his goal will somehow emerge from complexity. The stakes are too high and the problems too hard for Mark to make this assumption. He needs to act strategically – but what does it mean to have an effective strategy in the context of a goal like Mark's that requires effecting change through and across a system?

For an actor like Mark to have an effective strategy, he needs a picture of how to change the world that combines four elements. These same four elements apply equally to an individual like Mark, to a foundation with an endowment worth many billions, or to a large coalition making common cause to drive change.

- A picture of how the *central outcome* that Mark seeks – restoring function and movement to the victim of spinal injury – can be achieved
- A picture of the *higher-level context* that needs to be created to make this central outcome possible. In Mark's case, this includes how the relevant interventions will be developed, financed, tested and approved, taken to market, integrated into protocols of treatment, and so on
- A picture of the *journey* from the current starting place toward the world in which the necessary context has been shaped and the central outcome achieved at scale
- A picture of the 'we' that can complete this journey, what motivates and unites the individuals and groups who make up this 'we,' and how the smaller 'we' committed to action today can, over the course of the journey, evolve and develop into the larger, stronger 'we' required to achieve the goal

Of course, no actor begins their journey with a robust picture of how to drive change across these four dimensions. One must begin to act knowing one has an insufficient strategy, and sharpen strategy while taking action in the world. A working strategy establishes hypotheses concrete enough to test about how to drive change, paths to gain necessary resources, and frameworks for achieving cohesion across disparate actors. Some of these will be right, and some will be discovered to be wrong. Effective strategies create the experiences that fuel their own refinement. The imperative to learn isn't an argument against strategy; rather, a good strategy is a critical ingredient to learning how to achieve a goal that lies beyond the actor's reach as the journey begins.

To function as a *theory* of change, powerful in guiding action and guiding learning, a strategy must integrate into a larger whole the pictures of how a central outcome can be achieved, of the higher-level context that needs to be established for these levers of change to be effective, of the shape of the journey that the 'we' seeking change today will take, and how in the course of the journey this 'we' grows and develops in the ways needed to achieve the goal. All too often, strategies in the social sector – often called a 'theory of change' – articulate a vision of how the world could work better, without any clear picture of the causal mechanisms and the practical path by which the current world could be altered to work in this better way.[1]

In the pages that follow, we look closely at these elements of a strategy for systems change and how they come together. In The Rockefeller Foundation's work to bend upwards the curve of addressing youth unemployment, we see a team forming a *picture of the journey* that is rich enough to guide present action despite the many unknowns. In the case of the HCD Exchange – in which funders, NGOs, and designers are applying human-centered design to the persistent problem of supporting teens' sexual and reproductive health – we see that strategy requires a *picture of the big 'we'*: the full set of actors who need to be taking action and evolving to ultimately achieve the central outcome. Because these change-makers could not build this big 'we' in one leap, they also needed a picture of how smaller 'we's' – hubs of energy and shared learning among groups of actors – could, over time, grow into the big 'we,' with a level of reach commensurate with the scale of the problem.

The journey: From today's beginnings to a distant destination

A powerful picture of the journey needs to encompass three time horizons that orient action (Figure 2.1). The first time horizon is a *beacon*. Like the summit of a mountain, a beacon represents a destination and the completion of a significant journey: a big undertaking that nonetheless casts its shadow on the present, guiding current action.

The next time horizon is one level down from a beacon: a series of *eras*. Like the smaller hills leading up to the mountain's summit, each era represents a different

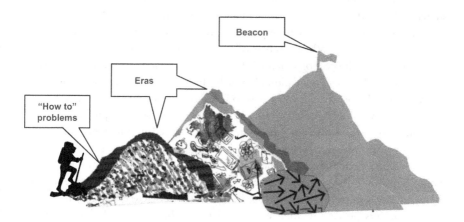

Figure 2.1 Picturing the journey at three horizons

stage in the journey, with distinct imperatives and challenges. Asking "What will it take to graduate into our next era?" enables changemakers to focus on the pivotal achievements – developments in the world and development of different actors' capabilities – that signal the arrival of a new stage and the ability to achieve greater impact. In guiding systems change work, an era should never be defined simply in terms of completion of a set of activities, but rather in terms of developments in the world and tangible development of capabilities that enable greater change.

Finally, beneath the horizon of eras are the *'how to' problems* that need to be solved. These are the critical questions most important to make progress on, to keep advancing toward the broader goal of era graduation. If thinking in terms of eras is like viewing the smaller peaks leading up to the highest summit, thinking in terms of 'how to' problems is like the view from the side of the hill. As one finds one's way to the hilltop, one views the core obstacles and opportunities on the path, and forms a view of the most important solutions to develop.

In the section that follows, we discuss how The Rockefeller Foundation's U.S. Youth Employment Initiative worked across these three time horizons to enable forward progress.

Tackling youth unemployment

As the financial crisis lifted and the labor market shifted back to historically low rates of unemployment, many young Americans were left out. Following the Great Recession, youth unemployment reached a 50-year high in 2010, and while it has dropped, it has remained more than double the general unemployment rate.[2] The Rockefeller Foundation launched its Youth Employment Initiative in 2013 with the commitment to focus on 'opportunity youth,' a vulnerable segment of young people who are disconnected from both school and work.[3]

From the beginning of this initiative, The Rockefeller Foundation had a clear strategic thesis. Most work on youth employment was driven from the 'supply side': investing in the employability of opportunity youth, usually through some form of education or training. While the best of these programs, such as Year Up, deliver measurable gains, the cost of supply-side interventions was far too great to achieve scale.[4] The Rockefeller Foundation's Youth Employment Initiative instead focused on the 'demand side,' acting as a catalyst to move the needle on how *employers* draw on opportunity youth as a talent pool, with the goal of unlocking significant unmet demand among employers for talent who could succeed in entry-level roles and grow inside the employer's career system.

This demand would directly benefit opportunity youth, and some of these youth would progress to more secure, higher-value roles, through the talent pipelines in their employers, improved skills and credibility, or the access to education that some large employers provide to their entry-level teams. In addition, The Rockefeller Foundation could promote steps that would extend the impact per unit of increased employment: for instance, influencing employers to design wraparound services to boost retention by helping young employees overcome challenges outside work, or influencing the spread of employer-sponsored programs to create access to higher education.

To act on the 'demand side' thesis required a clear picture of what would drive the *central outcome:* opportunity youth not only gaining employment, but building from entry-level roles to the point where they achieve a secure livelihood. No single intervention could achieve this goal. What was required was a chain of practices related to the following:

1   *Recruit:* how opportunity youth connect with opportunities and effectively navigate the hiring process
2   *Assess:* how employers evaluate opportunity youth in ways that surface their full potential to contribute
3   *Support:* how opportunity youth are positioned to succeed in their first role, address challenges outside work that could impede performance and grow professionally

The Rockefeller Foundation team came to see this chain of practices as an essential part of 'impact hiring,' which they defined as: talent practices that create business advantage through hiring and developing individuals who face barriers to economic opportunity. In the early phases of this work, certain aspects of each link in the chain were well understood and other critical aspects remained to be solved. The explicitness of the model made clear where further learning was essential.

This *central outcome picture* – of employer practices that would lead to the right kind of career trajectory within an employer and ultimately better economic outcomes – wasn't in itself sufficient to constitute a theory of change. A small group of employers – including major brands like Starbucks and mid-sized innovators like VILLA, an urban-inspired footwear and fashion retailer – had already begun to demonstrate the power of opportunity youth as a talent pool. How would a larger set of employers come to see this opportunity and invest in developing the practices of 'recruit, assess and support' required to achieve their business goals and in the process achieve the impact on youth The Rockefeller Foundation believed was possible? These open questions about the *higher-level context* reached beyond what anyone in the field knew at the outset of the work. And yet to act effectively, The Rockefeller Foundation team needed a *picture of the journey* specific enough to guide action and marshal investment while avoiding overconfidence and false precision.

The beacon: Picturing the destination

A picture of the journey needed to encompass three time horizons, as described above. The furthest of these horizons was an articulated beacon that would likely take several years to achieve. For the Youth Employment Initiative, 'crossing the chasm' of employer adoption and demand – to use the metaphor from Geoffrey

Moore's seminal book on technology adoption cycles – provided a bright, specific beacon.[5]

In Moore's model, left of the chasm are 'technologies' adopted first by enthusiasts who have an intrinsic passion for the technology, and then by early adopters who aim to achieve a strategic advantage by venturing beyond the frontier of current practice. Right of the chasm, more conservative decision-makers evaluate technologies based on whether there are proven, scalable solutions that have been successfully implemented by other companies they regard as credible peers.

The Rockefeller Foundation team understood impact hiring as a kind of technology, which would only unlock demand of the required magnitude if employers adopted it as a solution to a significant business need. Achieving systems change, beyond simply notching early wins with a few corporate champions, would require making the journey to the other side of the chasm.

The model of 'crossing the chasm' created a powerful beacon for The Rockefeller Foundation because it:

- Provided a rich picture of the journey, even in a period of many unknowns. The team could draw on analogies of how other technologies moved from initial kernels through early adoption and across the chasm – or failed to make this progress. For instance, the advent and growth of diversity and inclusion as a corporate objective and specialized corporate function provided one useful analogue of a successful chasm crossing.
- Built understanding of how the work of shifting the system would look different at different points along the way to crossing the chasm. For example, while the core demand side thesis was designed to achieve scale, the chasm model helped the team recognize that, counterintuitively, the early adopter stage necessitated highly bespoke focus on the specific needs of single companies.
- Established a frame of reference for the Foundation as an actor. In the early years, its funding and active engagement would be needed to do the more inventive, less predictable work of shaping a new domain. Later, as broad corporate adoption came into sight, a range of other actors would have a compelling signal to act and could build on established models and tools for impact hiring.

The era: Graduation to the next stage of the journey

A beacon alone is insufficient to navigate by when the journey is long and complex, as is the case in seeking to change a system. The second time horizon of an era is needed. What would it mean to graduate from the first era of demand-side work on youth employment? The launch of the 100,000 Opportunities Coalition – which The Rockefeller Foundation played a part in, along with Starbucks, the Schultz Family Foundation, the Walmart Foundation, and more than 20 national employers and other philanthropic funders – crystallized a picture of graduation. For the first time, a group of a few dozen significant employers had committed to focus together on advancing the hiring of opportunity youth, with the initial collective goal of 100,000 hires.[6]

Engaging with these employers made clear that while there was very real interest, and in some cases deep commitment to hiring opportunity youth, there was not yet a robust 'technology' and model for impact hiring that employers could readily adapt to their specific circumstances. For instance, many of the employers who joined the Coalition prioritized the successful retention of opportunity youth, and had research confirming that manager skills and behaviors were a major driver of retention. Yet, there was little sense among the employers that any of them had developed an explicit approach to changing manager behaviors that others could successfully apply. Looking at this landscape, a picture came into focus for The Rockefeller Foundation team of what graduation from the first era would require:

> Through pilots at specific employers, prove out a set of practices relating to recruitment, assessment and support/retention of hires. Ensure that the practices are beginning to generate meaningful uptake from the community of companies most interested in engaging with opportunity youth as a talent pool.

This graduation standard represents playing the game at the next level. On its own, it doesn't yet represent anything close to the far-away beacon of 'crossing the chasm.' But the goal at this stage couldn't be to 'cross the chasm' in one leap, i.e., convince the more skeptical mainstream adopters. Instead, the goal was to seed a set of practices that early adopters would readily adapt, further refine and prove out. Geoffrey Moore's model suggested this process would be a necessary step along the way to crossing the chasm, even if far from sufficient.

'How to' problems: Advancing along the journey's path

Clarifying as it was for The Rockefeller Foundation team to have this tangible picture of what was required to graduate from the first era, they still needed to think one further time horizon down: in a given era, they had to consider the specific questions that needed to be resolved and the results that needed to be demonstrated. We often call these 'how to' problems, because we find that framing problems in terms of 'how to' solve them creates the right balance of specifying what counts as a solution while allowing creativity about approaches. For instance, as The Rockefeller Foundation team's work and the work of their partners evolved over the first era, they faced different core 'how to' problems:

- *Initially:* how to secure a couple of partnerships with credible large employers who will co-create a compelling model for how managers can move the needle on opportunity youth retention, and be willing to share what they learn with a broad set of peers

- *Then:* how to execute a successful pilot with the employer HMS Host as an early partner, which will clear the hurdle of the business case required for HMS Host to scale the work internally and will elicit interest from a range of employers involved in the 100,000 Opportunities Coalition and beyond
- *And then:* how to create a forum for several companies advancing practices relating to opportunity youth retention to be able to share insights with one another, and through this evolve a compelling synthesis of this first generation of 'technologies' to improve retention

At any given time, The Rockefeller Foundation team had three to six 'how to' questions that were most important to progress on in order to keep advancing toward the broader goal of era graduation. These questions required intense focus – sometimes focus within the Foundation's own team, and sometimes focus by other actors (e.g., a working team inside HMS Host and an external consulting partner funded to drive the retention innovation work in the pilot).

The golden thread connecting the three horizons of the beacon, era graduation and the most critical 'how to' problems created a level of clarity and focus needed to act effectively amidst the vast complexity of trying to make a dent in a problem the size of youth unemployment in the U.S.

Building the critical 'we'

A theory of change answers the *what* and *how* questions most central to delivering on the *why* of a changemaker's deepest commitments. A picture of the journey provides a working model of *when* that guides action. Good answers to these questions remain inert without a clear picture of the *who* driving change and how these critical actors become an effective 'we.'

While there have been great advances in the field of sexual and reproductive health, most products and services are targeted at older women or women who are already married or have started families. Adolescents in regions such as East Africa and South Asia have been persistently hard to reach and engage. The application of human-centered design by innovation firms such as IDEO.org working in partnership with large implementer NGOs such as Marie Stopes International has demonstrated early promise. (In Chapter 6, Chris Larkin of IDEO.org discusses human-centered design as a method, including more on ways it seeks to address sexual and reproductive health.) For instance, in Zambia, where more than a third of women give birth by age 18, Marie Stopes saw very few teenage clients taking up contraceptive services. Marie Stopes and IDEO.org, with funding from the William and Flora Hewlett Foundation, applied human-centered design (HCD) techniques to understand the lives and aspirations of teenage Zambians and drew on these insights to develop Diva Centres as a radically new approach to connect with and serve teens. In IDEO.org's description:

> At the Diva Centres, girls do their nails while having informal conversations about boys and sex. They hang out with friends, learn about contraception in their own terms from trained peers, and, when they're ready, receive counseling and access to a variety of short and long-term birth control methods in a safe and judgment-free environment from a trained professional. In this safe environment, girls begin to connect birth control with their future aspirations and get the information they need to make smart decisions from a safe and trusted resource.[7]

Early results were promising. In the first three Diva Centres, 82 percent of teens who visited opted to adopt some form of birth control, many for the first time. More than a third returned to the Centre.[8] However, this was a small beginning. While these results were dramatically better than the results that adult-focused service models achieved with teens, the total cost to reach each teen was still high and scale was tiny relative to the magnitude of need. It wasn't clear how readily learnings from the metro area of Lusaka, a city of more than a million, would translate to rural areas or to other countries.

As the Hewlett Foundation, the Children's Investment Fund Foundation (CIFF), and the Bill & Melinda Gates Foundation (Gates Foundation) – three of the major funders of work applying HCD to adolescent sexual and reproductive health – took stock of the Diva Centres and other early efforts in the field, they confronted a challenging landscape.[9]

- Although promising, the early demonstration projects' rate of innovation and rate of scaling indicated they would take too long and be too costly to move the needle.
- The work didn't fit the traditional framework of replication: HCD as a process could yield quite different service model designs based on distinct 'user' needs, attitudes, and aspirations in different contexts.
- Successful scaling of models fueled by HCD would require integrating the capabilities of disparate actors with very different cultures and ways of operating. The working approaches of the design firms who had pioneered the methods of HCD differed sharply from the working approaches of large NGOs and ministries of health focused on delivering tested models at scale.
- For the field as a whole to advance at a faster rate, not only would diverse capabilities and cultures need to be brought together at a project level, but dots would need to be connected across geographies, up and down the levels of complex global organizations (e.g., global headquarters and field offices of implementers like Marie Stopes adapting learnings across countries) and across sectors (e.g., innovation born in the social sector building support from ministries of health).

Staring at these barriers, it was clear that the desired acceleration of progress for the field wouldn't just happen of its own accord. While of course there were a number of important questions about the *what, how,* and *when* of changing the system of adolescent sexual and reproductive health, the most pressing questions were about the *who*: which community of actors could bend upwards the curve of impact over time by applying HCD to the persistent problem of reaching and serving teens?

The structure of the challenge that CIFF, the Gates Foundation, and the Hewlett Foundation faced in creating an effective 'we' capable of accelerating the field's progress was a common one in systems change work. They could envision the outlines of the *big 'we'*: the many actors who would ultimately be needed, and the ways they would need to evolve, to change the system over the longer term. For example, the funders could picture how the large implementing organizations would need to evolve, how ministries of health would need to engage, and how design capabilities would need to be built in certain local markets. But there was no practical way to build this big 'we' in one giant leap. Even if all the relevant actors could be convened, the conditions weren't yet in place to create alignment and support. Early evidence wasn't yet sufficiently airtight. Questions about scaling hadn't yet been resolved. There wasn't even clear and sharp shared language about what the 'it' really was that one would seek to enroll a wide range of actors to support: a specific design, like the Diva Centres? A specific model for applying HCD to create new designs? HCD as a broad principle of engagement?

This big 'we' could only develop from a *core community* – a smaller group committed to advancing the field to the point where adolescents could effectively be reached and served at scale (Figure 2.2). This core community, in order to be an

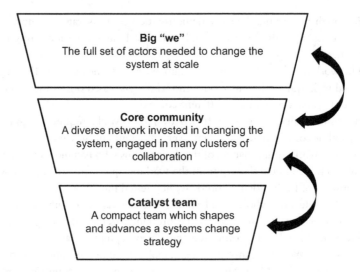

Figure 2.2 Three 'we's'

The big 'we' can't be built in one leap: smaller 'we's' need to form, which can draw in others over time, creating the full set of actors whose collective reach can bend upwards the curve of impact.

effective catalyst, needed to be both diverse and cohesive; large enough to have meaningful reach, but small enough to be tight and focused. The community needed to be made up of members with enough collective influence to build momentum toward the big 'we,' but with enough focus and enough investable time to take action and to build lateral connections with one another. Without becoming an organization – the essence of the core community being to integrate across many organizational contexts – the community needed to form enough of a shared picture of how to operate to advance their goals to be able to give one another's work real lift.

The barriers of geography, divergent professional cultures, and intensity of pressure to fund and execute the work at hand were too high for such a complex organic structure to simply emerge. In some instances, the requisite members of this 'we' were individuals working at organizations – design firms and public health organizations – that were competing with one another to work on projects, another barrier to organic formation.

Just as effecting the big 'we' necessary to change the system would require building an energized, effective core community, forming and nurturing this core community would require a tight *catalyst team* to generate the necessary activation energy. The program officers at CIFF, the Gates Foundation, and the Hewlett Foundation most deeply involved in early support for application of HCD to adolescent sexual and reproductive health between them possessed some of the critical ingredients to function as a catalyst team: a broad view of the field, convening power, capital to place behind promising work, and sufficient compactness as a group to be able to act effectively together.

This joint commitment among the funders was provisional. They resolved to convene a group of approximately 60 players from across organizations and disciplines, each already meaningfully engaged in the work of applying HCD to adolescent sexual and reproductive health, for a few days of intense work in Dar es Salaam, Tanzania. In preparation for this HCD Exchange in Dar, they would lay the foundations of understanding the needs and aspirations of different stakeholders – much as the process of human-centered design itself would suggest – and begin to sketch the outlines of a strategy for bending the impact curve that could be shaped more deeply through the thinking of a broader community. They would do the careful design work required to make space in Dar for subgroups to advance the areas of greatest mutual concern, such as how to apply monitoring and evaluation processes successfully to the often fluid, emergent intervention models developed through HCD. And they would let this gathering and the group's engagement feedback teach them whether the development of a core community could indeed represent a pivotal inflection point for the field.

As of this writing, a vibrant community is beginning to emerge in the months following the HCD Exchange gathering in Dar. Not only are the three funders forming a clearer picture of the 'we' than they had at an earlier stage of the journey, but this picture is now widely shared and emotionally resonant for a group of several dozen individuals who are critical 'repeat players' in the field. These individuals in turn are positioned to build the bridges to others in their organizations and professional communities who will be important on the road ahead.

Returning to the four elements of a strategy for systems change laid out at the start of this chapter, this picture of the 'we' is important but not sufficient. There remain many questions to solve about how to achieve the *central outcome* (e.g., how to reduce the cost to reach teens, how to increase the stickiness of interventions), how to create the *higher-level context* (e.g., what will be required to build more robust communities of design talent in the geographies critical to this work; how can the solutions developed through HCD be shaped to build the support of critical actors in the public sector?), and what should be the *picture of the journey ahead* (e.g., what are the three or four pivotal achievements in this era that would together unlock the next level of resources and capacity to scale?). The emerging strength of the core community of HCD Exchange provides fuel to confront these critical questions.

Conclusion: The power and limits of strategy

The course of work on systems change never did run smoothly. We have rarely seen or designed a strategy that got nearly all of its particulars right. We've seen and lived many instances of strategies arrived at thoughtfully that proved fundamentally wrong because some important dynamic was misunderstood in the conception – or, most often, because history took a different turn from what those shaping strategy imagined. In systems change work, our dreams and plans for a better world come up against our many frailties: limited understanding and limited vision; resources that, however large, are small in relation to the size of the need at hand; organizations and coalitions capable of only a fraction of what the road in front of them will demand. For all this, tough, imaginative and explicit thinking about strategy beats hands down the only alternatives, which are either to double down on whatever we happen to have been doing without a good theory of why this will have the desired effect, or to wander in the directions that beckon, without knowing whether we're pursuing a beacon or a will o' the wisp.

The value of having a just-clear-enough strategy – one that is as explicit about unknowns and unsolved problems as it is about commitments and convictions – manifests at least as much in crisis as in periods of smoother sailing. When surprises and reversals inevitably occur, explicit strategy enables effective reflection: should we revise higher-level beliefs close to the core of strategy or should we simply confront a new and perhaps difficult 'how to' problem that doesn't call the core of strategy into question? If, for instance, results from a few of the early projects applying HCD to adolescent sexual and reproductive health prove disappointing, or efforts to scale dilute the effectiveness of early programs, does this represent a reason to rethink the goal of bending the impact curve and the strategy for doing so – or does it simply point to specific practical challenges that must be overcome, efforts that the framework of a strategy place into context and crystallize into focus?

Good strategies guide us on what to expect, and by doing so, give us the potential to experience *as a* crisis conditions that we otherwise might calmly sail by. For instance, if The Rockefeller Foundation team proved slower in its work to seed demonstration cases of moving the needle on retention of opportunity youth, this would represent a troubling contradiction of its picture of what it would take to graduate from this era – and represent a potential crisis on the road to 'crossing the chasm' and creating sustained demand among large employers to engage with opportunity youth as a talent pool. With a picture of how to change the world, the team would be equipped to perceive the dog that wasn't barking and to reflect on how to interpret this silence.

In 2010, Mark Pollock lay in his hospital bed and formed a clear resolution that he'd find a way for victims of spinal injury to recover function and movement. At that moment, he had no answers and no resources beyond his own resolve. Less than a decade later, he is applying his fierce will to carrying out a training regimen powered by two innovative technologies for which he has raised funds and served as a leading test pilot: an innovative electrical stimulator placed over his spinal cord and a robotic exoskeleton technology. He is the founder of the Mark Pollock Trust, is on the board of the Christopher and Dana Reeves Foundation in the U.S., and an Ambassador for the Wings for Life Foundation in Europe. He has created a public platform, speaking from the TED main stage with his fiancée Simone and establishing Run in the Dark events in cities around the world to fund work in this field. He has built a global network of scientists and technologists, and made connections across disciplinary boundaries that could prove critical to future innovation.

As with all strategies, Mark has made substantive bets and substantive commitments that could prove wrong. We don't know if the path of treatment he has put his weight behind can in fact appreciably restore function and movement to the paralyzed. Even if such progress is in theory possible, links in the chain could fail. The spinal stimulation company or the exoskeleton company could stall out; the training regimens could prove too difficult to adhere to; regulators might not approve the treatments; physicians might not put their weight behind such treatments even if approved. Too many plans that are strategies in name only lack sufficient specificity to risk being wrong – and don't guide action. Good strategies wrestle with the true magnitude of the difficulties at hand, and arrive at the best path those who shape them can craft amidst their frailties and the world's unknowns. Good strategies demand and inspire action, and it is through action that their limitations can be discovered and, with luck and insight, transcended. This is the best we can do to guide the systems change work needed to tackle the significant problems of our time, and it is the least these imperatives deserve.

3 Toward new models of leadership and partnership

Jane Nelson

Jane Nelson is Director of the Corporate Responsibility Initiative at Harvard Kennedy School, and a nonresident senior fellow at Brookings. She was a director and senior advisor at the Prince of Wales International Business Leaders Forum from 1993 to 2012, and has been a senior associate with the Institute for Sustainability Leadership at Cambridge University and a track leader at the Clinton Global Initiative. In 2001, she worked with the United Nations Global Compact in the office of the Secretary-General, Kofi Annan, preparing his report for the General Assembly on cooperation between the UN and business. Prior to 1993, Nelson worked for the World Business Council for Sustainable Development in Africa, for FUNDES in Latin America, and as a Vice President at Citibank working for the bank's Financial Institutions Group in Asia, Europe and the Middle East.

Jane has co-authored five books and over 90 publications on corporate responsibility and public – private partnerships. She serves on the Boards of Directors of Newmont and Chevron's Niger Delta Partnership Initiative and on advisory councils for Bank of America, Abbott, ExxonMobil, the IFC, Pearson's Project Literacy initiative, APCO Worldwide, InterAction and the Rockefeller Foundation's Bellagio Center. She is co-chair of the World Economic Forum's Global Future Council on Food Systems Innovation and a member of the Forum's Stewardship Board for its Food System initiative.

★ ★ ★

The leadership challenge we face is clear – and it is urgent. It will be impossible to eradicate extreme poverty and increase prosperity within our planetary boundaries without fundamentally new approaches to problem-solving; new approaches that transform public policies, markets, and value chains to be more inclusive and sustainable; new approaches that influence the choices and behaviors of citizens and consumers; and new approaches that improve the quality and accessibility of research, innovation, data collection and evidence-based decision-making. There are thousands, if not millions, of projects underway around the world that are experimenting with such efforts. Yet, we are simply not achieving the speed, the scale or the systemic impact that are needed.

Three interconnected levels of leadership and partnership will be essential if we are to have any hope of achieving greater impact toward more inclusive and sustainable development:[1]

- Individual leadership skill sets and mindsets to drive change
- Institutional leadership structures to embed and sustain change
- Interactive or collaborative leadership platforms to accelerate and scale change

Remarkable individuals or small groups of individuals are the initial drivers of change in almost every context and period of history. It is their ability to galvanize others and to institutionalize this change in the structures and mechanisms of government, business and civil society organizations that is essential for sustaining any impact achieved. And it is the ability of both individuals and institutions to build broader, multi-stakeholder coalitions for change that determines whether new approaches are not only sustained, but also achieve more systemic impact at scale.

Increasingly defined as systems leadership, this requires leaders who can cultivate a shared vision for change, empower widespread innovation and action, and enable mutual accountability for progress.[2] Such individual and institutional leaders are needed in government and the public sector more than ever. At the same time, the role of civic, nonprofit and business leaders has grown dramatically in importance over recent decades. Today, they have considerable influence, access to resources and ability to support – or undermine – progress toward more inclusive and sustainable development. And their diverse roles are as important in industrialized economies as they are in emerging markets. As such, systems leadership is needed both within and across organizations, sectors and countries.

This chapter offers some hopeful examples that are emerging in all three levels of leadership and partnership. It concludes with an agenda for action to achieve more sustained and systemic impact in future.

Individual leadership skill sets and mindsets to drive change

The ability to achieve impact almost always starts with an outstanding individual or small group of such individuals. Although specific disciplines and skill sets will vary across different sectors and locations, and depend on the type of challenges that need to be addressed, there are common mind-sets and values that are essential for being an effective systems leader and driving positive change.

In almost any context, efforts to challenge, let alone change, the *status quo* require a combination of curiosity, courage, patience, and persistence. They require people operating within specific organizations or communities to be able to combine technical disciplines and expertise with empathy and strong listening, learning and relationship skills. They depend on the ability to build understanding and trust across traditional boundaries, whether these are disciplinary, sectoral or cultural, together with the skills to develop and sustain alliances both within and between organizations. And always, if the goal is to achieve more inclusive and sustainable development, there must be the questions, "to what purpose?" and "who is included in making the decisions and in sharing the risks and benefits?"[3]

In particular, there is a need for the interconnected and mutually reinforcing pillars of:

- Moral leadership and a commitment to serve the public good
- Inclusive leadership and the empathy to listen and learn from diversity
- Innovative leadership and a readiness to co-create, experiment and adapt
- Accountable leadership and an openness to transparency and evaluation

Moral leadership and a commitment to serve the public good

Moral leadership is the foundation for making a positive and sustained impact in helping to improve people's lives and protect the planet.

The Carnegie Council for Ethics in International Affairs invited participants in its online Global Ethics Network to comment on the question, "What does moral leadership mean to you?" The response from Bida Tamang, a secondary school teacher in Bhutan, captures it well. She states,

> Moral Leadership is a very different kind of leadership. Rather than aspiring to being followed, moral leaders aim to serve. Instead of showcasing their own skills, moral leaders tend to develop the capacities of others. Moral leadership is not about rank – any person holding any position can be a moral leader, but such individuals are always characterized by a deep sense of ethics, are driven by core ideals (such as justice) and are motivated by the pursuit of a higher purpose.[4]

As Jacqueline Novogratz, the Founder and CEO of Acumen, comments in the conclusion to this book

> . . . what separates the solutions that work from those that fail has less to do with the idea or the context in which we invest, be it a stable country or one in post-conflict. It has everything to do with character. Conversely, our failures are too often correlated with betting on entrepreneurs who chose to do what is easy, not right; or they lack moral imagination and curiosity about others; or they lose their resilience and don't stay the course.
>
> The kind of character that leads to success can be summed up in two works: moral leadership. Moral because we need leaders who care about the world, and not just themselves. Leadership to navigate our complex times.[5]

The key point is that anyone can exercise moral leadership. Relatively few of us will be called on to risk our lives as a result, although thousands of courageous people do so around the world every day to defend causes and policies that protect human rights and improve the lives of others. Yet, all of us can be more intentional about and committed to ensuring that moral leadership is the foundation for our decision-making and behaviors on a daily basis.

Beyond the personal responsibility of each individual to exercise moral leadership, professional oaths and voluntary pledges offer a way for diverse and dispersed individuals to build a common sense of purpose, community and mutual accountability to exercise moral leadership. The modern interpretation of the centuries-old Hippocratic oath is one example. While today's doctors do not swear to the original oath, the majority do take an oath to uphold ethical standards in their practice, usually when they graduate from medical school. The Four-Way Test developed almost a century ago by members of Rotary International is another – calling on Rotarians to ask themselves the following questions in all their activities: Is it the truth; is it fair to all concerned; will it build goodwill and better friendships; and will it be beneficial to all concerned? More recent examples are various shared commitments by MBA students to lead in the common interest such as Thunderbird's Oath of Honor, Columbia Business School's Honor Code, and the MBA Oath started by a group of graduating students at Harvard Business School in 2009 and currently supported by signatories from some 250 business schools.[6]

Institutions and networks can also help to provide supportive frameworks and operating environments where their employees or participants are empowered to exercise moral leadership and to hold each other to account for doing so or failing to do so. Frameworks include ethical codes of conduct, values statements, confidential whistle-blowing systems and institutional mechanisms to share good practices in areas such as ethics, safety, and respecting human rights. Yet, as too many examples of bad practice demonstrate in government, business and civic institutions, even the best frameworks on paper can be seriously undermined if the organizational culture or tone from senior leaders contradicts the values being espoused.

Ultimately, no amount of codes of conduct or professional oaths can make a difference if there is not a deep-seated personal commitment to ethics and to doing the right thing even when no one is watching.

While moral leadership is an essential foundation of driving systemic change towards more inclusive and sustainable development, other closely related leadership capabilities are also needed.

Inclusive leadership and the empathy to listen and learn from diversity

With a few notable exceptions, the vast majority of government cabinets and legislative bodies and the majority of corporate and university boards and management teams around the world, and to a lesser extent those of nonprofit organizations, still fail dismally to reflect the diversity of the populations they serve or represent. Related to this, they fail to include diverse voices, views and needs into their deliberative and governance processes and into deciding on where to allocate resources.

This is despite growing evidence and academic research that shows greater diversity and inclusion in government entities, companies, and NGOs improve the quality and rigor of decision-making, stakeholder engagement, and accountability, while also being the fair and morally right thing to do. Extensive research on the benefits of gender diversity offers compelling evidence. While more analysis is needed on other types of diversity, such as nationality, background, discipline, race, religion, age, sexual preference, and income, their positive impact is likely to be similar. This is especially the case when one considers the mutually reinforcing linkages between different types of inclusion and diversity.

In the area of gender diversity, there are hopeful examples of change in all sectors, but there is still a long way to go. In recent years, government leaders from countries as diverse as Ethiopia, Canada, Colombia, Rwanda, and France have made public commitments to achieve gender parity in their cabinets. Such leadership by individual presidents and prime ministers is essential, although experience in other countries, for example the United States since 2016, demonstrate how quickly such efforts can dissipate if they rely on commitments made by an individual leader rather than institutionalized commitments. Despite the progress being made at the legislative level in many governments, according to the Inter-Parliamentary Union, women on average only accounted for 23.4 percent of all parliamentarians in 2017.[7] Analysis of other types of diversity at the leadership levels of public sector institutions would be likely to show even less progress.

Much the same can be said for companies. There is substantially more diversity today at the entry level of most companies, but still not enough in corporate boardrooms and executive management teams, where the key decisions are made and resources allocated. In the 2018 Fortune 500 list of CEOs, for example, only 24 were women.[8] Some national and state governments, such as Norway, Germany, and California, have started to set targets for gender diversity on corporate boards. However, there is a long way to go in most companies and industry sectors to build truly inclusive and diverse workplaces and workforces. Individual leaders will be key to driving progress and impact.

In the absence of laws or direct market incentives, it is voluntary action by individual leaders that drives the organizational culture and sets the incentives to either enable or undermine greater inclusion and diversity. The tone from the top and the role modeling of leaders in government, business, and civil society have a remarkably strong impact on making a difference, whether positive or negative.

At the same time, bottom-up social movements led by outstanding individuals can also drive systemic change and impact. The #MeToo movement, for example, has been crucial in recent years to focusing the attention of public and private sector leaders on the need to tackle the negative impacts of gender harassment and discrimination, and on the opportunity to harness the positive benefits of gender diversity. The civil rights movement in the United States is another inspiring example. In the current polarized political circumstances, it also offers a sobering reminder that the work of individual leaders as champions and advocates for widespread inclusion and diversity throughout society never ends.

In efforts to tackle complex social and environmental challenges, there is also the need for multidisciplinary and multi-stakeholder diversity.

Individual leaders who aim to build coalitions must be effective at understanding the diverse skills and disciplines required to tackle a complex challenge. For example, they must be able to effectively bring together scientists and technologists with financial and business people and with humanitarian and social experts.

They must also be able to map and engage the various stakeholders who need to 'be at the table' to achieve more inclusive and informed decision-making. Most of these stakeholders will come from different sectors and backgrounds, and have little understanding of the motives or contributions of the others. Sometimes there will be active distrust. The leaders convening them must be adept at facilitating dialogue to develop mutual understanding, respect, and trust, before a shared vision can be developed, let alone implemented. This rarely happens at scale without intentional design of more inclusive and diverse processes and institutional structures.

One of the most important types of diversity when it comes to building coalitions for change is the ability to connect and build empathy among grassroots leaders and on-the-ground practitioners with elites and senior level decision-makers and resource allocators. This requires careful management of power dynamics and sustained efforts to ensure that all participants are able to engage as equal and mutually respected partners.

The United Kingdom's Business in the Community organization, for example, operates the Prince's Seeing is Believing program. Established by HRH The Prince of Wales nearly 30 years ago, the program facilitates on-the-ground engagement between business and community leaders through a structured process of experiential learning and opportunities to co-develop solutions and initiatives.[9] Another example is the World Economic Forum's New Vision for Agriculture, which has brought smallholder farmers from Africa and Asia to engage directly with ministers of agriculture, corporate executives and UN officials in a number of its design workshops and programs.

Innovative leadership and a readiness to co-create, experiment and adapt

In order to achieve more inclusive and sustainable development, we urgently need innovation in public policies, institutional arrangements, financing mechanisms, business models, and in technologies, products, and services. None of this is possible without individual innovators.

From scientists, technologists, and academics to politicians, corporate executives, and community activists, we need leaders who have the imagination to see what is possible and whom they need to engage to achieve it. We need leaders who have the courage to take risks in experimenting with new approaches and non-traditional partners, and the persistence to keep trying and adapting. Above all, we need leaders who have the curiosity and empathy to listen, learn, adapt, and understand the needs of others, especially those whose voices and aspirations are often excluded.

As author J. K. Rowling commented when she received an honorary degree at Harvard University,

> Imagination is not only the uniquely human capacity to envision that which is not, and, therefore, the foundation of all invention and innovation. In its arguably most transformative and revelatory capacity, it is the power that enables us to empathize with humans whose experiences we have never shared.[10]

While individual innovators with the above skill sets and mindsets are essential for driving new ideas and approaches, they usually require a multi-stakeholder ecosystem of supporters in order to implement these new models and to achieve impact at scale. As already outlined, it is rare for such an ecosystem to evolve in the absence of intentional and creatively curated design processes that are able to convene, inspire, and mobilize diverse stakeholders to take action. If the achievement of social and environmental progress is a key goal, then these processes must be people-centered and/or planet-centered.

Much progress has been made in the field of human-centered design over the past few decades. As Patrick Frick at Value Web comments,

> At this time in history, we know so much about how humans work (or don't) that we can increase the odds for success. Psychology, sociology, architecture, systems dynamics, social physics, economics – we can draw from these bodies of knowledge to experiment with how we come together to solve problems and grasp opportunities.[11]

Over a ten-year period, Patrick and his colleagues at Value Web have worked with a small team at the World Economic Forum to build the networks and commitments that have underpinned the New Vision for Agriculture (NVA). Together, their teams convened diverse stakeholders from business, government, farmers organizations, and civil society through a series of more than 15 intense and interactive gatherings. These were crucial in building the social fabric or relationships that enabled a shared vision and sense of co-ownership to emerge despite widely differing interests and resources. This in turn led to hundreds of specific commitments and on-the-ground partnerships. NVA currently operates in more than 20 countries, has gained support from more than 650 private and public organizations, engaged more than 1,200 senior leaders and practitioners, and reached millions of smallholding farmers. Yet, the initial vision and impetus came from a tiny group of individuals who saw the potential for institutional innovation and took the personal risks to make it happen.

The Breakthrough Energy Coalition inspired by Bill Gates offers another example of a few individual innovators who have come together to build a multi-stakeholder platform for change. Since 2015, Gates has worked with 28 fellow high-net worth investors to build a team of financial, energy, transportation, agricultural, buildings, and manufacturing innovators alongside governments, corporations, and financial institutions. Their goal is to improve access to reliable and affordable energy, food, goods, and service without emitting more greenhouse gases through investing public and private resources into new technologies.

Underpinning the coalition's activities is what they describe as their 'Landscape of Innovation' – which maps out an ecosystem of grand challenges and specific scientific pathways or technical quests, and then a combination of public investments, scientific research, companies, products, and private investors that are needed to advance progress in each of these technical quests. While still relatively new, the coalition illustrates how individual innovators with convening power can build a comprehensive ecosystem of actors to achieve systemic change.

The development of the 100,000 Opportunities Initiative outlined by Niko Canner in Chapter 2 offers another compelling example of an emergent design process aimed at convening diverse stakeholders to influence systemic change. Supported by leading foundations alongside more than 20 companies, and facilitated by the collective impact team at FSG, this initiative aims to create innovative new pathways to employment for unemployed American youth. To date, they have jointly implemented programs in a variety of demonstration cities, hosted catalytic events and built an employer-led learning coalition.

There are common lessons in these three different examples of small groups of people who have built networks or ecosystems for innovation: first, the crucial role of individual innovators who are able to convene and inspire others to take action; second, the intentional use of emergent design or systems design methodologies, drawing on inclusive and human-centered design processes that are experiential, generative, and iterative in nature (such approaches often require experienced facilitators or backbone organizations that can work with participants both individually and collectively over an extended period of time); third, the flexibility to adapt and course-correct as the processes and participants evolve and new approaches are tested that are either proven to work or not; and fourth, the importance of building a sense of co-ownership among participants so that each supports innovation according to their capabilities and so that they hold each other mutually accountable for results.

Accountable leadership and an openness to transparency and evaluation

Trust in political and business leaders remains low. The Edelman Trust Barometer has tracked trust in and credibility of leaders across sectors in more than 20 countries for the past 18 years. The 2018 Trust Barometer concluded that the general public in 20 out of 28 countries distrust their leaders.[12] In an era of fake news and social media – driven information bubbles or echo chambers where people are able to restrict what they hear and learn and thereby reinforce their own views and prejudices, there is also an alarming growth in distrust of information. This includes information provided by what have been traditionally regarded as reputable news media.

The onus is increasingly on individual leaders and institutions at all levels of society to be more transparent about their failures as well as successes, and to be open to independent evaluation. This is easier said than done, especially in the context of high levels of mistrust and political polarization and increasingly competitive markets and political cycles. Yet, it must be a focus for any leader who aims to achieve social impact.

Despite skepticism of scientific data and evidence among a substantial number of the general public in many countries, ongoing efforts are needed by individual leaders to collect and share such data. This includes finding ways to make complex scientific data on topics such as climate change, rising non-communicable diseases, nutrition, and the employment implications of digital technologies more relevant and directly connected to people's lives.

Developing mechanisms whereby citizens can participate more proactively in monitoring the performance of their political, business, and civic leaders is another way to raise levels of transparency and accountability. Technology can play a useful role in enabling such participatory monitoring to occur.

Civicus, the global alliance of civil society organizations, which has more than 4,000 members in some 175 countries, has developed a Participatory Governance toolkit for use by citizens and civil society organizations. The Initiative for Equality is another example of a network of activists and civil society organizations in more than 130 countries that is spreading the concept and the practice of Participatory Monitoring and Accountability.

There is also an urgent need for individual leaders, including at the level of local communities and cities, to convene conversations among citizens of different backgrounds and beliefs to better understand different perspectives, explore areas of shared interests and responsibilities, and be more accountable for results.

At an institutional level, the heads of government departments and companies can also make a more concerted effort to increase their levels of transparency and accountability. This can range from regular, independently verified reports and evaluations on social, economic, and environmental performance to the establishment of grievance mechanisms and citizen or stakeholder advisory panels. It is rare for any of these mechanisms to be established without support from the top, and the active engagement of individual leaders who believe strongly in the importance of their personal and institutional accountability.

Institutional leadership structures to embed and sustain change

Individual leaders who are moral, inclusive, innovative, and accountable are essential for setting the tone for change and acting as champions and role models for that change. Yet, individual leaders come and go. Their influence waxes and wanes. It is their ability to galvanize others and to institutionalize change in the structures and mechanisms of government, business, and civil society organizations that are essential for sustaining any impact achieved. In short, two of the most important legacies that any individual leader can leave in achieving social impact are through inspiring many other people to take action and through embedding new models into institutional structures and mechanisms that can sustain change over the longer term.

What do such institutional structures and mechanisms look like in practice? To a certain extent they will vary across different sectors, such as government, business, and civil society. Yet, in all cases they involve the creation of structures, mechanisms, and incentives that are dedicated to embedding and sustaining more responsible, innovative, and accountable practices.

In governments, for example, they include the setting of public goals and targets for more diverse executive and legislative bodies, such as the governments of Rwanda, Ethiopia, Canada, and Norway have done in establishing gender targets. A number of governments are also establishing cross-ministerial working groups to address key sustainability challenges. In Peru, for example, the 2030 Water Resources Group is supported by a coalition of five different government ministers ranging from environment to energy and mining. Governments can also create multi-stakeholder consultation processes to engage business and civil society more systematically in contributing to policies for sustainable development. A number of them are developing national action plans and public campaigns to support global frameworks such as the Sustainable Development Goals (SDGs), the Paris Climate Agreement, and the UN Guiding Principles on Business and Human Rights. A growing number of regional and national governments are also requiring companies to publicly disclose their social and environmental performance, ranging from initiatives such as the EU's Corporate Responsibility Directive to the Modern Slavery Acts in the UK and Australia.

A few pioneering governments have also set up or supported the establishment of national or global challenge funds for cross-sector innovation in a variety of social and environmental issues. In the UK, for example, the government was instrumental in establishing Big Society Capital, following a pledge by the prime minister in 2010 to use dormant account money in British banks and building societies to make new finance available to dynamic social organizations. Big Society Capital was launched in 2012 as a private sector entity independent of government with a trust governance structure. Grand Challenges Canada is another example. Established in 2010, it is funded by the Canadian government and now other partners, with the explicit goal of funding innovators in low- and middle-income countries and in Canada that address a variety of social and environmental issues by integrating science and technology with social and business innovation. To date, it has supported a pipeline of over 1,000 innovations in 95 countries, with the estimated potential to save some 1.6 million lives and improve 35 million lives by 2030. Similar initiatives to scale social innovation are underway with direct support from the U.S., Danish, Dutch, and Australian governments, to name a few.

In companies, institutional leadership to drive social and environmental change includes a variety of models from the boardroom to stakeholder engagement initiatives. Examples include boards of directors hiring directors with social, environmental, and community expertise and establishing board committees that are focused on addressing these issues. CERES and the World Economic Forum, for example, have developed useful tool kits and good practices for climate-competent boards. Companies can also be more explicit and strategic about identifying and then integrating material social and environmental risks and opportunities into their corporate strategies and risk management systems, making these a core pillar of strategy rather than an add-on. Unilever's Sustainable Living Plan, Bank of America's Responsible Growth Strategy, Nestlé's Creating Shared Value framework, and Royal Dutch Shell's commitment to halve its carbon footprint by 2050 are all examples.

A growing number of companies are creating cross-functional working groups and decision-making teams that include both business unit leaders and functional leaders to drive social and environmental change. They are also developing internal incentives and accountability processes for driving social performance through their executive compensation and reporting activities. Many are becoming more ambitious and strategic about supporting employee diversity, inclusion and engagement through changing their human resource policies and practices, establishing employee resource or affinity groups and community engagement councils, and creating internal social venture finds and award programs for employees who are driving social change. A small vanguard of companies is also setting up external stakeholder engagement mechanisms, such as advisory councils, community participatory monitoring initiatives and grievance mechanisms.

Civil society organizations and research and educational institutions are also developing similar structures to achieve more multidisciplinary and multi-stakeholder approaches to learning and problem-solving. They are exploring market-based approaches and new alliances with the private sector, while at the same time working to balance this with the need to remain independent of corporate interests in their governance and decision-making. They are also experimenting with new technologies and engagement mechanisms to ensure better understanding and representation of the communities they represent – from low-income households to students – and to give these communities a stronger voice and 'place at the table' when it comes to decision-making.

In short, new institutional leadership models are emerging in every sector aimed at embedding and sustaining social impact and being more inclusive, innovative, and accountable in achieving this goal. Yet, it is still a small vanguard of pioneers who are making these changes. While these institutional pioneers are demonstrating what is possible, much more concerted effort is needed by more institutions in the public, private, and civic sectors.

Interactive or collaborative leadership platforms to accelerate and scale change

Outstanding individual and institutional leadership are necessary but not sufficient. Efforts by individuals and even institutions to drive scale and systemic impact in achieving more inclusive and sustainable development are often impeded by governance gaps. These range from inappropriate or insufficient policies and regulations or lack of political will to repressive regimes, conflict, and corruption. Market failures are another obstacle to large-scale system change. Examples include the lack of a price on carbon and other vital natural resources as well as failure by the global capital markets to reward good social and environmental performance by companies or to penalize bad performance. Cultural or social norms and behaviors may also be an obstacle to achieving large-scale impact among citizens and consumers in the drive toward greater inclusion, diversity, and sustainability.

Few of these obstacles can be overcome without concerted and collective effort by interested stakeholders – preferably in large numbers and on a multi-stakeholder or cross-sector basis.

The following three types of collective action can be especially effective in driving policymakers, markets, norms, and behaviors towards more inclusive and sustainable development:[13]

- Collective action to spread responsible values, norms, and standards
- Collective action to catalyze innovation and investment
- Collective action to advocate for progressive policy reform

Collective action to spread responsible values, norms, and standards

Global frameworks such as the Universal Declaration on Human Rights, the Sustainable Development Goals and the Paris Climate Agreement provide an essential foundation for promoting and implementing shared global values, norms, and standards at national and local levels. Alongside global treaties negotiated and implemented by governments, there are growing examples of multi-stakeholder platforms aimed at providing a voluntary mechanism for spreading more responsible practices by companies, civil society organizations, and in certain cases governments. In some situations, these are a response to public governance gaps. In others, they are a complement to government efforts to regulate and incentivize systemic change in markets or in public behaviors on social and environmental issues.

Examples of a few well-established multi-stakeholder platforms with these objectives, which have been in existence for a number of years and have undergone independent evaluations include:

- *Improving human rights, social, and environmental performance in consumer goods, electronics, and apparel supply chains:* The Fair Labor Association; the Ethical Trading Initiative; the Global Network Initiative; the Better Work program; the Bangladesh Accord and Alliance initiatives; and the ACT (Action, Collaboration, Transformation) initiative on living wages.
- *Improving natural resource governance and impact on people and the environment:* The Extractives Industries Transparency Initiative; the Voluntary Principles

on Security and Human Rights; Marine and Forest Stewardship Councils; the 2030 Water Resources Group; and a number of commodity-specific certification programs in agriculture, forestry, and minerals.

- *Tackling corruption and money laundering:* The Partnering Against Corruption Initiative hosted by the World Economic Forum; Transparency International's sector and country-based Integrity Pacts, especially in large-scale construction, infrastructure development, and public procurement; and the Wolfsberg Group (a coalition of major banks focused on developing frameworks and guidance to tackle financial crimes).

Collective action to catalyze innovation and investment

A growing number of multi-stakeholder coalitions are being established with the primary goal of mobilizing financing from public and private sources, increasingly called blended finance, alongside expertize and other resources to meet crucial sustainable development needs. Collective action has been particularly strong in efforts to improve the productivity, incomes, livelihoods, and resilience of low-income producers and to improve access to health, food security, nutrition, energy, education, training, technology, and financial inclusion.

Some well-known examples, most of which have been independently evaluated, include:

- *Health and nutrition:* GAVI – the vaccine alliance; the Global Fund to Fight AIDS, Tuberculosis and Malaria; the Global Alliance for Improved Nutrition; Scaling Up Nutrition; and a number of other disease specific or population-specific global health funds (for example, Medicines for Malaria Venture, the TB Alliance and TB Accelerator, and Every Women Every Child).
- *Biodiversity, food, agriculture, and forestry:* The Global Environment Facility; the New Vision for Agriculture; the New Alliance for Food Security and Nutrition; Alliance for a Green Revolution in Africa; the Tropical Forest Alliance; and commodity-specific value-chain coalitions, such as the World Cocoa Foundation, Aquaculture Stewardship Council, Better Cotton Initiative, Roundtable on Sustainable Biofuels, Global Roundtable on Sustainable Beef, Roundtable on Sustainable Soy, and Bonsucro.
- *Clean water and sanitation, energy access, and infrastructure:* Sustainable Energy for All; the Global Infrastructure Facility; the Global Alliance for Clean Cook Stoves; the Global Water Partnership; the 2030 Water Resources Group; and Power Africa.
- *Financial and digital inclusion:* The Consultative Group to Assist the Poorest; the Better Than Cash Alliance; the Alliance for Affordable Internet.
- *Humanitarian assistance:* NetHope; Logistics Emergency Team; Partnership for Quality Medical Donations.

Collective action to advocate for progressive policy reform

A third type of collective action that is becoming increasingly important in efforts to accelerate and scale systemic change is coalitions focused on advocacy. These are coalitions where civil society and business leaders are joining forces, either in their individual or institutional capacities, to advocate for progressive policy reforms, or to change public attitudes and behaviors.[14]

Ultimately, large-scale and sustained impact on social and environmental issues is unlikely to be achieved without effective government interventions, whether in the form of policies, laws and regulations, fiscal incentives, or public sector investment and procurement vehicles. There is a growing need for sub-national government entities, companies, NGOs, and academic institutions to join forces to advocate for greater government leadership on these issues.

In particular, in the current era of political polarization, populism, and fake news, there is a need for leaders in civil society and business to step up and speak out publicly for the causes and for the policies that they believe can make a positive impact on people's lives, especially on the lives of people who do not have the same public voice or ability to influence policymakers that civic and business leaders have. In some cases, there is also a need to publicly challenge certain government policies or practices that undermine the core values of inclusion, diversity, social justice, and environmental sustainability.

Such public advocacy positions can be difficult and politically risky for individuals and even institutions to undertake alone, no matter how influential they are. There is great potential to share the risks of public advocacy, to amplify the voices for such advocacy, and to increase overall influence by working collectively.

There are a number of successful and long-term advocacy alliances in the area of global health. The 30-year commitment to eradicate polio, led by Rotary International and supported by the United Nations and Gates Foundation, among many others, is probably one of the best examples of a successful global advocacy campaign. Its success has depended not only on targeted advocacy with key national governments, ministers of health and inter-governmental organizations, but also on the fact that the advocacy campaign has been anchored by on-the-ground action and innovation, and enabled by a network of tens of thousands of local Rotary Clubs and hundreds of thousands of volunteers, working in partnership with others.

Other global health coalitions such as GAVI – the Vaccine Alliance, the Global Fund to Fight AIDS, Tuberculosis and Malaria, and the London Declaration for Neglected Tropical Diseases have strong public advocacy platforms, anchored by on-the-ground implementation.

A number of pioneering coalitions have also emerged in the area of climate change. They include the We Mean Business coalition, which is a business-led coalition initially focused on providing a common and progressive business voice to support the Paris Climate Agreement. This coalition, among others, was instrumental in establishing the We Are Still In campaign in the United States after the federal government withdrew from the Paris Climate Agreement. This is a network of state governments, mayors, corporations, universities, and civil society organizations that have all made specific commitments to action, supported by data collection and analysis of their progress. They aim to provide both evidence and advocacy for ongoing American leadership in the global climate agenda, despite the absence of presidential leadership.

A final example of multi-stakeholder collective action to advocate for progressive policies is the U.S. Global Leadership Coalition. This is a network that brings together leaders from more than 500 companies and nonprofit development organizations, as well as retired military generals and state-level chapters. Together, they are making a collective case for the U.S. government to sustain its commitment to international development assistance. Learning from the model and effectiveness of this U.S.-focused advocacy coalition, a similar alliance has also been established in the United Kingdom called the Coalition for Global Prosperity.

These collective action leadership platforms are not without their critics and challenges. Not surprisingly, they are the most challenging types of partnership to build and sustain. They face particular challenges in terms of governance and accountability, especially given the power dynamics that are often involved and the combination of public sector resources with potential private sector benefits. They are also operationally challenging to manage and usually require a backbone organization or intermediary to facilitate alignment, mediation, communication, and coordination of the many participants and levels of engagement.

Despite these challenges, emerging evidence suggests that they offer high potential to drive the type of transformational or systemic change that is needed. This is especially the case with those that target a specific sector and/or a clearly defined set of sustainability goals, and that cover a range of both market interventions and financing mechanisms with public policy engagement and advocacy.

Conclusion: An agenda for collective action

The year 2015 marked one of history's high points in multilateralism and international cooperation with the signing of the Sustainable Development Goals and the Paris Climate Agreement by over 190 nations in each case. These two global agreements, together with the longstanding Universal Declaration on Human Rights (UDHR), provide a shared framework for norm setting and practical action around the world. This framework is fundamental for good governance. Implementation and accountability should be a core responsibility of national governments everywhere, while at the same time being increasingly relevant for sub-national public entities, such as states and cities, as well as civil society organizations and business.

There are few countries in the world that come close to achieving the aspirations of the UDHR, the SDGs and the Paris Agreement, and in too many places the direction of change is going backward. Growing empirical evidence points to many environmental indicators that are continuing to deteriorate, from climate change to water insecurity and biodiversity loss. Technological disruption is happening at a speed and scale that is unprecedented, with the potential for both benefits to human progress and serious dislocation between those who can effectively harness technology versus those who cannot. In addition, due to a combination of rising inequality, fears about job losses due to technology disruption and globalization, distrust in established institutions, and populist politics, we are witnessing a rise in nationalism and tribalism. In turn, these are creating a threat to democracy and global economic integration.

There is much to be concerned about. Yet, the UDHR, the SDGs, and the Paris Agreement, and what they should mean for people every day in every place, must remain our 'North Star'; our vision for what is possible with the right leadership and partnerships. More than ever, we need to work together to support, promote, mobilize, and develop leaders who not only understand these societal transformations and the risks and opportunities that they create, but who can also bring together the necessary stakeholders and resources to help address them. Four areas of action are particularly important:

First, our schools and universities must do a better job at educating future leaders who have some of the individual characteristics outlined and illustrated throughout this book, and who will be able to lead institutions in all sectors that aim to be more responsible, inclusive, innovative, and accountable.

Second, companies, governments, and NGOs should become more creative, inclusive, and diverse in their hiring practices and their employee training and volunteer programs. They should identify and support the social and environmental intrapreneurs within their ranks, and empower their employees to establish innovation networks and affinity groups. They should explore opportunities for exchanges and experiential learning programs across sectors and traditional boundaries.

Third, public donors and private foundations should place a greater emphasis on finding, funding, and promoting the systems leaders who display the right combination of moral, inclusive, innovative, and accountable leadership – and supporting them both individually as well as through their institutions. They should also explore ways to work together in establishing and scaling innovation funds and facilities.

And fourth, some of the collective action or multi-stakeholder initiatives that are currently operating at a global level should explore ways to replicate their models at national and city or regional levels, in terms of both governance structures as well as resource mobilization and implementation.

In all cases, there is the need for us to be more ambitious about developing systems leadership at the individual, institutional, and collective levels. There are many good examples to illustrate what is needed and what works. These efforts must now be accelerated and scaled to achieve the type of impact that will support more inclusive and sustainable development for more people around the world.

4 Measuring for insight

A new paradigm for measurement in the social sector

Fay Twersky

Fay Twersky is the Director of Effective Philanthropy at the William and Flora Hewlett Foundation. The team, which she shaped and launched in 2012, guides strategy, evaluation and organization learning within the Hewlett Foundation, and also leads grantmaking in support of organizational effectiveness and a strong philanthropic sector. Fay spent 2010–2011 working in Jerusalem, advising Yad Hanadiv (The Rothschild Family Foundation) on issues of strategy and organization. She served for four years as director and member of the leadership team of the Bill and Melinda Gates Foundation, designing and developing the impact planning and improvement division. She was also a founding principal of BTW (now Informing Change), a strategic consulting firm.

Fay is a frequent author and commentator on trends in philanthropy. Her publications include the 2014 Stanford Social Innovation Review article 'The Artful Juggler,' on what it takes to be a successful foundation CEO, as well as Listening to Those Who Matter Most, the Beneficiaries *and* A Guide to Actionable Measurement. *This chapter builds on her many different roles and experiences in the sector and her passion for making measurement relevant to the people and communities we are seeking to benefit through nonprofit and philanthropic efforts. She serves on the boards of The Center for Effective Philanthropy and the UBS Optimus Foundation in Zurich, Switzerland. She is one of the founders and co-chair of the Fund for Shared Insight. Fay holds two bachelor's degrees in Middle Eastern Studies and Rhetoric, with high honors, from the University of California, Berkeley, and a master's degree in City Planning from the Massachusetts Institute of Technology.*

* * *

People enter the social sector to make a meaningful, positive difference in the world.[1] It is almost a job requirement that they bring passion and conviction to their work. Such passion is essential to achieving impact. But, that same passion necessitates ongoing measurement – to ensure that we are appropriately challenging our strongly held beliefs about how and whether change happens, and to ensure that we are learning along the way.

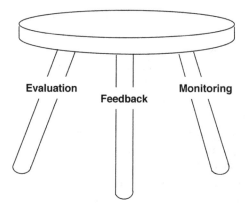

Figure 4.1 The new measurement stool

When it comes to the measurement of impact in the social sector, there have been two complementary pillars for the last 50 years: Monitoring and Evaluation, or 'M&E.' Monitoring is the routine data collection and analysis conducted by an organization about its own activities and progress. Evaluation typically means the kind of systematic data collection and analysis conducted by an independent third party to assess how and to what extent goals or objectives are achieved.

M&E are necessary to any effort to achieve impact, but insufficient, as I hope to make clear. We need to add a new leg of the measurement stool in the social sector – one that adds more balance and is more human-centered. The leg is 'F' for the 'feedback' leg of the measurement stool. I know, I know: there are lots of claims of 'new-ness' in the nonprofit world that really aren't new, just old ideas dressed up for a new party. And in truth, this new leg is the product of evolution – a cycle of try and try again until you get it right. So, let me begin with a brief history of measurement in the social sector. This is a history as seen through my eyes and experience, and so it may be incomplete, but serves the purpose of explaining why I have reached the conclusion that we are ready for a new measurement paradigm.

A brief history of measurement

The field of evaluation came into being in the 1960s, largely to assess the effectiveness of government funded social programs. In the '60s and '70s, the U.S. federal government funded large independent field studies often conducted by social science researchers at universities or independent research institutes, using largely quantitative methods. When I began my career in the late 1980s, the evaluation field was still largely government funded and focused on accountability. The animating value for the field at the time was that independent evaluators use dispassionate technical skills to offer independent, objective assessments of merit.

Evaluators wanted their efforts to add value to programs, to help them improve. They were honing their technical skills and desperately wanted to contribute to understanding – not just whether something worked or not – but what made for successful programs. They wanted to make a difference and they wanted to matter. But oftentimes, there was a bit of an adversarial relationship between nonprofit practitioners and evaluators. Practitioners often felt judged and misunderstood, and it seemed to me that the evaluation field suffered from an inferiority complex, because evaluators were typically invited late to the table and their evaluation reports were often put up on a shelf and not used.

I suspect part of the problem with evaluation in the early days was a result of a disconnect between different stages of program planning. Evaluation designs were often based on strategies or program descriptions that had been written many months earlier and were out of date. This was true both for government funded programs and later, for foundation funded efforts. Here is a typical scenario I faced in my early days as an evaluator: a nonprofit or foundation leader would call me to inquire about commissioning an evaluation for their work. I asked them to send me the description of the program they were interested in having evaluated so I could review it before we met to discuss. At our meeting, I would say something like, "I read your write-up and before we talk about an evaluation design, can you tell me if this is what you are now doing in your program?" And the staff person would inevitably say something like, "Well, not exactly." They would go on to explain that they had made changes to accommodate this factor or that one, or that their timing had changed, or, quite often, that they were being unrealistic in terms of their expectations for progress.

This kind of mismatch between evaluation design and program implementation led to an important development in the field in the 1990s – a more integrated approach to strategy and measurement. Enlightened evaluators realized that everything begins with strategy – and they developed the term of art 'theory of change.' A theory of change is a clear articulation of the change you are seeking, how you expect to achieve that change, the key assumptions underlying those expectations, and the short-term outcomes you expect to achieve along the way. Theories of change have had many permutations, but at their core they provide a kind of roadmap for strategy and measurement to follow hand in hand. It was now that evaluators began to routinely use these theories of change and their more labor-intensive cousin 'the logic model' to guide development of M&E plans. These more integrated plans led evaluators to use both formative and summative approaches meaning they were contributing to the development of programs as they were forming and they were also summing up results about successes and shortcomings at the end of a program or period of implementation. This important shift made evaluation more relevant in the nonprofit world.

The 1990s also marked a surge in bringing business thinking and MBA students into the social sector, particularly in the field of social entrepreneurship. This catalyzed some new trends as well. First, social entrepreneurs were somewhat obsessed with 'metrics,' a vague term that means different things to different people, but in general refers to a robust internal monitoring system. These monitoring systems were designed for organizations to collect lots of data about the frequency and intensity of their services, and about the characteristics of those they were serving. These systems were aided by the development of better and more ubiquitous technology, enabling more organizations to track their own data, especially with quantitative measures.

A related development of the time, one with which I was personally involved, was the push to measure 'Social Return on Investment' (SROI). For many, this was simply a term of art with no distinctive definition. The Roberts Enterprise Development Fund (REDF), however, was a trailblazer on SROI. REDF supported nonprofit enterprises – like landscaping, commercial bakeries, silk screening shops and the like – seeking to create both social benefit through employing vulnerable populations and generate financial returns to support their social programs (what is commonly referred to as a 'double bottom line'). As an independent third party, I led REDF's evaluation efforts for over a decade and during that time we developed a robust data collection to track a range of outcomes like income, employment, housing stability, use of welfare supports, educational attainment, self-esteem, and more. This was unique because we were not just counting exposures – we were calculating results. We used these data to calculate a sophisticated SROI that estimated the savings to society each social enterprise was producing. It was an exciting time and a heady affair. We prepared the equivalent of stock reports for each organization in the REDF portfolio, integrating the M&E data into a short report that summarized in a number the dollars returned to society for each dollar socially invested.

This period in evaluation history was a generative one. It inspired new foundations and nonprofits to invest in measurement systems of various stripes and engendered a lot of enthusiasm and a proliferation of software, frameworks, pilot initiatives, and new organizations devoted to evaluation. But, it also came with a downside which was an emphasis on demonstrating success, and too often demonstrating success came at the expense of learning for improvement. REDF offered a bit of a lesson in this regard as the 'stock' reports looked great and reflected well on the participating nonprofit enterprises but they didn't much inform program decisions. The underlying data were useful both at the enterprise and portfolio levels but the SROI measure turned out to be a bit for show and to demonstrate success with respect to cost-effectiveness. In truth, it had limited utility in day-to-day decision-making.

In terms of the emphasis on demonstrating success, there is one experience I will never forget. I was working with a large nonprofit in San Francisco on a significant evaluation project. The evaluation was funded by a foundation and the evaluation findings were intended to inform funding decisions. I worked closely with the nonprofit CEO and his leadership team to clarify the strategy, the evaluation design, the data collection tools, and analysis plan. The evaluation was to be independent but in good alignment with program goals, approach, and expected outcomes. During a planning meeting, the CEO was talking about future programming plans that to me sounded like he was assuming the evaluation results would be positive. I turned to him and asked, "What will you do if the evaluation shows negative results?" Without skipping a beat, the CEO said, "I will question your methods." I was shocked, not just at the brazen admission that he expected to demonstrate success at all costs (after all, it is the cheapest of tricks to question methods when you don't like the results), but also that he could make such a claim after collaborating so closely on the choice of methods in the evaluation design.

This kind of relentless questioning of evaluation's methodological credibility led to the emergence of increasingly rigorous methods to generate more certainty about what works, in particular the proliferation of Randomized Controlled Trials (RCTs). In the 1990s and into the early 2000s, RCTs earned the moniker 'the gold standard' of impact evaluation because they were designed to determine causality. Simply put, social scientists borrowed from the medical field to design controlled experiments where people were randomly selected to participate in a treatment or a control group and by measuring both over time, researchers could isolate effects and determine attribution – that is, if those who received the treatment changed in desired ways more than those who did not receive the treatment, then one can conclude that the treatment, or the program in the case of development, was causing the change. RCTs had been deployed in the social sector since the 1960s and especially in the 1970s when MDRC (formerly the Manpower Demonstration Research Corporation) began using the methodology, but they really took off during the early 2000s, attracting much greater attention and resources, especially on the global stage where there had been a long history of failed development projects. Development professionals and global funders were feeling urgency to get beyond stories and wanted greater certainty about how to deploy resources to achieve results.

RCTs and the push for greater certainty came with its own up- and downsides. On the upside, RCTs did help to shed light on programs that were working and those that were failing. Policymakers and funders were increasingly paying attention to those results. On the downside, not all programs or interventions lent themselves well to an RCT either for practical or ethical reasons and those efforts were sometimes critiqued or undervalued as 'unproven.' Also, RCTs at that time often did not include measures to understand why an intervention worked or didn't which made them less useful when thinking about replication in the real world.

Pitting themselves against the primacy of RCTs was a new class of evaluators who brought what they considered to be a more holistic approach to evaluation, especially to evaluation of complex systems change efforts. This led to an unfortunate period of 'evaluation wars,' including attacks on evaluator quality and integrity. There were a group of evaluators, led by Michael Quinn Patton, who argued against RCTs as the ubiquitous gold standard, making the argument that not all programs are meant to be fixed and studied in a static format. Many programs are intended to evolve and develop over time in a continuous fashion, he argued. He coined the term 'developmental evaluation' as a new line of practice that is almost the opposite of RCTs. Developmental evaluation involves an independent evaluator providing more real time flexible measurement for programs that are meant to be constantly evolving, often working in complex systems where the context is changing and so too must the programmatic approach. This developmental evaluation approach in some ways helped set the table for this third leg of the measurement stool.

In this admittedly oversimplified history, there is one clear theme that shines through all the permutations of evaluation and monitoring: the pursuit of technical relevance. Since the earliest days, with only good intentions, evaluation and monitoring have been largely focused on methods, frameworks, systems, tools, and analytic accuracy. These are obviously important and in many respects, they have matured and strengthened over time. The evaluation field has become more nuanced with new approaches to answer a wider array of questions about outcomes, impact, and the key features that enable or inhibit change. And monitoring has also developed, aided by technology, to collect information about who is being served, with what level of frequency and intensity, and even sometimes short-term outcomes – to be more useful in real-time decision-making.

The evolution all made sense at the time and I didn't realize what was missing from this picture until the mid-2000s.

The third leg of the stool

It was a grey autumn late afternoon in Seattle. I was sitting at my desk, lost in thought about how I would go about the job I had just stepped into. I had moved my family from California up to Seattle and my children were starting at new schools. I had signed on to help the Bill & Melinda Gates Foundation build a brand-new team – Impact Planning and Improvement. This was a pivotal moment for the young Gates Foundation. Warren Buffett just made his famous pledge to double the foundation's giving, from $2 billion to $4 billion per year, compelling the fast-growing Gates Foundation to be even more strategic in its results orientation. Inspired by Buffett's gift, Patty Stonesifer, the foundation's CEO, decided it was time to launch a team that would help bring more shape and discipline to how all foundation programs practiced strategy and measured results.

I had come into the role confident about the strategy and measurement components. I had spent my career advising foundations and nonprofits on ways to achieve impact and how to engage in purpose-driven measurement. That is not to say that it was easy. The Gates Foundation was a complex organization with great ambition and global reach. But still, I had a sense of the steps to take to build a strategy life cycle for the foundation and associated measurement efforts.

But there was also a third remit for this new team – 'hearing from outside voices.' This was a new piece of the puzzle. Why outside voices, and which voices matter? And, how should we listen? The foundation was excellent at hearing from experts. And, it felt like we were making slow but steady progress on hearing from grantees, too. But, as I was sitting in my office in that late afternoon light, nestled in the picturesque Pacific Northwest, thinking about the foundation's grantmaking all over the world, I had a feeling in the pit of my stomach that we were far away from all the people and communities we were seeking to help. And that feeling led me to the realization that those were the outside voices we were missing. I had a strong intuition that we needed to hear from the students in the schools we were funding to reform, from the smallholder farmers whose yields we were hoping to improve, and from the women who wanted to better plan for their families and their futures. I wasn't sure what we would learn, but I was pretty sure we would learn some new things.

That insight led me to explore different ways to listen, systematically and authentically to the people and communities we are seeking to help with our funding, products, and services. This journey of listening began with a student voice initiative at the Gates Foundation, beginning in 2007, to understand the student experience of the small schools the foundation was supporting. I realized that by that time, the foundation had invested in more than 2,500 small schools across the nation and had collected a lot of data about those schools. Some were traditional monitoring data the foundation gathered directly from the schools, like numbers of students, matriculation, and graduation rates. The foundation also commissioned independent evaluations including many RCTs, to understand the impact that small schools were having on students. But, none of that included asking how students were experiencing the schools. On the face of it, that was stunning. Would a customer-facing business never ask its customers for feedback? Of course not. The fact that a business tracks inventory and profit and loss is great but those measures are not the same as customer feedback. The foundation was collecting the equivalent of profit and loss data but no customer feedback. We knew that not all schools were succeeding at closing the achievement gap but we had never asked the students themselves to gain insight into *why*. We decided to experiment with the ask.

Our initiative started small, with 20 schools to test the feasibility of student feedback. It grew to become Youth Truth, a premier student feedback survey in the nation, and is ably run out of the Center for Effective Philanthropy. It includes questions to get at things like, did the students feel: safe? Challenged academically? Supported by their teachers? Bullied by their peers? Did they experience discipline, and was it practiced fairly?

That initial experiment showed that asking students for feedback was not only feasible; it was also useful to the schools that participated. There were a few key ingredients to this early student feedback experiment that came to exemplify what we now call a high-quality feedback loop:

1   Framing simple questions for the students to understand
2   Benchmarking the data for one school with a comparison set of schools to help with interpretation
3   Sharing the data with both teachers and students – to get their ideas on interpretation and applying the ideas in practice
4   Closing the loop about what actions were taken as a result of the feedback

Scott High School in Taylor Mill, Kentucky participated in Youth Truth early on. The high school had very poor Youth Truth ratings from the students. Their scores ranked near the bottom percentile on many questions. But the result that haunted the principal, Dr Brennan Sapp, was the question "Do your teachers care about you?" His school rated on the bottom one percentile for that question! It was an upsetting finding that gave Dr Sapp, as a new and passionate leader, the push he needed to make changes to the school culture. His reflection is

> Youth Truth gave us the proof and the hard facts that we could not argue with. That's how the students felt and because it was comparative with schools around the country, it was even more of a hit. And there were schools in the district that were doing better than us.[2]

Youth Truth gave Dr Sapp the ammunition he needed to make changes to the way teachers engaged with students. And, it made a difference. He took a variety of steps to improve culture and student outcomes and in short order, reduced the student failure rate from a high of 24 percent to just 5 percent.

Listening to students is the right thing to do because you gain insights you wouldn't otherwise have as demonstrated by the Scott High School experience. But we also now know through the Gates-funded Measures of Effective Teaching study that student perceptions are in fact predictive of student outcomes. If a school can know early on whether a student is on the right track simply by asking them a few questions, that can be hugely helpful in informing teaching and classroom management. It can also help inform funders of education reform to know whether those efforts are on track. So, getting feedback from students is not just the right thing to do; it also the smart thing to do.

The Youth Truth experience set me on a path to explore more ways to systematically hear from nonprofit customers. And I have seen the incredible power that comes from a more balanced approach to measurement in the sector, one that includes a third leg of the nonprofit measurement stool. This third leg, as a complement to evaluation and monitoring, is 'feedback.'

Feedback, simply put, is distinctly focused on the 'customer experience.' Feedback involves systematically soliciting, listening, and responding to the experiences of the nonprofit clients, participants, and customers about their perceptions of a service or product.[3] By listening to nonprofit customers about their experiences, preferences, and ideas, we gain unique insights that we would otherwise have no way of knowing. And, at its essence, it is so simple just to ask!

The power of the feedback leg

Feedback from the ultimate nonprofit customers, clients, participants, and beneficiaries can be helpful in many ways. For organizations that are resourced with monitoring and evaluation systems, feedback can be a powerful balance to the information gathered through traditional M&E, can help source innovation, empower participants, and amplify voices that may be least heard. For other organizations that are perhaps smaller and/or where third-party evaluation is either less applicable or out of reach financially, feedback can offer useful, robust information to drive ongoing improvement.

Sourcing innovation

Organizations leading the way in building this leg of the measurement stool have embraced feedback and the amplification of 'customer voice' as a crucial component of their work. And they are using it to source innovation and surface hidden problems identified by those most affected and least heard in our typical systems of service delivery.

Among organizations that have begun implementing all three legs of the stool, Nurse Family Partnership (NFP) stands out for using feedback to source innovation. An evidence-based program operating in 42 states and six tribal communities, NFP pairs young, first-time mothers with nurse visits for two years, to learn the basics of parenting. Recently, NFP experienced feedback as 'transformative' when they asked the moms it serves what they actually wanted, and used the answers to adapt and create programming. From its genesis 40 years ago as a research project in Elmira, New York, NFP has used evaluation to document outcomes such as healthier births, improved parenting, early child development, and so forth. But a few years ago, new CEO, Roxane White and new Chief Communications and Marketing Officer Benilda 'Benny' Samuels thought that even evidence-based programs needed periodic innovations to reach new moms and retain participation. So, NFP decided to participate in Listen for Good, a systematic feedback tool to ask the moms about their experiences with the program – from whether they would recommend to other new moms, to what they saw as the strengths and improvable areas of the program.

Some staff were skeptical that the moms would want to participate; that moms, who would receive the Listen for Good survey via text message, wouldn't want to use their data plan minutes in this way. However, when they sent out the feedback survey to 10,000 women, they received almost a thousand responses in 20 minutes. The first thing they noticed was just how much the moms appreciated being invited to participate; they saw it as a sign of respect. While they provided positive feedback about the nurses and the program overall, the moms also had innovative ideas for improvement, such as connecting the participating moms with each other and not just with the NFP staff, creating an app for NFP's print materials, and, counter to the staff's expectation, the moms asked to be able to communicate with the nurses via text and not just in person.

These recommendations led to innovations now being tried at NFP, along with a newly created feedback team where feedback from moms is a central component, in addition to feedback from staff, volunteers, and partner organizations. NFP, the paradigmatic gold standard evidence-based program, has integrated feedback as a third leg of its measurement stool to unlock new insights and drive continual improvement.

Empowering participants

The Center for Employment Opportunities (CEO) is a nonprofit that also now uses all three legs of the measurement stool.[4] CEO works with formerly incarcerated individuals to help them transition to a job and life circumstance after they exit the criminal justice system. CEO had commissioned an RCT of its program which demonstrated reduced recidivism among participants. It also has an extensive internal monitoring system where they track all encounters with participants, services provided, the nature of conversations and job placements. For 30 years, they have had a data-driven culture.

But, a few years ago, their CEO Sam Schaefer took a fresh look at their program and decided to add a third leg of their measurement stool – feedback from the participants. He reasoned that CEO staff give feedback to participants all day long – about how to behave in certain circumstances, how to dress, how to interact with peers, and he thought it was time to turn the tables a bit and ask the participants for feedback on how CEO could do better.

It wasn't easy at first because of the power dynamic. They tried different approaches to encourage candor. The most important thing they did was make changes in response to some of the ideas they heard. For example, one participant said that a 7:00 am start time was too early. He was trying to restart his life at home and if he had to be at work at 7:00 am, he had to leave home at 5:00 a.m., which meant he couldn't see his family in the morning before he left for work. This was counter to his ability to reintegrate to life outside of prison. Based on that feedback, after 30 years of a 7:00 am start time, CEO changed to an 8:00 am start, making the logistics better for everyone. Once participants saw that their feedback was taken seriously and that changes were in fact being made, more feedback poured in.

Epiphany Community Health Outreach Services (ECHOS) in Houston also discovered problems they needed to address by listening to voices seldom heard. A ministry of the Episcopal Diocese of Texas, ECHOS provides health and social services to the growing population of immigrants and refugees in the city. Its safety net services include English language learning classes – and more recently, Hurricane Harvey relief services. Through its first efforts at customer feedback, ECHOS heard loud and clear that clients are waiting excessive amounts of time – often multiple hours – which makes ECHOS' support extremely difficult to access. Representative of many, one client said, "I would love to have a way to make an appointment so I did not have to wait so long . . ."

This was counter to ECHOS' intention to treat those they served with respect. Because of this feedback, ECHOS overhauled its service process – changed the registration system, expanded hours and adjusted workflows – who did what – to increase efficiency and timeliness. Participants are so pleased with the new positive and respectful customer experience that they wonder whether they will be invited to provide feedback to other institutions in the community.

Surfacing hidden problems

Other nonprofits are using feedback to surface hidden problems in their programming. The Second Harvest Food Bank serves millions of people each year in Silicon Valley – the dirty secret of a highly affluent community – but it had never asked customers how they experienced the food or the service. When they rectified this in a feedback campaign across ten locations, they learned that customers from different cultural communities had vastly different experiences. The white and Latino clients were far more content than Asian clients. That insight led them to seek more culturally sensitive approaches to their work, including recruiting volunteers with Asian language skills, adapting training for volunteers to heighten cultural sensitivity, and establishing a new food pickup location in an Asian neighborhood to improve accessibility.

Second Harvest routinely monitors the amount of food provided and the number of people served. But like many nonprofits, Second Harvest may never be able to commission rigorous, third-party evaluation. They were, in a sense, balancing only on one leg of the measurement stool. By adding systematic feedback, they are now bolstering their understanding of client experiences and preferences. If they can improve food bank clients' experience, and reduce the shame that many feel in seeking help with food, they can use those insights to advance their mission to reduce hunger in all local communities.

Going global on three legs

Internationally, some new and interesting feedback efforts are afoot. Chief among them is an effort of the Omidyar Network and Acumen Fund called 'lean data sprints.' That involved collecting feedback from 68 Omidyar investee organizations (nonprofits and small businesses). They surveyed approximately 30,000 customers across 18 countries. Like Listen for Good, the Acumen tool uses the Net Promoter system, which asks customers to rate their experience from zero to ten on likelihood they will recommend the service or organization to a friend. Because of the effort, Omidyar and its investee organizations generated a list of needs common to different sectors – independent media, education or financial inclusion – as well as discrete areas for improvement for their specific organization.

The Omidyar Network still relies on traditional impact evaluation where it can, bringing third-party evaluation in to critically assess results. It also has elaborate dashboards to monitor the progress of the organizations and businesses they support. But the addition of customer feedback as a third leg of their measurement stool makes listening to those they seek to help a priority both for themselves and their investees and is deepening their understanding of true progress as well as places for redress.

Calling all funders

A recent study by the Center for Effective Philanthropy found that foundation CEOs believe that listening more to the people they are seeking to help is key to having greater impact. The Fund for Shared Insight, a philanthropic collaborative that has been the driving force behind the Listen for Good system and other feedback efforts, has grown rapidly in the past four years, from six original participating funders to 78 co-funders and counting. They range from large, global funders like the Bill & Melinda Gates Foundation, the Ford Foundation, and the William and Flora Hewlett Foundation, to national funders like the Rita Allen Foundation to smaller, local funders such as the Plough Foundation in Memphis Tennessee.

The Plough Foundation was started by Abe Plough to serve the people of Shelby County in Tennessee. Last year, the Plough Foundation supported two grantees to participate in a Listen for Good feedback process. Diane Rudner, the board chair and Plough's youngest granddaughter, describes the learning from that feedback, particularly from an organization serving people with developmental disabilities as ". . . so valuable . . . the organization had never asked their populations what they wanted . . . They had never been asked their opinions about anything. It's amazing!" Rudner was so impressed that the insights could translate into immediate operational improvements that the foundation is now routinely asking its nonprofit partners how they listen to participants and incorporate their perspectives.

The Plough Foundation isn't abandoning the first two legs of their measurement stool, though. They will continue to commission independent evaluations when appropriate, and monitor their work, but they are balancing those legs with the third leg of the stool – feedback – which, according to Rudner, "is just perfect for us to ensure a truly complete assessment."

Conclusion: A new day for measurement

When I started out my career 30 years ago, I was taught to denigrate 'client satisfaction surveys.' They were seen to be 'lite' in contrast to 'hard outcomes.' Because of the power differential between nonprofit and client, evaluators made assumptions that satisfaction measures would always be positive and therefore not meaningful.

It is a new day.

Throughout the social sector there is a growing recognition of the importance of being 'human-centered.' The problems we are trying to solve are, after all, social problems – they are complex and involve humans – and so too must our solutions. It is time to apply that human-centered design principle to nonprofit measurement.

Many new initiatives these days are targeting systems change – the kind of change that typically requires new policies, allocating resources in new ways and implementing programs that bring about material changes in people's lives. Systems change is clearly important. But, if we change systems and people don't feel treated with dignity and respect, what have we really accomplished? Feedback balances our measurement schemes and helps provide a unique view into *how* people are experiencing the products and services nonprofits work so hard to provide.

I am not arguing against evaluation or monitoring. They are both critically important tools for our sector. Evaluation helps us gain deep understanding of what works and why (or why not) and monitoring helps us keep track of our progress, providing useful signs for course correcting. But, not every organization can invest equally in each leg. Evaluation can be expensive and monitoring can only take you so far in identifying needed improvements. It is time to embrace a third leg of this nonprofit measurement stool that is both affordable and rigorous so that all nonprofits – from the most endowed to the least – can learn about what matters most to people we are seeking to benefit. Insights, ideas, and preferences from our ultimate beneficiaries can unlock new possibilities for operational improvements, programmatic innovation, and more respectful engagement.

As a mentor of mine advised, "Let not the abuse of a thing be an argument against its proper use." It is time to stop denigrating the satisfaction surveys of old and unleash the power of feedback in new ways. Let's strengthen our feedback tools to be reliable, comparative, simple to use, with both quantitative measures and qualitative verbatim comments. And, let's start listening – to gain insight, to improve, to innovate.

5 'Antidisciplinary' and the practice of change

Joi Ito

Joi Ito is the Director of the MIT Media Lab, Professor of the Practice of Media Arts and Sciences at MIT, and the author, with Jeff Howe, of Whiplash: How to Survive Our Faster Future *(Grand Central Publishing, 2016). Ito is a Visiting Professor of Law from Practice at the Harvard Law School, and chairman of the board of PureTech Health. He serves on several other boards, including The New York Times Company, the John D. and Catherine T. MacArthur Foundation, and Knight Foundation. He is the former chairman and CEO of Creative Commons, and a former board member of ICANN, The Open Source Initiative, and The Mozilla Foundation. Ito is a serial entrepreneur who helped start and run numerous companies, including one of the first web companies in Japan, Digital Garage, and the first commercial Internet service provider in Japan, PSINet Japan KK. He has been an early-stage investor in many companies, including Formlabs, Flickr, Kickstarter, littleBits, and Twitter. Ito received a PhD from The Keio University Graduate School of Media and Governance in 2018 for his thesis 'The Practice of Change.' Ito has received numerous awards, including the Lifetime Achievement Award from the Oxford Internet Institute and the Golden Plate Award from the Academy of Achievement, and he was inducted into the SXSW Interactive Festival Hall of Fame in 2014. In 2017, he received the IRI Medal. Ito has been awarded honorary doctorates from The New School and Tufts University and is a member of the American Academy of Arts and Sciences.*

* * *

Over the last century, civilization has systematically supported a market-based approach to developing technical, financial, social, and legal tools that focus on efficiency, growth, and productivity.[1] In this manner, we have achieved considerable progress on some of the most pressing humanitarian challenges, such as eradicating infectious diseases and making life easier and more convenient. However, we have often put our tools and methods to use with little regard for their systemic or long-term effects and have thereby created a set of new, interconnected, and more complex problems. Our new problems require new approaches: new understanding, solution design, and intervention. Yet we continue to try to solve these new problems with the same tools that caused them.

In this chapter, I ask: *How do we break down the silos that academic disciplines have become and the funding mechanism that supports them so that we can better understand, design, and deploy the ideas and strategies necessary to tackle the complex modern problems of society?*

In particular, I argue that we need an anti-disciplinary approach and paradigm shifts that recognize how and why we must change the values of society from the measurement of financial value to a focus on flourishing and robustness.

As I have written previously, one of the first words I learned when I joined the Media Lab in 2011 was 'antidisciplinary.'² It was listed as a requirement for applicants for a new faculty position. At the time, I was transitioning from the world of Internet entrepreneurship and open-source governance, and initially it didn't make sense that I could fit in at a huge academic institution like MIT. But the Media Lab was different. Its students and researchers had (and still have) the freedom to explore and to fail, and it has produced some groundbreaking innovations that its corporate members – more about that later in this chapter – have gone on to commercialize with great success.

The 'antidisciplinary' requirement listed in that job posting captured the beating heart of this very different kind of organization. *Interdisciplinary* work is when people from different disciplines work together. But *antidisciplinary* is something very different; it's about working in spaces that simply don't fit into any existing academic discipline – a specific field of study with its own particular language, frameworks, and methods. Ed Boyden, a researcher at the Media Lab, for example, brings together nanotechnology, robotics, chemistry, biology, electronics, music, machine learning, just about any technology or theory that he finds useful in understanding and interacting with the brain to solve problems like migraine, motor disabilities, dementia, and other difficult neural disorders.

For me, antidisciplinary research is akin to mathematician Stanislaw Ulam's famous observation that the study of nonlinear physics is like the study of 'non-elephant animals.' Antidisciplinary is all about the non-elephant animals.

When I think about the 'space' we've created at the Media Lab, I like to think about a huge piece of paper that represents 'all science.' The disciplines are little black dots on this paper. The massive amounts of white space between the dots represent antidisciplinary space. Many people would like to play in this white space. But there is very little funding for work there, and it's even harder to get tenured positions without some sort of disciplinary anchor in one of the black dots, or disciplines.

Yet it appears increasingly difficult to tackle many of the interesting and 'wicked' problems via a traditional disciplinary approach. With funders and researchers focused on the disciplines, it takes more and more effort and resources to make a unique contribution. While the space between and beyond the disciplines can be academically risky, it often has less competition; needs fewer resources to try out promising, unorthodox approaches; and provides the potential for tremendous impact by unlocking connections between existing disciplines.

So, let us return to the question I posed at the outset of this chapter: *How do we break down the silos that academic disciplines have become and the funding mechanism that supports them so that we can better understand, design, and deploy the ideas and strategies necessary to tackle the complex modern problems of society?* I believe the Media Lab's antidisciplinary approach to solving complex problems offers a valuable example for all kinds of organizations – research labs, companies, even academic institutions, that are challenged to adapt to the tidal waves of change sweeping over all of us.

The Media Lab method

Though important for tackling wicked challenges, operating an organization in this antidisciplinary way poses the same challenges I faced growing up. I've always been most comfortable in an antidisciplinary 'space,' so it's probably not unexpected that I have learned almost everything through working on projects and being mentored along the way. But the question becomes how do you manage wanting to learn about everything without the structure and the boundaries that traditional disciplines impose? For individuals and organizations, the best approach is passion-based constructionism.

The Media Lab has deep roots in constructionism – learning through doing – beginning with founding faculty member Seymour Papert, who defined constructionism in his 1987 National Science Foundation grant proposal, 'Constructionism: A New Opportunity for Elementary Science Education.'[3]

I have learned through experience that learning by doing can be hard at first, especially if you have very little learning before you start. You may lack the frameworks that traditional educational models convey. Also, what you learn by doing depends on what you happen to be doing, so it may lack the coherence that traditional discipline-based systems provide. It can be difficult to build a coherent view, and it's easy to go wrong if you don't know the extent of what you don't know – a lack of discipline and absence of the guardrails of traditional disciplines can lead to attempts to 'boil the ocean' in pursuit of a single unified theory of everything.

Over the years, however, one's model of the world may begin to come together, as one's influence and trust in a variety of networks mature; as one's ability to translate and connect ideas across networks and disciplines increases; and as opportunities and problems present themselves from odd but often useful perspectives.

My years as the Media Lab's director (I became director in 2009) have tested my natural affinity for constructionism, for now I'm expected to lead one of the most highly respected research centers in the world. The Media Lab is able to keep moving across disciplines because we don't define ourselves by any specific technology or field of study; rather, we define ourselves by a point of view, a way of doing things, a sensibility. In the late 1980s and 1990s, we focused on personal computing, interfaces, and displays. As time progressed, we built on that work by moving into email and networks. Later, we pivoted again into big data and physics.

Most academic institutions are not particularly comfortable with 'learning by doing,' or the community-based, antidisciplinary approach I have long advocated. They tend to stick to their traditional disciplinary silos, attempting to shoehorn new fields of study and technological developments into them. Providing an environment like the Media Lab at relative scale – about 800 people are in our extended community – required learning how to hop back and forth across the boundary that separates traditional institutional mechanisms and the 'heterotopia' that has made the Lab so highly regarded externally, and so cherished by MIT and its community members.

The Media Lab model

One of the key elements of the Media Lab approach is its embrace of both design and science. On the Krebs Cycle of Creativity that Professor Neri Oxman designed to show the relationship between disciplines, design and science are opposite one another on the circle and the output of one is not the input of the other, as is often the case of engineering and design or science and engineering (Figure 5.1). I believe that by making a 'lens,' a fusion of design and science, we can fundamentally advance both.

This connection includes the science of design and the design of science, as well as the dynamic relationship between these two activities. By bringing together design and science, we can produce a rigorous but flexible approach that will allow us to explore, understand and contribute to science in an antidisciplinary way.

The kind of scholars we therefore look for at the Media Lab are not traditional 'scientists.' I often say that if you can do what you want to do in any other lab or department, you should do it there. Only come to the Media Lab if there is nowhere else for you to go. We're the new Salon des Refusés.

This approach is peculiar, even within a highly diversified, somewhat quirky university like MIT. The Lab's history gave rise to that peculiarity. It was founded in 1985 by former MIT president Jerome Wiesner and a young faculty member named Nicholas Negroponte. Wiesner was retired but wanted to continue working in areas about which he was passionate, including bringing the arts and sciences together at MIT. Negroponte, working in the Architecture Machine Group in MIT's School of Architecture and Planning, was promoting a vision of a digital future that included a computer-aided design system on everyone's desktop. Together they created the Media Laboratory, now known as the Media Lab.

They did something you can only do when your partner is the former president of MIT: they broke a bunch of institutional rules. Typically in universities like MIT, you have labs and you have academic programs, and they tend to work like church and state in a healthy or unhealthy balance. The academic program offers classes to students and grants degrees. The labs focus on raising funds to conduct specific research aimed at real-world impact. The Media Lab does both. It has its own

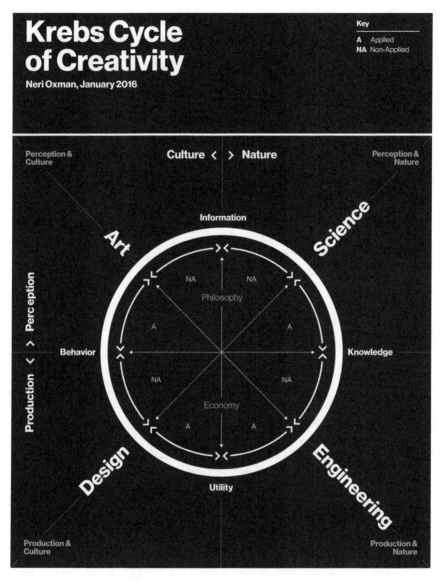

Figure 5.1 Krebs Cycle of Creativity

academic program – the Program in Media Arts and Sciences within MIT's School of Architecture and Planning – and it is also home to a wide variety of research labs where students learn by working on projects.

The other unique aspect of the Media Lab is its funding model. When the Lab opened, about 80 percent of MIT's funding came from government sources and 20 percent from private sources. The Media Lab was the exact opposite – 80 percent of its money came from corporate sources. This was partly a result of Wiesner's history. As science advisor to President John F. Kennedy, he was dispatched to Japan to help that country rebuild its technology and research infrastructure. As a result, many in the Japanese business world felt a real debt to Wiesner, and when he and Negroponte were planning the Media Lab, these companies had money to spend. As a result, much of the money to launch the Media Lab came from the chief executives and chairmen of Japanese electronics firms. In the protectionist atmosphere of the late 1980s, the Media Lab was even criticized for undermining American competitiveness by 'selling' technology to the Japanese.[4] It wasn't, of course.

The way the Lab handles corporate support is also atypical in academia. Money from corporate members does not support directed research but rather goes into one Lab-wide fund we call the consortium. Thus, any intellectual property, or IP, resulting from Lab research is available to be shared among all the corporate members.

The total lab budget is currently about $75 million, the majority coming from the consortium with a bit from government and other non-IP-generating research grants. As director, I distribute the consortium funds to around 25 research groups, working on everything from synthetic neurobiology to the future of opera. Each research group is made up of students and faculty members. Crucially, the research groups have almost full license to spend the money on whatever they want, at their discretion. This enables them to explore, fail, learn, and explore some more.

How the Media Lab works

This structure has major consequences for the way the Media Lab works.

First, it helps to create a strong sense of community.

In a typical lab, if you're a faculty researcher, you write a grant proposal, your students work with you, and together you deliver the required results. Such a system makes it difficult for people from different labs or departments to work with one another. It can even make it difficult for corporate donors to work with one another. Everybody works on their own projects, using money from grants specific to them, and the IP generated by that research must be protected from all the other research groups.

At the Media Lab, the consortium owns the IP, so there's no barrier to collaboration. Twice a year, hundreds of people from our member organizations – from LEGO to Lockheed Martin to governments – come to the Lab to learn about its current research efforts. Amazingly, even companies that are normally fierce competitors, such as LG, Samsung, Toshiba, and Google, join together in this unique member community.

The pooling of IP gives us the freedom to fund things that others wouldn't. The member companies aren't supporting us so we'll help them do what they're already doing, only better. Instead, they support us because we might do something they would never have thought to do on their own. That's what makes working in the white spaces core to the Media Lab's 'business model.' In fact, we try to exit research areas when they become mainstream.

Membership model and growth

One of the first things I did when I joined the Media Lab was change the label for our funders from 'sponsors' to 'members.' I wanted to make it clear that the companies who support us are members of our community and to be respected as colleagues, not bosses telling us what to do or simply 'dumb money' that stands on the sidelines.

I also initiated a price increase because the consortium membership, $200,000 a year, had not been raised for 15 years. We increased it to $250,000 a year. We had significant pushback from member companies at first, because we didn't communicate the price change well. We got together, regrouped, tweaked the contract and reintroduced it with much greater success.

While this process damaged our relationship with some members and we lost a significant number of them, it turned out to be critical for building a tighter relationship with the companies that stayed. Many of the companies that left didn't think they were getting value out of the Lab. We quickly replaced them with companies that were excited and more engaged with the Lab, and we learned how to communicate the value we were giving them. We turned them into engaged members of a unique research community. Today, including incremental funding that companies provide to projects of specific interest to them, the average member spends well over $300,000 a year with the Lab.

The consortium model has continued to thrive. Our membership numbers and overall revenue have increased every year since 2012 (See Figure 5.2).

Recently, we presented these numbers during a meeting of the entire Lab. I was proud to report that we had 475 full-time staff and graduate students, and nearly 800 people in our ecosystem, including part-time undergraduate researchers (Figure 5.3).

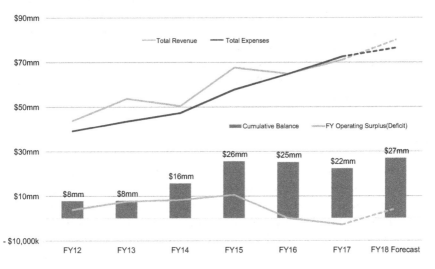

Figure 5.2 Media Lab consolidated profit and loss

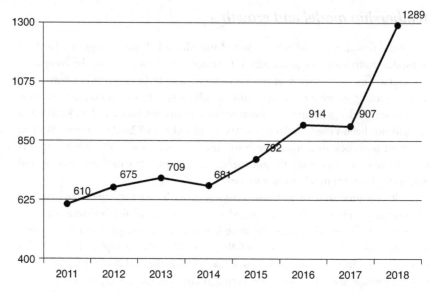

Figure 5.3 Total number of applications (master's and PhD)

Later that evening, though, a long-time researcher who has a good sensibility about the Media Lab culture approached me and asked, "When are we too big?" He also mentioned that it's virtually impossible to know 800 people's names, much less to know those people well.

The question surprised me. I noted that we had 30 tenure track slots and 26 research groups, and as I said that, I realized that some groups had become quite large. I realized that while I espouse the limits of growth and warn about the danger of focusing on growth, I had pushed for growth of the Lab myself. One significant question for me now is, "What is the right size for the Media Lab?" How do we decide what to do and what not to do? How do we increase quality over quantity? How do we determine quality? We were, in fact, facing one of the core dilemmas in the age of connected technology: how to scale community?

Community

When I got to the Media Lab, women had represented about 20 percent of the student population for as far back as we could see. For the past four years, the Visiting Committee, an external committee of experts from inside and outside MIT that audits the Media Lab's performance biennially, had called out this unacceptable level of gender diversity at the Lab. The number of underrepresented minority students was also unacceptable, because it's not enough just to have a community in the anti-disciplinary model; it's necessary to have a diverse community so that a broad range of insights, attitudes, and expertise is available.

We hired Monica Orta as the assistant director of diversity, but her first task wasn't to increase diversity – it was to find ways of making the Media Lab a safer, more welcoming place for a diverse student body. She immediately stopped unacceptable behavior on mailing lists, and harassment and other issues were dealt with quickly and firmly, including inappropriate comments by visitors from our member companies.

Gender diversity at the Lab has increased markedly (Figure 5.4).

We haven't yet met our goals for ethnic and racial diversity, but Danielle Wood, a recent faculty hire and an African-American woman, is working to improve these statistics (Figure 5.5).

Since we hire faculty members one at a time, and they do not turn over as quickly, it is more difficult to increase diversity among the faculty than with students. This is now one of my most important areas of focus, and we are making progress in this area, including with our most recent faculty hires, Ekene Ijeoma and Deblina Sarkar.

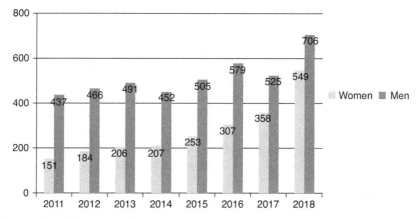

Figure 5.4 Master's applications by gender

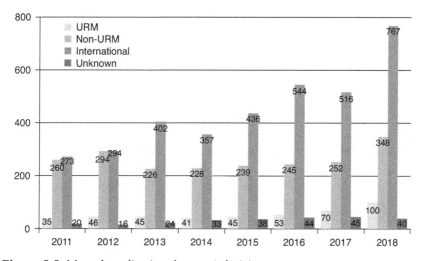

Figure 5.5 Master's applications by race/ethnicity

The Media Lab mindset

The companies that interact with the Media Lab are seeking its discovery sensibility; they're looking for exploration rather than a problem-solving kind of thinking. In a book I co-authored with Jeff Howe, *Whiplash*, I tried to capture the core principles that drive the Media Lab.[5] *Whiplash* grew out of nearly five years of discussion between my colleagues and me as we worked through the collision between the Media Lab's peculiar DNA and the DNA I brought with me from the Internet world. In those discussions, we developed a set of principles, iterated on over multiple faculty meetings, by asking two questions: what are the principles that define the Media Lab? And what are the principles that drive innovation on the Internet?

Among the most far-reaching changes brought by the Internet was the recognition that the Newtonian laws that had governed how companies operate were now just local ordinances that only worked for certain things. Everything moved faster, everything was hyper-connected, and some operating models didn't survive, while others thrived. Some companies – some big companies – were able to survive this transition, and a whole new set of players entered the scene – Google is just 20 years old, Facebook only 15. The old rules no longer applied, and a new set of guiding principles emerged. We began to see agile, bottom-up systems outperforming those built around more rigid, top-down authority. Organizations with a more creative vision and culture were more likely to succeed than those with elaborate, well-documented, time-tested plans. The ever-decreasing cost of innovation allowed for – in fact necessitated – taking more risk. These are the principles that we talk about in *Whiplash* (see Table 5.1), and they are the principles that drive much of what the Media Lab is doing now.

Table 5.1 Innovation principles for the age of the Internet

Emergence *over* Authority	Complex, bottom-up systems beat out top-down authority.
Pull *over* Push	Resources and innovation should be pulled from the edges rather than controlled from the center.
Compasses *over* Maps	Detailed plans (maps) become less valuable than vision, values, and culture.
Risk *over* Safety	With the cost of innovation coming down, the focus should be on taking smart risks rather than seeking safety.
Disobedience *over* Compliance	Agile, effective innovators will question authority and think independently.
Practice *over* Theory	Focus less on theory and more on learning by doing.
Diversity *over* Expertise	A nontraditional team approach will be more productive than the abilities of any one individual.
Resilience *over* Strength	Resilience will come from failure, especially with complex, adaptive systems.
Systems *over* Objects	Everything is connected to everything else; to succeed, you must understand the full ecosystem.
Learning *over* Education	Fixed educational systems must be replaced with lifelong learning.

Permissionless innovation

The first thing the Internet did was drive down the cost of innovation. In the early 1990s, a company I founded was running a magazine website for the *Asahi Shimbun*, a major Japanese newspaper, off a server in the bathroom. One day the server's fan failed, then the hard disk failed, and then we were taking turns blowing on the hard disk while somebody ran to get a new fan. In the Internet world, we called this 'best effort': you couldn't guarantee your hard disk would never fail, but you promised that you would do your very best to fix it if it did.

A telephone company trying to create an Internet service provider then would probably have spent millions of dollars building an infrastructure. What we did took a bathroom and a couple thousand dollars.

This is permissionless innovation. We didn't ask if we could do it and we didn't check what the rules were. We just did what we could do. For the first time, a handful of students could actually compete with a telco. The openness of the ecosystem made that possible: everything we ran on those servers was free and open-source software. This kind of activity forces competition by driving the price down to functionally zero compared to where it was before. When you add Moore's Law to that, you get very low-cost technology continuously increasing in power without increasing in price. Network these powerful computers and it creates an explosion of free and open-source software, which further lowers the cost of innovation.

Lowering the cost of innovation doesn't just change what it costs to do something. It also changes how you do it, as well as what you can think about doing. In the old days, the cable companies and the telephone companies tried to do multimedia over set-top boxes or kiosks, such as the Minitel system in France. These systems cost hundreds of millions – if not billions – of dollars because every company had to do it all: the lines, switches, computers, database, software and content. This kind of complexity required a tremendously detailed plan with lots of dependencies that made the plan extremely complicated to implement correctly. I call this MBA-driven innovation. Its opposite is engineer-driven innovation.

An MBA-driven innovation system has money, permission, jobs, and a system of authority that generates whatever capital is required for a project or program. Talent chases money because you need so much money to even get started. With engineer-driven innovation, a bunch of college students (or dropouts) can run around making cool things that make money in the form of venture capitalists hoping to get in on a good deal. The money chases the talent. It's a very different dynamic.

For projects where cost is substantial, spending some percentage of that cost to minimize risk makes sense – building roads or designing airplanes, for example. But if a project is inexpensive – say only a couple hundred thousand dollars – and if the cost of failure is just the failure of that thing, permission costs can exceed actual costs. Permission granting can be expensive. I once had a company for which I was trying to get an investment of $600,000; the potential funders spent about $3 million deciding not to do it. If they had just given me the $600,000, I could have demonstrated whether it worked or not; if it had, they'd have made some money. Failure would have cost very little. If an attempt to build something fails, you've nonetheless learned something that will help the next project succeed. In general, my rule of thumb is that if the cost of assessing risk and providing permission exceeds the cost of just trying to do it, why not try?

At the Media Lab, we think of every failure as an opportunity to gain information. In considering whether to pursue a project, we ask if the information we might get out of it is worth the investment. No one asks me as director for permission to start a project, though twice a year everyone is required to demo the things they're working on so the entire community can learn from each other's advances and setbacks. This constant interaction among the researchers and member companies is perhaps the main value of joining the consortium at the Media Lab.

Of course, it's key to have the right facilities and equipment to keep innovation and iteration inexpensive. At the Media Lab, when there's a conversation and someone hits on an idea, they're in the shop making it by the afternoon, and by the end of the week, there's a photo of it with a video, a rough demo, and all the files needed for somebody else to replicate it.

Permissionless innovation is only feasible when the costs are low enough. The Internet and digital revolution have dramatically lowered costs, but it helps to have the backing of a research center that can provide material support, as well as a community and culture that encourages antidisciplinary innovation in the white spaces.

Motivations of researchers

Increasingly competitive offers from businesses, especially in fields like cryptocurrency and computer science, are draining research universities of talent. Large companies and even nonprofits hire researchers for millions of dollars and provide them with labs equipped more lavishly than any university lab.

While MIT and the Media Lab are of course still able to attract talent, in some fields it has become more of a challenge. An important part of the Lab's response has been to advance a counter argument to the conventional wisdom about why people take jobs. We generally have assumed that job applicants are rational, self-interested actors looking to enter into a new contract that compensates them for their work by paying them money. But academics traditionally have been motivated less by money than by other values, including intrinsic values like the joy of teaching, discovery, and collegiality.

Intrinsic rewards, I believe, are the most robust motivators, though it's important to note that even intrinsic motivation must be nurtured and supported – it doesn't have a completely solitary effect.[6]

Benefiting from intrinsic motivation requires discovering what truly makes one happy. Without necessarily announcing it as such, the Media Lab tries to make an offer that appeals to the intrinsic motivations of potential community members: this is a place rich in intrinsic values and goals, such as the excitement of learning in the white spaces, the joy of community, and the ability to contribute to the intrinsic values of others outside of the community. You can build something that will make people healthier, improve the planet, provoke someone's curiosity – *and* bring delight.

The Lab is fortunate to be able to make such offers to those thinking of joining us, for our community includes businesses as well as researchers. Spaces for open innovation such as the Lab should not be sheltered enclaves. Researchers need to be part of the bustling world around them so that their work addresses real needs and can be adopted and have an effect. That is a boundary that needs to be made permeable, and not just at research centers like the Media Lab.

I believe that understanding intrinsic and extrinsic motivators and how we can manage communities to strengthen healthy versions of both is a key piece, if not the key piece, of improving our institutions as well as society.

Leadership

I often describe my role at the Media Lab as a gardener, not a commander: I'm focused on providing nourishment, pruning, and cultivating the community to increase its flourishing. While I try to have vision and a strategy, I aim to support the community, not push it. I try to be a participant, not just a director. I try to be decisive but inclusive. Rather than laying out a crisp, definitive mission for the Media Lab, my job is to manage a vibrant ecosystem of groups, each with different goals and sensibilities, that somehow manage to interact with one another and improve the flourishing of the whole institution – more akin to a rainforest than the Starship Enterprise.

Conclusion: The next generation

I'm now less focused on scaling the Lab itself and more interested in scaling what I have learned by transferring my experience to the next generation of leaders and community organizers. Many of the Lab's students and faculty are building communities themselves, and it is my great pleasure and mission to support their growth.

One question I'm often asked is whether we can make more Media Labs.[7] I think the Media Lab is difficult to replicate exactly – we have our own academic program inside of a research lab; we have a critical mass of funders and projects that makes the math work, and we have the MIT brand to attract talent and provide 'air cover' for students to work on strange things without their parents being worried that they're wasting their time on wacky projects instead of getting a useful college education. That said, many schools are experimenting with elements of the Media Lab model in their own way, such as project-based learning and design programs that are massively interdisciplinary. My hope is that the Media Lab can inspire innovation in higher education and beyond, and create other experimental research and development projects that take advantage of the unique opportunities and assets of different regions and institutions.

I think that the key challenge to the Media Lab model is that it is difficult to measure its success. Nicholas Negroponte often said that if you can measure something, it isn't interesting, but that notion is too radical for most traditional organizations and funding agencies. Also, while antidisciplinary research can have impact and flexibility, building a body of knowledge without structure is difficult, and how antidisciplinary research scales beyond a single lab is as yet an unanswered challenge.

II

Bringing disciplinary approaches into dialogue

6 Design for impact

Bringing empathy and creativity to social change

Chris Larkin

Chris Larkin joined the world of design several years ago, following a journey through the fields of social and organizational psychology, social research, and behavior change programming. She has led research and evaluation with a number of creative organizations that leverage media, communications, and digital technologies for social impact. These have included BBC Media Action and Girl Effect, where she has worked extensively in Africa and Asia on programs tackling gender equality, political participation, climate resilience, and health. At IDEO.org she supports design teams with integration of impact theory, measurement, and systems thinking in the creative design process. She is inspired by the transformative potential of design for social impact.

* * *

In 2015 the American Refugee Committee (ARC) embarked on a journey. Starting with one of the largest refugee settlements in East Africa – Nakivale, Uganda – they wanted to know, at any given moment, how well services were being delivered and received across the camp. They already knew how many liters of water were being delivered on a given day, and whether the water points were operating as they should be. But what did camp inhabitants think about these services? Were they happy? They wanted to position the refugee population as active participants in shaping the services they needed, and to do this they needed to hear their voices. As Daniel Wordsworth, ARC's CEO, believes: "If you're thinking of a refugee as your customer, it just makes sense then that they get to tell you if what you're doing is good or not."[1] ARC had worked with design in their programs before, and believed there could be an efficient and human-centered solution to their challenge. They engaged a team of designers and set to work together, on the ground in Uganda.

I arrived in Nakivale in April 2017, right as prototypes of the new model were being rolled out. A simple, interactive tablet experience captured feedback from

Figure 6.1 Kuja Kuja interviewer collecting feedback at the water pump
Source: Courtesy of IDEO.org

camp inhabitants waiting in water pump queues. They could swipe left or swipe right to express their satisfaction with the services and then offer suggestions for improvements to their interviewer (Figure 6.1). ARC staff across the globe could see what sentiment levels were like in real time via a digital dashboard. Looking beyond the data component, the designers found that a truly customer-centric approach would require changes to how ARC's customer-facing staff, the Kuja Kuja team, appeared in the camps. *Kuja Kuja* means 'Come, Come' and the designers created a brand around this welcoming message. Physically, it would be highly visible across the settlement through the team's bright yellow T-shirts and hats, featuring a logo that was itself a beaming smile. On a deeper level, the brand provided the Kuja Kuja team with a set of values that they could rally behind, as they undertook a transformation from service providers to customer agents. The designers introduced narratives and rituals, captured in a *Big Yellow Book*, that helped staff internalize and bring these values to life in their work. My favorite example, a daily habit of stopping before a mirror when exiting the morning meeting to practice the same smile that they would bring to their customers in the camp.

This was the first time I'd seen designers in the field. I had joined IDEO.org just three months prior, tasked with strengthening measurement in the design approach, and building evidence and learning around the value of design for social impact. I was in Nakivale to learn about prototyping. With a background in social research and behavior change program measurement, I arrived with some preconceptions about what this should look like. I expected to see sampling frames, pre-printed discussion guides, and numerator training sessions. Instead, I observed a business designer sitting with Kuja Kuja team members, diving deep into how the customers should feel; a digital designer making changes on the fly to the tablet app as the first morning's tests revealed the colours were barely perceptible in the glaring, equatorial sunshine; and a communications designer observing that the Kuja Kuja team needed to be more energized around their values, and then working until 2:00 am on new content for the *Big Yellow Book* for a retrain the next day. The designers also empowered the Kuja Kuja team to do their own rapid testing at water points across the site, helping them to pick out diverse customers who looked willing, shy, busy, relaxed, old, young. We gathered at the end of each day to download what we'd seen, heard, sensed that day and what the focus of the next needed to be. It was intense, immersive, and exhausting.

As we drove back to Kampala at the end of the week, I felt uneasy – we did not have a stack of interviews to transcribe and analyze back at the office or Excel files with each day's data points neatly ordered. But then I reflected on the model that we had left with the Kuja Kuja team. In the space of one week the tools had become more usable, the team ethos more purposeful, the customer experience more meaningful. The team were excited to keep testing and felt ownership to find fixes for their own processes. I realized that this was unfamiliar territory. I had glimpsed a very different approach to developing a program and needed to momentarily suspend my critique while I learned more about the workings of design, and its value, in the social impact space.

Consensus on this value is slowly but steadily forming through numerous design partnerships, a small, but valuable, set of process evaluations, and a collaborative community of funders, implementers, and design firms. Design can offer a more nuanced framing of problems, generation of new ideas and concepts, meticulously crafted user experiences, and, for some, organizational transformation. However, there are also examples of where design has fallen short of achieving its promise, which point to ways that designers can iterate upon their own approach to become a more effective and integrated practice in driving impact at scale. This chapter explores some of these insights, illustrated through applications of design in the adolescent and youth sexual and reproductive health sector (AYSRH, introduced in Box 6.1) and the ongoing work of ARC.

Box 6.1 Moving the needle on adolescent reproductive health

Despite a vast increase in availability of modern contraception in recent years, more than 200 million adolescent girls in low- and middle-income countries remain underserved. Taboos around discussing sexual health and restrictive social norms relating to girls' sexual activity limit the extent to which girls can freely and comfortably access services. The cultural value placed on fertility, geographic and economic barriers, and inadequate policies on adolescent and youth sexual and reproductive health (AYSRH) in some countries, make the challenge a complex one.

In recent years funders, such as the Bill & Melinda Gates Foundation, the Hewlett Foundation, and the Children's Investment Fund Foundation, have looked to design to increase adoption of contraceptive methods amongst 15-to 19-year-old girls. These investments have prompted numerous collaborations between leading health organizations in sub-Saharan Africa and design firms. The result has been a series of interventions that place the girl at the center and position contraception as something in line with, not at odds with, her life.

In Kenya, Future Fab is a movement that celebrates teens, their talents and their potential, and positions contraception as a means by which young people can achieve their goals. In Zambia, the Diva Centres are spaces where girls are invited to hang out, paint their nails, talk about boys, and get to know their health options and providers in an informal setting. Kuwa Mjanja, in Tanzania, is a brand deeply rooted in Tanzanian culture and puberty rituals, that speaks to girls about growing up strong and smart. All have strong value propositions for girls, communicated through role models, mantras, and bold, fun brands. Girls engage in events and activities that are tailored to their contexts and in some cases designed to mobilize boys, parents, and communities around them, too.

Within 18 months of Marie Stopes International launching their Future Fab program in 2016, they had reached more than 100,000 people through mobilization events and had seen a seven-fold increase in the average number of adolescents served through clinics and outreach. Marie Stopes Zambia saw similar early success with their Diva Centres, reaching more than 11,000 girls in the capital, Lusaka.

In 2017 the *Adolescents 360* program,[2] led by Population Services International (PSI), took design one step further with their launch of AYSRH programs in Nigeria, Ethiopia, and Tanzania. Kuwa Mjanja mentioned above was one of these, and the Ethiopia program – Smart Start – is discussed later in this chapter. With design as a core methodology, A360's transdisciplinary approach integrates expertise from public health, adolescent development science, cultural anthropology, and social marketing. Within the first seven months of project scale-up, more than 96,000 girls had engaged in A360 activities with over half of those adopting a contraceptive method for the first time. A360 is striving for 257,000 new adolescent contraceptive adopters by 2020, and the trajectory right now is looking good.

This work has created momentum to strengthen the practice of design for the AYSRH sector. To this end, a group of funders initiated the HCD Exchange, a convening of more than 70 funders, practitioners, evaluators, and designers in Tanzania in January 2018. From this a Community of Practice has been born, dedicated to bolstering partnerships, strengthening measurement, and ensuring design can tackle outcomes for girls at even greater scale.

As to my first experience of design, the Kuja Kuja team have collected almost one million responses from camp inhabitants, on water, health, safety, and other needs as of the end of 2018. The data feeds through to a map at the ARC's service team headquarters and to a public digital platform, where they can quickly pinpoint problems to be addressed across the sites. As ARC's CEO sees it:

> I think our whole industry overcomplicates this stuff. In the end, we just ask them, did you like it or not? Then, by making it transparent, we hope that it will bring about change. And it has brought about great change.[3]

The organization has scaled the model to sites in Rwanda and Somalia, with plans for further expansion in the Middle East. In a sector where the human experience is sometimes lost in the scramble to keep up with the ever-increasing needs of displaced and migrating populations, ARC is changing the face – literally – of humanitarian service.

The value in a design approach

Design is a creative approach to problem-solving that starts with people and arrives at solutions tailored to their needs. It is premised on empathy – the capacity to step into other people's shoes, to understand their lives, and solve problems from their perspectives. Design has its origins in the creation and shaping of objects and symbols – from pattern making in textiles and ceramics in the sixteenth century to the production of industrial, business, and household products in the twentieth. As the last century progressed, however, design's applications evolved beyond cars and vacuum cleaners to tackle challenges that require less immediately tangible solutions. Through brands, services, business systems, and strategies, each step has seen an expansion from shaping objects to giving shape to decisions.[4]

When we tackle a challenge through design we work through iterative cycles of divergence and convergence (Figure 6.2). Rather than a sequence of orderly

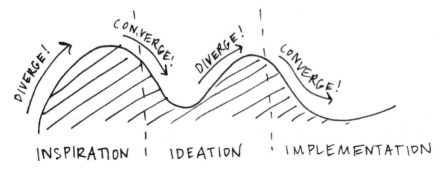

Figure 6.2 Inspiration, ideation, implementation

steps, the approach can best be understood as a system of overlapping spaces, which Tim Brown (IDEO's CEO) and Jocelyn Wyatt (IDEO.org's CEO) describe as inspiration, ideation, and implementation.[5] Individual designers and design firms have their own ways of mapping and naming their design approach, but the core principles are generally similar.

During the inspiration phase we frame the problem to be addressed through immersive research with users to understand their needs, experiences, and contexts. In ideation we identify design opportunities, generate ideas, and quickly get tangible prototypes into the hands of users. By implementation we have learned what users value and are confident that our solution can influence the intended outcomes. Only then do we put a fully formed solution out into the world, to establish how to make it feasible and viable for implementation at scale. Projects will often loop back into ideation from implementation, or inspiration from ideation, as a design team gains new insights or considers ways to refine solutions. The people a solution aims to serve remain at the heart throughout, and we continually look to them as discerning customers, co-designers, and constructive critics of what we create.

As a practice, design has its own underlying philosophy that goes beyond these make/test cycles. At IDEO.org, this philosophy is brought to life through *design mindsets*, which include empathy, embracing ambiguity, and creative confidence. Others have codified these as *design attitudes* – a composite of distinct skills, capabilities, and aptitudes that designers apply during the process of designing.[6] Some design attitudes that are recognized across the literature are described in Box 6.2.

Box 6.2   Design attitudes

- *Empathy:* the ability to arrive at a deep understanding of how others see, feel, and experience
- *Ambiguity tolerance:* the ability to embrace change, take risks without fully knowing the outcomes, and be exploratory when faced with complex or unfamiliar situations and stimuli
- *Creativity:* the capability and confidence to produce novel and useful ideas
- *Engagement with aesthetics:* an orientation towards integrating aesthetics in design, recognizing beauty as a door to function
- *Connecting multiple perspectives:* the capability to reconcile multi-dimensional meanings, make connections, and recognize patterns

Designers have always been compelled to tackle social challenges, and the demand for design has soared in the social impact sphere in the past ten years. An appetite for experimentation and a recognition that fresh approaches are needed to meet the ambitious goals of complex social challenges have driven interest from funders and implementing organizations exploring social innovation. The designer's toolkit offers a new approach. These are a number of the ways in which we have seen design bring immediate and obvious value in getting to more engaging and impactful models for change.

Design reframes problems

A design approach resists defining a solution pathway too quickly. The expectation is that the solution – be it a messaging campaign, a digital product, or a service refinement – will emerge through the design process. Very often the problem framing itself is allowed to be emergent, as designers flux between divergent and convergent thinking. They will go wide to understand an issue and explore avenues beyond what immediately appears to be the focal problem, and then converge on potential new directions. Boyer, Cook and Steinberg of Helsinki Design Lab eloquently describe this in their book *Recipes for Systemic Change*:

> When working in mysterious territory, we gently reject the assumption that one first defines the problem and then creates a solution as separate elements to be addressed in sequence. We prefer to describe them as existing in a continuous feedback loop . . . the hunch of a solution inspires new questions about the problem space and that is where the cycle begins again.[7]

The A360 team in Ethiopia started out asking: how might we design SRH services that can more effectively reach adolescent girls? As designers immersed in girls' experiences they discovered that young Ethiopians are anxious about their financial futures in a rapidly developing economy and that they want to talk about this. This insight (among others) gradually reshaped the problem framing to: how might we position contraception as an asset for newly married couples as they start their lives together? This *how might we* question format is one commonly used by designers. The phrasing is intentional – suggesting that a solution is possible, and allowing for a broad challenge framing without suggesting a solution.

The resulting program – Smart Start – introduces contraceptive counseling to young married couples through financial planning. Health Extension Workers are equipped with engaging visual materials and interactive exercises that help couples think through the costs of raising a child and understand contraception as a tool that can help them align their financial goals with those of starting a family. The counseling messages are scaffolded in a precise way, to match message delivery to girls' and their partners' cognitive and emotional life stages. The Health Extension Workers delivering the counseling have reported a new-found understanding and ease of connection with the young clients they previously struggled to reach.

Design is generative and iterative

I remember how unsettling my first brainstorm with designers felt. Coming from a highly analytical training in psychology, my instinct was – and often still is – to accompany a fledgling idea with a series of caveats or to point out that others' ideas have been tried before, have failed before, or could pose risks. This is a mode I'm still working to unlearn, as I've come to understand that it is through uninhibited contribution of simple or wild ideas, a temporary rejection of the 'expert,' and a bias towards *building* rather than *critiquing* that innovative concepts can surface.

Design offers many tools to nurture ideation, brainstorming being just one of them, and experienced designers each have their own well-honed methods and facilitative techniques for this. All are underpinned by the assumption that experimentation will follow, where the wild idea thrown out in that brainstorm or co-creation session can be prototyped, pulled apart, and iterated upon before one commits to a final direction. Prototyping is a physical manifestation of divergent and convergent thinking, where designers quickly make concepts tangible for end-users and implementers. Early prototypes are multiple, scrappy, and often sacrificial – intended to convey an idea rather than be perfect. Designers are not aiming to determine empirically whether a concept, in all its scrappiness, does or does not work – rather they are still in research mode, using physical prompts to observe how people respond. Mariana Amatullo describes this 'making' competency of designers as:

> a mechanism for discovering unforeseen opportunities, and exploring and mediating what alternative options may be taken forward, providing a foundation for collaboration, and building a common point of view in team learning.[8]

Before landing their couples financial planning model, the Smart Start team prototyped different hooks to discussing contraception. The concepts tested included a celebratory box for newly married couples, a marriage counseling session, and a baby cost calculator. When the baby cost calculator proved most resonant the designers moved into the next learning loop, and played with ways to visually communicate the annual cost of raising a child to potentially illiterate and under-educated girls. Through further prototyping in villages they landed on bags of teff, a common grain in Ethiopia, as a metric of comparison whose value could be interpreted immediately by any young person in the region. The result is that girls can recite back the content unaided after the session to their parents and other gatekeepers, who can in turn understand the relevance of the message and thus more easily support girls' decisions.

Design elevates experiences

Designers are commissioned to develop *interventions*, but to do this they create *experiences*. In the Smart Start example, the designers probed questions such as 'What style of illustration will feel aspirational yet relatable in the materials?' and 'How can we make the counseling session more rewarding for the Health Extension Worker?' These framings can feel superfluous, and even jarring, to those new to a design process and carrying the burden of scale timelines or accountable reporting to a funder.

In fact, at a recent workshop to develop a design toolkit for the global health sector a designer shared that they had stopped using the word 'delight' in conversations with their implementing partner as it was causing eyes to roll.

But the truth is that delight matters. People are universally more likely to use a new service or adopt a new behavior if the experience is enjoyable. More than 30 years ago practitioners in the social and behavior change communications field argued that distributing condoms and telling people that they should use them would not prompt safe-sex behaviors. Rather, approaches needed to speak to people's hearts as well as their minds. Design takes this principle one step further, considering how to create a positive experience for users at every touchpoint of a solution and then executing that experience with finesse. This includes the experiences of those who will implement a service, who must feel equipped and motivated to deliver to a high standard for a solution to be a success.

This is often where innovation emerges through design. Rather than inventing totally new products or services, innovation actually infers evolutionary changes or contributions to existing solutions. This could be a rebranding of a service to attract a new customer segment, or a reconfiguring of how products and processes come together so as to better engage stakeholders across an ecosystem. An independent process evaluation of the Hewlett Foundation's investment in design for MSI's AYSRH programs found that while the components of the solutions were not perceived to be particularly innovative (branding, peer counseling, and youth-friendly spaces), the way in which they were implemented had the potential to be transformative.[9] As Margot Fahnestock, then Program Officer at Hewlett, reflected:

> We were most surprised by the contribution design craft and quality seem to be making to the popularity and effectiveness of the models. The evaluators had difficulty determining how much design quality matters, but our hunch is that designing delightful places for young women to get birth control is a marked improvement over traditional public health approaches and contributes to how girls react to the services. One leader of a community-based organization in Homa Bay, Kenya, said even the quality of the paper used to print the Future Fab magazine was important; the quality, he said, made the community and girls feel valued.[10]

Design can transform organizations

In his book *Design Attitudes*, Kamil Michlewski highlights that role that designers can play as agents of change within organizations.[11] Through socialization and enculturation, Michlewski argues, designers "transmit their ways of doing things, their thinking and crucially, their attitudes to the people that they work with." The culture that designers produce can potentially influence the capacity of an organization to achieve impact beyond the processes or products that they initially partnered with designers to create. The experiences of partners at ARC and PSI's A360 program certainly resonate with this assertion.

The A360 team have reported that working with design not only provided a structured means of ensuring their program was girl-centered, but had a knock-on effect of building trust and greater systems of collaboration within teams as they also changed how they listen to each other.[12] Taking a design approach ensures that learning, and failing, moments are plentiful early on, and once programs have originated from this type of model teams tend to be more excited and equipped to continue with an adaptive method of implementation. As then Program Director of A360 Manya Dotson reflected in a blog post following the 2018 HCD Exchange:

> Certainly, while nobody I spoke with felt that the experience had transformed them into professional designers, everyone said they had seen their teams becoming much more responsive to the needs of young people and willing – and able – to adapt and course correct through implementation.[13]

Such organizational growth is by no means immediate, though. In the case of ARC, the Kuja Kuja project followed several years of working with design on projects such as I am a Star in Minneapolis and Asili in Democratic Republic of Congo, an enterprise that provides clean water, health care and agricultural support to underserved communities. The commitment of the organization's leadership to innovation and a learned trust in the process of experimentation created space for an initiative like Kuja Kuja to start small, weather some failed prototypes, and flourish in time.

Evolving design for greater impact

Social problems are complex problems. Challenges of education, health, and violence involve multiple actors and deep, interconnected drivers that are often systemic and hidden. Scholars in the 1960s used the term 'wicked' to describe this class of social system problems that are "ill-formulated . . . where there are many clients and decision makers with conflicting values, and where the ramifications of the whole system are thoroughly confusing."[14] Much has been written about design's capacity for tackling wicked problems, but in reality design initiatives are not always scoped or structured in a way that fully enables this to happen.

While the application of design in manufacturing and business pushed its evolution from patterns through to products and then strategies, the success of design for social impact will be in how it evolves to truly tackle systems and scale.

Tackling complexity

To effect real change, design needs to be both human-centered and systems-oriented. In addition to understanding what drives and engages users, we need to ensure that we are considering the balance between short- and long-term outcomes of solutions, and designing within or around the right levers in social and structural systems.[15] Knowing where to act within a network of stakeholders takes more than social scientific theory – it requires deep, institutional knowledge on a hyper-local level, and ideally personal or organizational connections with decision-makers within those networks. Transdisciplinary programs like A360 present a promising model for tackling complexity, but such cross-expert, cross-organization, cross-location endeavors are no easy feat. Teams have had to feel their way, become super-translators in each other's technical languages, and inevitably make trade-offs in deciding the most critical paths to address.

For example, the question of whether shifting societal norms around girls' use of contraception should be part of the intervention arose several times. A social norms approach that influences the expectations and discourse of communities at large could influence deep and sustained impact around AYSRH. However, it would be a much longer-term mechanism for change than the four-year project term of A360 was scoped for. Solutions tailored towards targeting girls' individual knowledge and motivations, and creating more seamless connections to girl-friendly service providers, would prompt more immediate results.

Integration – of more explicit systems mapping, of existing theory and evidence, of data, and of the place-based expertise of implementing partners and stakeholders – will be crucial for design to better grapple with complexity. The network of designers I've engaged with at HCD Exchange are already building on how they do this. Jessa Blades, Managing Director of IDEO.org's health practice, explains:

> HCD is a discovery driven process. It necessitates continuous alignment amongst partners and experts, not just at the start or mid-point but all the way through, to ensure we're all on the same boat, navigating the same course together. We've had to strengthen our communication systems and refine our project blueprints to embed this in our approach. An external AYSRH advisory board is also helping to bring the right checks as we make decisions.

There is space for innovation too in how we delve into ecosystems and select design directions. The behavioral sciences hold huge promise for driving precision in solutions. These social scientific approaches adhere to evidence-based problem scoping and decision-making principles, the empirical nature of which is somewhat at odds with the intuitive basis of design. Effective integration of empiricism and intuition into everyday project models presents an exciting design challenge in itself. Data science is also increasingly leveraged to surface hypotheses for critical impact pathways in complex systems, with machine learning in particular strengthening our ability to predict trajectories and prescribe action to optimize for scale. The field of *Arte Util* (or 'useful art'), which draws on artistic thinking and the rise of networked cultures, also holds inspiration. *Arte Util* rejects the conventional idea of users as just consumers of knowledge or services, and instead considers them to be producers of their own information, meaning and value. This opens up a conversation about how designers might harness policy loopholes, piggyback on corporate distribution channels, or empower users to hack and repurpose product and service offerings to meet their distinct needs.[16]

Optimizing for scale

When IDEO.org partnered with Marie Stopes International (MSI) to reimagine adolescents' access to contraceptive services in Zambia, the resulting solution brought delight, not only to the adolescent girls who engaged with it but also to observers from across the public health and development sector. The Diva Centres, vibrant spaces for girls to socialize and paint their nails while learning about contraception with trained peers, presented a radical new approach to connect girls to AYSRH services. However, the program did not scale nationally.

During prototyping, the design team had found that the differences between urban and rural girls and their health service models were significant, and that the project budget and timeline would not allow for adequate prototyping of solutions in both contexts. They decided to focus on an urban setting and the centers, while effective in driving an 84 percent uptake of contraception amongst urban girls, were considered impractical and costly for rural locations.

This is a challenge that many well-designed initiatives face. While all solutions are assessed against how well they meet the criteria of desirability, feasibility, and viability, the parameters for these shift once the question of scale comes into question. Feasibility (which largely looks at the implementing partner's operational capacity) and viability (which considers sustainable funding and cost models) are difficult to assess in small-scale tests. Solutions need to live in the real world for a time and at relative scale, to establish more clearly where more resources are needed or where costs can be saved without impacting effectiveness.

The A360 program has scaled in increments, from small live prototypes to larger pilots, with additional design sprints along the way to iterate and bolster for the next level of scale. PSI have built in formal phases of optimization six to eight months into their pilots, to conduct experiments for cost-effectiveness and replication in new regions. In Ethiopia, Smart Start is working to reduce costs and lighten the workload for Health Extension Workers that implement the model, so that it can be adopted by the Ministry of Health who plan to integrate it into their national family planning service delivery system. Successful scale will depend on ensuring not only that the experience delivered to young couples continues to be a positive one, but that any adaptations to the delivery model feel meaningful and efficient for the Health Extension Workers who need to be on board to deliver it. Marie Stopes Zambia have since undertaken a similar optimization sprint, to adapt the Diva Centres for national implementation by the Zambian Ministry of Health.

This incremental and adaptive approach to scale is not specific to design but resonates completely with the spirit of experimentation that underpins the approach. Formalizing optimization as a distinct phase can help to set expectations for success and make the challenge of designing for broader systems more achievable.

Getting data-driven

Much has been written about the promise of design for social impact, largely within the burgeoning social innovation media but also within the academic design and innovation literature. However, we still lack a volume of evidence that validates the contribution of design by the standards that have come to be expected in the social and development sector, that is, rigorously gathered, peer-reviewed, and employing experimental study designs. This paucity is to be expected, for design is still a relative newcomer to a space carved out by pioneers in public health, community development, social and behavior change communication, and others in the history of change-making. Until recent years, many funders still saw design as an experiment in sparking innovation or a creative injection into a larger program of work, and so expectations (and budgets) for measurement were secondary to understanding process and how to integrate design in the first place.

To move forward, we need to view design not as an intervention or solution in itself, but rather a means by which we get to a solution. When those solutions are rolled out in the real world they can, and should, be more data-driven and validated by evidence. It is simply a question of timing. In early prototyping, designers need the freedom to experiment in fast, fluid, daring ways. But as we move closer to a final solution and start making decisions for scale, we need to be more scientific and precise in these experiments, tinkering with one program component at a time and drawing on quantitative data to identify strengths and weaknesses in models. Determining the right moment in the design cycle where the solution has been formalized and stress-tested enough to be ready for a formal evaluation (generally entailing larger n sample sizes and investments) should be a conversation that starts from the outset between designers, implementers, and funders. Just because we adopt principles of experimentation as we innovate, does not mean that we cannot leverage experimental measurement methods as we implement.

It is across a suite of these well-measured solutions that we will establish a case base – of successes and failures – from which to make stronger inferences about the value of the design. That said, true to its nature, design cannot wait for multi-year studies or meta-analyses of individual evaluations to strengthen how it serves the social impact sector. These early insights have already set a course for change.

Acknowledging design as its own practice

The designer Nigel Cross wrote in 1999, "We have come to realize that we do not have to turn design into an imitation of science, nor do we have to treat design as a mysterious, ineffable art."[17] Twenty years later this dichotomy of 'art versus science' is one that we do in fact grapple with in design for social impact. In efforts to apply design to the social and international development sectors, it has sometimes been simplified to a linear sequence of steps with an associated toolkit of activities. To explain and validate these steps, practitioners – like myself – have tried to map them like for like to more familiar development models, resulting in confusion and critique when a phase of immersive design research does not follow the methodological principles of a qualitative social study.

The propagation of design thinking in the commercial sector has brought a similar pressure, against which there has been some backlash in recent years. According to John Kolko, founder of the Austin Center for Design:

> [There are] two paths of design, diverging. There are people and firms practicing design thinking by making things, driven by practitioners aware of the history of making things and skilled in the craft of making things. And then there are people and firms practicing design thinking by, well, thinking about things.[18]

Design, as it has been practiced by and brought value to all of the organizations referenced in this chapter, has always been of the making kind. It indexes high in design attitudes such as engagement with aesthetics and creativity. In a post on her excellent blog, designer Dr Stefanie Di Russo likens design aptitude to that of a musician, whose muscle memory, established through years of formal training and continued practice, allows them to pick up their instrument and play a never seen before piece of music with ease and skill.[19] Without elevating design to an elitist pursuit, which democratization efforts were specifically aimed to counteract, it is important to acknowledge that there are some aptitudes that only dedicated practice and a design education can hone.

Design firms have a role to play in better articulating their unique offering. They must also manage capacity-building expectations, and be transparent and realistic about how far a design engagement can take a partner along a trajectory of awareness, fluency and mastery in design. Optimizing the involvement of professional designers where they are really necessary, and clarifying for partners where they can be relied on less, will be key to scaling the practice of design in the future.[20] As we do this, it will be crucial to keep sight of the qualities of intuition, aesthetics, and depth of craft that were intended to drive new ways of working when design was first looked to as a tool for social innovation.

Conclusion: A new value proposition for design in social impact

No doubt, this landscape will have already changed in the window between writing and publishing these reflections. Designers, implementers, funders, and evaluators are rallying to align on how they are framing, practicing, and measuring design for social impact. In 2017 and 2018, summits such as HCD Uncut in Berlin and the HCD Exchange in Tanzania (as mentioned in Box 6.1) brought these stakeholders together, resulting in the establishment of a Community of Practice for Design in

AYSRH and a Global Health public good toolkit.[21] These efforts are driving debate and guidelines for what constitutes best practice and effective collaboration.

There is a necessary focus right now on improving how we integrate design into existing program development approaches. However, design as a futures technique, leveraged widely in the commercial sector, has yet to be granted the space to demonstrate its potential in the social impact realm. How might looking ten to 50 years ahead, through speculative and design fiction exercises, to an economic, technological, or social future that might exist, illuminate new possibilities and avenues for change? Designers have the skills to make products and services for the most vulnerable and marginalized more effective, but they are still tasked with narrowly defined briefs and often operating within a space that is tightly constrained by existing service and system barriers. Truly radical thinking and transformative innovation start from a higher point of departure, where those barriers can be treated as opportunities for redesign rather than constraints to be designed within. This is a difference between using design to help set the vision for impact and scoping the brief accordingly, versus delivering against a predefined strategy to nudge a rigid set of outcomes believed to contribute to that impact.

The ARC's reframing of how they serve refugees and determine the effectiveness of their humanitarian efforts is one example of where design has influenced a vision for change. Through a deep understanding of the people they serve and years of co-designing with their users, they've recognized dignity, self-sufficiency, and a return to normalcy as their markers of meaningful change. These are outcomes that have human experience at their core. Eudaimonism, a moral philosophy stemming from the ancient Greeks, puts the complete life of the individual at the center of ethical concern. It positions action that leads to well-being, human flourishing, and happiness as having essential value. Design, as an empathy-based approach to problem-solving, is imbued with this philosophy. How might it influence the change we see in the world if design aptitudes – of reframing and elevating the experience of the user – were applied to reimagining the future of women's empowerment, climate resilience, or healthy families?

In the meantime, we can apply design's own principles – namely learning from failure and iterating – to the practice itself, and bolster the evidence base that should, in time, validate its role and value in creating meaningful and sustainable change.

7 Product development for impact

Creating impact at scale in the digital age

Prem Ramaswami and Craig Nevill-Manning

Prem was at Google for 12 years, where he led the Search Social Impact team, founded Google.org's Crisis Response Team, and launched products like Health Search. He is a computer engineer by training, founded and taught a Product Management course at Harvard and Stanford, and is currently Head of Product at Sidewalk Labs.

Craig spent 15 years at Google, where he founded its first remote engineering center, in New York City. There his team built products like Google Local, which became Google Maps, and Froogle, which became Google Shopping. He has a PhD in Computer Science from Waikato University in New Zealand, and is currently Head of Engineering at Sidewalk Labs.

★ ★ ★

This chapter is concerned with product development for social impact. Of course, engineering inventions have always had profound impacts on society – never more so than the current concerns over the impact of technology on politics and public discourse. However, although they have an *impact*, traditional engineering projects are usually not conceived with the express purpose of impacting society. In contrast, this chapter describes an application of technology where the primary motivation is to have a *social* impact: to improve response to natural disasters. What we learned – and are continuing to learn – is that the way products are developed in the technology industry has utility in the social impact context. However, technology developers often have less experience and intuition about the context of these technologies' application when the goal is social impact than when the goal is to build an Internet search engine, an online marketplace, a social network, or other products where the developer is representative of a typical user.

Success, then, depends on tackling these problems as a tightly integrated multidisciplinary team. In our specific example, partnering with responders who have firsthand experience of the aftermath of natural disasters makes the difference between success and failure.

A crisis on our doorstep

At 5:00 pm on January 12, 2010, a magnitude 7.0 earthquake rocked Port-Au-Prince, Haiti's capital. It claimed the lives of over 200,000 people and caused over $15 billion in damage.[1] Some 1,500 miles away, we were in Google's New York office listening to news reports, but as night fell on Haiti, news from the island also went dark. As the human toll unfolded, we realized that a humanitarian crisis was taking place right on our doorstep. Haiti is a 4-hour flight from JFK airport – closer to New York than Google's headquarters in Mountain View, California.

We had to do something – but our skill sets as product managers and software engineers seemed a world away from the horrors seen in news reports. Regardless, dozens of Google engineers around the world quickly dropped what they were working on to spend their '20 percent time' building tools they hoped would help the recovery effort.[2]

We created a website that showed updated satellite imagery from Haiti, aggregated news and relevant links, provided a way for people on the ground to upload user-generated content such as YouTube videos, and featured organizations that were accepting cash and in-kind donations. The site was launched in 12 languages and featured on the Google.com homepage for over a week to raise awareness of the impact of the earthquake and provide practical ways for people to help.

From previous disasters like Hurricane Katrina, we knew that geographically referenced information is critical in the aftermath of a disaster. We worked closely with the Google Maps and Earth teams to collect and display up-to-date, high-resolution imagery over the disaster region.[3] People used this to assess damage, identify refugee camps, and find navigable routes for rescue and medical crews.

Our servers detected a precipitous drop in Haiti's Internet traffic to Google services at the time of the earthquake, caused by widespread power outages and loss of the main undersea fiber link. Google donated networking hardware to Haitian Internet Service Providers, as well as to NetHope, who provided other nonprofits with stable Internet connections.[4] Within a week, three major Internet service providers were serving customers, and traffic levels had risen to half the pre-earthquake level. Google assisted the United States Agency for International Development (USAID) by preparing a white paper detailing a plan for Haitian Internet reconstruction and growth.[5]

A group of '20 percent' engineers built the Google Person Finder tool within 72 hours of the earthquake.[6] They noticed that in order to find out about a missing friend, colleague, or family member, it was necessary to locate and consult many different, uncoordinated, 'missing persons' lists. Working closely with numerous nonprofits and news organizations as well as the U.S. State Department, the Google team created a federated database that amalgamated information from missing persons databases compiled by the Red Cross, CNN, the *New York Times*, the *Miami Herald*, and more. This made it possible for victims and their families to consult a single up-to-date source for information on over 60,000 individuals. The Person Finder Interchange Format, which had been developed after the September 11th attacks in New York City and used after Hurricane Katrina, was used to communicate this data between services – and then to redistribute it back to each service. In this way, Person Finder not only offered comprehensive information, but enabled all the other services to incorporate that data as well.

Numerous nonprofits such as NetHope, Ushahidi, and FrontlineSMS also deployed technology to help earthquake victims. Ushahidi, along with FrontlineSMS, launched the 4636 SMS short code to allow victims trapped in rubble to request help – resulting in over 150 individuals being saved. The American Red Cross launched an SMS short code for donations in the U.S., raising $32 million dollars – a record at the time for any single collection effort.[7] Supporting the larger effort, for-profit companies like Cisco, Microsoft, and Walmart provided digital hardware, consulting, and logistics support. Google donated $1 million and raised donations from the public.[8]

Two weeks into the disaster, I (Prem) led a team of Googlers to the affected region to better understand how technology could help in crisis response. We stayed next to the Petionville Golf Course, which had become one of the biggest Internally Displaced People (IDP) camps in Haiti.[9] We embedded with Partners in Health, a global health care delivery nonprofit with deep roots in Haiti. We were awed by the work of doctors, rescue workers, and servicemen and women who put themselves in danger to help. We conducted user interviews and set up Google Earth servers to provide locally cached geographic information. The expertise of a Google product manager, Roni Zeiger, himself a medical doctor, was critical in understanding how best to support medical personnel.

We learned some important lessons. First, use of Google Maps and Google Earth was widespread across many of the organizations on the ground. In a crisis, people don't have time to learn new tools; instead they use those they already know. Second, situational awareness is a constant challenge. The UN Development Programme (UNDP) ran daily stand-up meetings with all organizations working on the ground. Still, the basic question 'who is doing what, where?' was difficult to answer. Third, many victims of the earthquake didn't know where to turn, who to trust, or which rumors they heard were true.

On our return, Craig and I proposed the formation of a Google Crisis Response team. Questions we had to answer included:

- *In a crisis, aren't clean water and medical expertise more important than technology?* True, but technology plays a vital role in making basic necessities available – communications and information sharing are critical for getting help to people who need it.

- *Isn't the Internet unusable in the wake of a disaster?* The Haitian power grid is unreliable even under normal circumstances, while mobile telephone networks are designed to be robust to power outages – each base station has generator backup with plenty of fuel. In addition, Internet protocols are designed to be robust to partial failure. Although the story that the Internet architecture was designed to survive a nuclear war is apocryphal, it is still true that its operation withstands loss of individual transmission paths. In fact, although Internet access over cellular networks is a relatively recent development, these protocols mean that data traffic is more reliable than phone calls or text messages.[10]
- *Doesn't using Internet technology further disadvantage people who can't access it?* Mobile is eating the world.[11] The last decade has seen massive penetration of mobile technology, and especially smartphones. In 2010, most phones could only SMS, Nokia's feature phone (with the 'killer feature' of also serving as a flashlight) was most popular globally, but Android and iOS were rapidly gaining market share. Today, over 1.4 billion smartphones are in circulation.[12] The Reliance Jio sells for 150 rupees ($2.25) per month for a 4G connection.[13]
- *Do you really think technology is the solution to all the world's problems?* Of course not.

Over the last eight years, the Crisis Response team has responded to earthquakes, floods, mudslides, tsunamis, forest fires, and most recently terrorist attacks. In that time, it has grown from an informal band of '20 percent' engineers, product managers, and designers to a fully staffed and funded team. It has built better tools to help provide information in the aftermath of these crises. Perhaps even more significantly, the lessons from these efforts have been integrated into Google's mainstream products: search and maps, for example, now incorporate features originally built to solve specific crisis response issues. In this way, point solutions are available much more widely to people in need.

The product development process

To understand product development in an impact context, it's useful to first discuss product development as a discipline more generally. Good products solve a fundamental user need, but the process of getting there can be long and arduous. The product development process can be (over)simplified into three steps: why, what, and how.

Why?

It is the responsibility of a product manager, and potentially a user experience researcher, to first understand 'Why are we solving this problem?'[14] Successful products reflect the actual pain and needs of users, not just what they say they want – urban legend pins Henry Ford as stating, "If I had asked people what they wanted, they would have said faster horses."[15] Clay Christensen in *The Innovator's Dilemma* refers to this as 'The Job to be Done.'[16] Numerous research methods ranging from ethnographic research (following and recording a user's actions in their natural environment), interviews, and surveys are used to focus a problem statement and hypothesis. In addition, product managers survey existing solutions to learn how they satisfy (or fail to satisfy) the user need, hoping to discover truly effective solutions.[17]

Geoffrey Moore's *Crossing the Chasm* provides a template for the positioning statement that one should be able to write after the 'why' stage: "For [target customer segments] who must [problem to be solved], our product is a new [category name] that provides [solution to the problem]. Unlike [current solutions], we offer [key differentiating factor]."[18]

What?

Once convinced of a need, product managers, working closely with engineers, start to design a solution. This often results in a product requirements document that describes a minimum viable product (MVP). The MVP is the first step to gaining real user validation with an end-to-end product that involves a manageable amount of engineering work. To supplement the MVP, the team will define metrics for success that will help determine whether there was truly a need or whether the team should pivot towards a different solution. Product managers help ensure that teams stay focused, and prioritized, on the key tasks to deliver the MVP.

How?

Building the product is the responsibility of engineers. They design the architecture and estimate how long it will take and what it will cost. Simultaneously, product managers help figure out how to introduce the product – the 'go to market' plan – to ensure that users find, love, and share the product.

There are two approaches to MVPs: (1) Work on the hardest part of the problem first in order to fail quickly; and (2) Take the easiest path to success to demonstrate that a market exists. Each comes with its own dangers. The most common failure points for both types are: false positives, if the MVP users aren't representative of the eventual user base; and false negatives, if the MVP is too minimal and fails to solve the real problem.

Product distribution

The World Wide Web significantly changed the product management process and accelerated the development cycle. The creation of companies like Google, Facebook, Amazon, and Netflix emerged. Open standards mean that anyone can launch innovations. In the last few years, cloud computing and devices like Arduino and Raspberry Pi have reduced development costs to near zero.[19] Before the Internet, software was sold on physical disks, giving start-ups a single shot at creating a complete, flawless software package. Today, distribution costs have also dropped to near zero. With capital costs so low, the barriers to entry have disappeared. Now a developer can create prototypes quickly and gain immediate user feedback. Social media allows good products to be disseminated almost instantaneously, avoiding high-overhead traditional advertising channels.

Creating social impact products

We define social impact products as those that have a clear and primary social mission. The social mission need not exclude profit, but has as its primary motive the betterment of community, the environment, culture, or a cause.

Like products in general, good social impact products solve a user problem. A product manager should not try to answer 'how' before fully understanding 'what,' and should not try to define 'what' before fully understanding 'why.' This process is more time-consuming up front when defining user and market needs, but without it, the rest of the process is unlikely to succeed. 'Garbage in, garbage out.'

Many nonprofits use a theory of change framework to structure their approach, tracking inputs, outputs, outcomes, and broader impact towards their goals. This helps these organizations evaluate and validate their approaches and supports iteration and evolution of their strategy. In contrast, the product development cycle starts by discovering a need, paying little attention initially to outcomes. Of course, once that need is identified, technology products very quickly begin taking a similar structured approach working backwards from a broader vision or hypothesis. This stepwise iteration is essentially the MVP process.

Analysis of a failed product

After the Haiti earthquake, our team embedded with a field hospital in Port-au-Prince and interviewed numerous aid workers. We empathized with an anguished doctor who had amputated a child's leg, not realizing an orthopedic surgeon was at the clinic next door. The doctor did his best with the limited information available, but we thought it should be possible to improve information sharing to avoid this outcome. We heard numerous similar stories about the challenge of finding blood banks, functional x-ray machines, and more during the earthquake's aftermath. We decided to build a tool, Resource Finder, that aggregated medical information on a map, including where clinics were, what type of doctors they contained, and what materials and equipment existed at those facilities. We used an open standard for medical information (EDXL-HAVE: Emergency Data Exchange Language Hospital Availability Exchange) and Google Maps as the user interface. We spent time calling clinics in

Haiti and collecting the initial data to seed the map and created metrics and goals around the number of views and database updates that would constitute success. We even came up with a go-to-market plan, working closely with the UNDP and a group of clinics to help evangelize the tool. Still, after a week, we had no more than a few views, and within a few weeks the data was completely stale.

We used the why/what/how approach but still failed – so what went wrong? We can break our mistakes into two categories – regular product mistakes and social impact product mistakes. In terms of regular product mistakes, we suffered from our own optimism bias. We heard what we wanted to hear, specifically that doctors wanted to go to Google Maps and search for local x-ray machines. We failed to listen carefully enough: doctors wanted to go to Google Maps, not *resourcefinder.appspot.com*! The tool also depended on people entering data, and we assumed that doctors would keep it up to date. We then interviewed medical staff and found that the employees running the clinics didn't have access to desktop computers.

We tried again: we made sure the website worked on smartphones, delivered Android phones with data plans to a select set of clinics, and even had an SMS short code that the facilities managers could text to update the database. We relaunched the tool, convinced that we had learned the right lessons, and waited for updates. But once again, a few weeks in, failure.

What went wrong this time? The success of our tool depended on the freshness of the data and updates, but users had no real incentive to enter data. The hospital managers who needed to keep the data up to date had different needs to the medical doctors who needed the data. We failed to distinguish the two different users and their needs, and properly connect them. Similarly, even though signing people up for regular SMS pings seemed like a great way to onboard people, we also failed to understand how many spam SMS messages existed already in Haiti. Users there routinely ignore SMS messages. We made another fatal error – designing for people like us who don't deal with the problem of spam SMS messages and read every SMS we receive. A large part of social impact work revolves around communities in need. Users have different mindsets, geography, culture, socioeconomic status, and needs from those of us who create tools for them.

There were also some lessons unique to being in a crisis zone and working in the social sector.

Sometimes, obvious solutions are still best. As an example, when thinking of the market landscape and competitors for a to-do list application, people often forget 'writing on one's own hand,' a competitor which doesn't require battery power or a learning curve.[20] Digitizing an existing process doesn't guarantee its adoption, especially in the social impact sector where the cost and time to learn new tools or train people may exceed the savings gained. This is amplified in a disaster where everyone is busy and under-resourced. It's not an ideal time to learn a new workflow.

We suffered from being 'a hammer looking for a nail,' especially as we kept pivoting deeper when the initial solution wasn't viable.[21] When you have a solution in mind and go seeking problems, you're often destined to fail.[22] Boring, incremental solutions can still be extremely useful, even if they are simple process or operational improvements. After numerous iterations with Resource Finder, we found Google Spreadsheets to be an adequate solution, enabling responders on the ground to share information without the overhead of learning new tools, and providing the flexibility to adapt to new uses as they arose. Resource Finder just served to define appropriate initial column headers!

Still, one of the biggest lessons from the social impact space is that you'll have more failure than success – not unlike the wider world of technology product development. Technology is by nature experimental and risky. This sense of risk is especially pronounced when compared to the immediate and direct impact required by more conservative approaches of the philanthropically funded aid sector. When developing products for impact at scale, most ideas don't pan out, but the cost of failures are outweighed by the massive successes. The venture capital industry is built on the understanding that it takes hundreds of investments for one positive outcome. Especially when dealing with complex social challenges rather than rapid-response-based crisis relief, there is a lot of merit in the iterative, experimental approach taken by the venture world. We need to get more comfortable with failure in the impact space, because it is from these learnings that we will find a revolutionary solution.

Even if we accept the value of a high failure rate, it's useful to know when a product is failing so it can be evolved or abandoned. This requires a thoughtful approach to measuring the impact of products. Our team had planned to measure page views and interactions, how many people actually viewed the tool, as well as updates to data, as a way of showing its utility. Still, this data was a distant proxy for actual utility. Did the tool save a life? Did it help deliver blood on time? Many digital tools are layers removed from the offline impact they have in the real world. We faced a very similar challenge more recently when working on Google's Health Search, a way of navigating high-quality medical information when searching for health information.[23] Here, using things like clicks and views were far proxies from our actual goal of improving population health.

The gap between measuring online behavior and offline actions is slowly closing with mobile phones constantly with us and offline processes becoming more data-driven. But most social impact projects have long timelines for change, creating the difficulty of separating correlative and causative factors. One might conclude that the launch of Google Health Search four years ago actually *reduced* the life expectancy of Americans if only those two events are correlated without understanding the opioid epidemic and spate of recent suicides in the U.S.[24]

When prioritizing, teams have to make difficult decisions between scale and impact. For example, offsetting the saving of a single life against changing the minds of an entire population introduces tricky ethical prioritization decisions. As technology becomes more pervasive in our lives, we need to recognize the potential harm caused by apparently 'small' experiments. As an example, in 2012, Facebook briefly altered the news feed to show happier or sadder stories, to understand the emotional impact on users, without engaging an Institutional Review Board

(IRB).[25] IRB processes are largely outdated for the Web, but as tech companies move into spaces like health, psychology, and well-being, appropriate IRB processes and informed consent procedures need to be devised.[26] In addition to the effect of algorithms, the effects of data and user privacy must be carefully considered early in the product process to ensure individuals in need, need not give up their privacy.

So, why did Person Finder succeed where Resource Finder failed? The former was simple – and it answered a burning need. Incentives to provide data and to search for data were strong. And it fit into an existing, if imperfect, ecosystem of missing persons lists. And maybe it helped that we were closer to the user – we were better able to put ourselves in the shoes of someone outside Haiti looking for a loved one in an information-poor environment.

Making product development for social impact sustainable

In the case of Crisis Response, we were initially embedded inside Google.org, a corporate philanthropy set up by Google's founders to invest 1 percent of the company's net profit in innovative nonprofit partners.[27] Google.org helped bridge the divide between the way that nonprofits adopt technology, and the way that technologists think. The challenge of interdisciplinary collaboration like this is one of the central issues in achieving positive social impact with technology: for technologists tend to provide solutions without sufficient appreciation of the problems to be solved, and domain specialists tend to hew too closely to conservative approaches that have worked well in the past. In order to succeed, technologists must resolve the conflict between risk aversion and impulsive experimentation to create an organizational approach that integrates the iterative, fail-quickly methodology into the more highly planned style favored by nonprofits. It turns out that if a technology works well in one context, the social sector is much more likely to adopt it. This permission does not come easily – nor should it. After all, as in the case of Resource Finder, the cost of wrong information could be life-threatening. But the interdisciplinary collaboration that Google.org prized – a collaboration that brought out the best in both philanthropists and technologists – is an important concept that should be taken forward as product development for impact continues to evolve.

Google is not alone in their impact-minded work – a large portion of impact engineering happens under the auspices of commercial companies. This adopted model is similar to Google.org, with impact engineering taking place not just inside the corporate social responsibility arm. This is an exciting and much-needed development in our opinion. While many social impact efforts require philanthropic input (or at best eliminate the priority of profit), we believe that in the long run profitability is critical for sustainability and scalability. But how can capitalistic forces of shareholder value and profit be reconciled with the social aim of doing good?[28]

Tesla, the electric car company, is a great example of the corporate coupling of profit and impact. Elon Musk's initial goal with Tesla was to prove the viability of electric cars in the U.S. because of the threat posed by climate change. Today, every major car company produces at least one electric car model, because Musk has not only been able to reduce carbon emissions, but also to run a profitable business.[29] While nonprofits often have a hard time allocating budget towards capacity building given funding pressures and the immediate needs of the populations they serve, for-profit companies, like Musk's, have a role to play in continually improving products because of market demand – but also pushing market demand in a particular, in this case sustainable, direction, with the products they invent.

Businesses like Tesla that are focused on positive social impact often have a 'double bottom line.' The primary one still focuses on fiscal needs while the secondary one focuses on social impact. In the case of Crisis Response, as the product matured and became part of the Search team, we endeavored to also have a double bottom line, one serving victims of disasters and another serving user needs on Search. We used the same page view and click metrics as other Search teams and organized our team to align well with the rest of the organization. This ensured the team wouldn't get reallocated to higher-priority projects and set proper expectations inside the organization. Even with these safeguards, Crisis Response still needed executive support to ensure that the team is sufficiently resourced for success.

Conclusion: The future of product development for social impact

Technology is a significant force in the global economy. Seven of the top eight companies by market capitalization are tech companies.[30] Computer science is becoming a literacy requirement for new jobs – and some universities offer it as a language credit.[31] Inevitably, technology is becoming important for social impact. The growth of B Corporations and Social Enterprises shows how thinking has shifted; Y Combinator, the Silicon Valley start-up incubator that produced Dropbox, Airbnb, and Reddit, accepts several social enterprise start-ups each year.[32]

Technologists themselves are becoming more excited about their ability to create social impact. Jeffrey Hammerbacher, an early Facebook data scientist, said, "The best minds of my generation are thinking about how to make people click ads. That sucks."[33] And Jennifer Pahlka from Code for America, exhorts us to "try to solve overcrowding in jails or climate change . . . and I think those minds will find themselves pushing for more-innovative solutions."[34]

The same technically ambitious product development approaches and the same talented people that have created valuable companies can produce valuable social impact. We can't help but be optimistic that the best is yet to come!

8 Behavioral science for impact

The new science of designing for humans

Piyush Tantia

Piyush Tantia is Chief Innovation Officer at ideas42, and a board member. Since joining ideas42 in 2009 he has worked closely with leading academics from Harvard, MIT, Princeton, and others to design and implement solutions in various areas including consumer finance, education, international development, poverty, criminal justice, and health care. As ideas42's founding Executive Director until June 2018, he transitioned the organization from a research initiative at Harvard University to an independent 501(c)(3) nonprofit. Prior to joining ideas42, Piyush was a Partner at the leading strategy consulting firm, Oliver Wyman. He has been a visiting lecturer at the Princeton Woodrow Wilson School and frequently lectures at Harvard, Wharton, and Columbia. Piyush has served on the World Economic Forum Global Agenda Council on Behavior and various boards. He holds an MPA from the Harvard Kennedy School of Government, a B.S.Econ from the Wharton School, and a B.S.E. in Computer Science from the University of Pennsylvania.

★ ★ ★

Today the design of things that involve human interaction, such as programs, product delivery, and services, is more art than science. Here is how it typically works: we use our creativity to brainstorm a few big ideas, experts decide which one they like, and then investors bet on the winner, often with billions of dollars at stake.[1]

This way of design should be replaced by a superior method that can enable us to innovate with more success and less risk. Specifically, we can use scientific insights to generate new ideas and then systematically test and iterate on them to arrive at one that works.

Advances in two academic fields afford this opportunity. The first is behavioral science, which gives us empirical insights into how people interact with their environment and each other under different conditions. Behavioral science encompasses decades of research from various fields, including psychology, marketing, neuroscience, and, most recently, behavioral economics. For example, studies reveal that shorter deadlines lead to greater responsiveness than longer ones, that too much choice leads people to choose nothing, and many more observations, often counterintuitive, about how people react to specific elements of their context.[2]

The second academic field is impact evaluation. Economists have used Randomized Controlled Trials (RCTs) and other experimental methods to measure the impact of programs and policies. Such impact evaluations are becoming more and more common in the social sector and in government. These methods allow us to test whether an innovation actually achieves the outcomes that the designer sought.

Taking a scientific approach also solves another common problem: sometimes we do not even realize that there is something in need of rigorous, thoughtful design. When we look carefully, the success of most of what we design for people depends as much, if not more, on the human interaction as on the physical product. For example, the first iPhone offered essentially the same functions (phone, calendar, address book, etc.) as a BlackBerry, but it totally changed the experience of using those functions.

In the social and public sectors, programs and services are made up largely of human interactions. And yet anything involving human interaction can be designed more scientifically, and more successfully, when behavioral science and impact evaluation are applied. For instance, a vaccine is a technological product, but how and when parents get their children vaccinated, and how they are reminded to do so, is as much a part of the innovation as the vaccine itself. Poorly designed interactions make products less successful and can also underlie serious social problems.[3]

By putting behavioral science and impact evaluation together – a methodology we call behavioral design – we can design more like engineers than like artists. We can use behavioral science to develop ideas that are much more likely to work than those relying entirely on intuition. And we can rigorously test those ideas to determine which ones truly work. Following the model of engineering and scientific progress, we can build on prior success to make enormous advances that, under previous approaches, would not be possible.

A better methodology

At ideas42, in the behavioral science innovation lab I co-lead, we encounter many different approaches to innovation among our partners. I have also spent considerable time comparing notes with experts in design thinking, attending design workshops, and reading about design methodologies. The typical approaches for innovation range from quickly brainstorming some ideas in a boardroom to using some version of human-centered design (HCD). Fundamentally, all of these approaches aim to generate 'big ideas' that appeal to the intuition of a few decision-makers considered experts in the area where the idea is to be implemented.

HCD appears to be the methodology of choice for a significant, and growing, number of organizations. The most advanced version begins with defining the problem or design mandate, and then conducts qualitative research with potential users and proceeds through a series of structured exercises to promote creative thinking. The design team may also test some crude prototypes to get feedback along the way. This approach is called 'human-centered' because it focuses on users' and other stakeholders' needs and preferences.

In the qualitative research phase, designers use ethnographic techniques such as qualitative interviewing and observation. They not only interview potential users but also may talk to others, such as program administrators and front-line staff involved in delivering a program or product. In the design phase, HCD employs several techniques to enhance creativity (which remain useful in the next-generation behavioral design methodology as well). Finally, HCD ends with trying a few prototypes with a handful of potential users. Some ethnographic research methods are incorporated into HCD, but on the whole the approach is still much closer to an art than a science.

It is time to build on HCD with a better method. Let us begin our investigation by comparing how engineers invent new technology. Two features stand out. First, engineers rely on a rich set of insights from science to develop new ideas. Every invention builds on countless previous attempts. For example, the Wright brothers are credited with inventing the airplane, but the key parts of their design leaned on previous inventions. The wing was based on science that went back to 1738, when Daniel Bernoulli discovered his principle about the relationship between pressure and the speed with which a fluid is moving. The engine design was borrowed from automotive engines invented more than 25 years earlier. They were able to test model wings in a wind tunnel thanks to Frank H. Wenham, who had invented that critical apparatus 30 years before that, in 1871.[4]

Second, contrary to popular belief, inventions do not come simply from a single flash of insight, but rather from painstaking refinement in small steps. Sir James Dyson, the famous vacuum cleaner tycoon, went through 5,126 failed iterations of his new wind tunnel design to separate dirt from air before he landed on the right one.[5] Inventors sometimes iterate only on particular components before working on the complete invention. For example, the Wright brothers tested some 200 wing designs in a wind tunnel before settling on the right one.

Why do engineers work so differently from those of us who are designing for human interactions? Until recently, we did not have a sufficiently large body of scientific insights that describes how humans interact with their environment, and each other, under different conditions. True, the field of user experience design offers some insights, but it is very new and is still restricted to certain elements of digital interactions such as Web page layout and font size. Direct marketers within for-profit businesses have experimented with letters and phone scripts for years, but those findings also cover a very narrow set of interactions and are often not public.

The second engineering feature – experimenting and iterating – is also hard to replicate, because measuring whether something 'works' in this case is more complex than simply turning on a piece of technology and playing with it. We must first clearly define what outcomes we want from the design, devise a way to measure them, and finally run a test that reliably tells us whether our design is achieving them.

More rigorous testing of ideas

The problem with HCD and similar approaches to innovation is that they depend too much on intuition. Research has repeatedly shown that our intuitions about human beings are often wrong. Take the commonsensical idea that penalties always help prevent people from engaging in bad behaviors; this notion may have intuitive appeal, but it has proven false. For example, in a study of Israeli day-care centers that sanctioned parents for being late to pick up their children, researchers found that penalties made parents *even more likely* to be late.[6] This is because they viewed the penalty as a cheap price for the option to be late, versus feeling bound by a social obligation to be timely.

Not only do the social and behavioral sciences give us better starting points, but it also enables us to prototype and test ideas more readily, because we can measure if they are working using impact evaluation methods as well as lab testing procedures from experimental psychology. We can then iterate and improve on the idea until we have a solution ready for implementation.

The behavioral design methodology incorporates HCD's fundamental approach of being human-centered and thoughtful, but adds scientific insights and iterative testing to advance HCD in three significant ways. First, it applies observations about people from experimental academic research. HCD's reliance solely on self-reported and intuitive insights presents a risk, since so much human behavior is unconscious and not transparent. Also, psychology research shows that people's self-perception is biased in several ways.[7] When we do supplement academic insights with qualitative research, we can use behavioral science to make the latter less vulnerable to bias. For example, we can get more unvarnished answers by asking subjects what their peers typically do rather than what they themselves do. When asked about themselves, subjects may be embarrassed to admit to certain behaviors or may feel compelled to give what they assume the interviewer thinks is the 'right' answer.

Second, behavioral design can enhance HCD in the design phase. The behavioral science literature can contribute ideas for solutions based on previously tested interventions. As behavioral design becomes more widely used, more and more data will become available on what designs work and under what conditions. In filtering ideas, we can use behavioral science to anticipate which solutions are likely to suffer from behavioral problems such as low adoption by participants or misperception of choices.

Third, this new approach improves upon HCD by adding more rigorous testing. Many HCD practitioners do test their ideas in prototype with users. While helpful, and part of behavioral design as well, quick user testing cannot tell us whether a solution works. Behavioral design leverages experimental methods to go much further without necessarily adding considerable cost or delay.

Using this approach, we test whether something works – whether it triggers a desired behavioral result – rather than whether the subject thinks something works. We can also test a single component of more complex designs, such as whether a particular piece of information included on a Web page makes a difference, in a lab setting with subjects from our target audience. This is analogous to aeronautical engineers testing wing designs in wind tunnels. By testing and iterating in the field, we do not need to bet on an untested big idea but instead can systematically develop one that we know works. Testing is also what makes it possible, in the design phase, to build on previous successful ideas.

ideas42's work includes many examples of using behavioral design to invent solutions to tough social problems. For example, we recently worked with Arizona State University (ASU) to encourage more eligible students to apply for a special federal work-study program called SEED. In fall 2014, before we started working with ASU, only 11 percent of eligible students were applying for SEED jobs, leaving nearly $700,000 in financial aid funds unused. ASU wanted our help to increase this proportion.

Diagnosing the problem through a behavioral lens, and interviewing students and staff, we learned that students mistakenly believed that SEED jobs were menial and low-wage. Some thought that a work-study job would interfere with their education rather than complement it. Others intended to apply but missed the deadline or failed even to open the email announcing the program. We designed a series of 12 emails to attempt to mitigate all of these barriers. The emails dispelled the misperceptions about work-study jobs by stating the correct facts. They made the deadline more salient by reminding students how many dollars of aid they stood to lose. Behavioral research shows that losses loom larger than gains, so the loss framing promised to be more impactful than telling students how much they stood to gain. The emails asked students to make a specific plan for when they would complete the work-study job application to reduce the chance that they would forget or procrastinate past the deadline. These behaviorally informed emails were compared against a control group of 12 emails that contained only basic information about how to apply to the SEED program.

With the redesigned emails, which ASU has now adopted, 28 percent more students applied for jobs, and the number of total applications increased by 56 percent. As we were sending 12 emails, we used the opportunity to test 12 different subject lines to try to maximize the number of students who opened the email. In five out of the 12 cases, the rate of opening increased by 50 percent or more, relative to a typical subject line. A subject line that increased the open rate from 37 percent to 64 percent made students feel special: "You have something other freshmen don't." The control in this case was commonly used language to remind the recipient of impending deadlines: "Apply now! SEED jobs close Thursday."

The behavioral design methodology

Efforts like this one may sound like nothing more than trial and error, but a systematic and scientific process underlies them that tracks the success of engineering or medicine more closely than HCD. It begins with *defining* a clear problem, *diagnosing* it, *designing* solutions, *testing* and refining the effectiveness of those ideas, and then *scaling* the solutions.[8] It also starts from a body of knowledge from behavioral science, rather than intuition and guesswork, so that the solutions tried are more likely to succeed.

Let us now take a closer look at these steps.

1. Define

The first step is to define the problem carefully to ensure that no assumptions for causes or solutions are implied and that the desired outcome is clear. For example, organizations we serve commonly ask: "How do we help our clients understand the value of our program?" In this formulation, the ultimate outcome is not explicitly defined, and there is an assumption that the best way to secure the outcome is the program (or product) in question. Say the relevant program is a financial education workshop. In this case, we do not know what behaviors the workshop is trying to encourage and whether classroom education is the best solution. We must define the problem *only* in terms of what behaviors we are trying to encourage (or discourage), such as getting people to save more.

2. Diagnose

This intensive phase generates hypotheses for behavioral reasons why the problem may be occurring. To identify potential behavioral hurdles, this approach draws insights from the behavioral science literature and what we know about the particular situation. For example, in the ASU work-study project, we hypothesized that many students intended to apply but failed to follow through because they procrastinated past the deadline or simply forgot it. Both are common behavioral underpinnings for such an intention – action gap.

After generating some initial hypotheses, the next step is to conduct qualitative research and data analysis to probe which behavioral barriers may be most prevalent and what features of the context may be triggering them. Here, 'context' refers to any element of the physical environment, and any and all experiences that the consumer or program's beneficiary is undergoing, even her physical or mental state in the moment.

Qualitative research usually includes observation, mystery shopping (purchasing a product or experiencing a program incognito to study it firsthand), and in-depth interviews. Unlike typical qualitative research that asks many 'why' questions, the behavioral approach focuses on 'how' questions, since people's post-hoc perceptions of why they did something are likely to be inaccurate.

3. Design

Having filtered down and prioritized the list of possible behavioral barriers via the diagnosis phase, we can generate ideas for solutions. Here many of the structured creativity techniques of HCD prove useful. When possible, it is best to test a few ideas rather than to guess which solution seems best. Solutions also change during their journey from the whiteboard to the field, as numerous operational, financial, legal, and other constraints invariably crop up. Such adaptations are critical to making them scalable.

4. Test

We can then test our ideas using RCTs, in which we compare outcomes for a randomly selected treatment group vis-à-vis those for a control group that receives no treatment or the usual treatment. Although RCTs in academic research are often ambitious, multiyear undertakings, we can run much shorter trials to secure results. An RCT run for academic purposes may need to measure several long-term and indirect outcomes from a treatment. Such measurement typically requires extensive surveys that add time and cost. For iterating on a design, by contrast, we may only measure proximate indicators for the outcomes we are seeking. These are usually available from administrative data (such as response to an email campaign), so we can measure them within days or weeks rather than years. We measure long-term outcomes as a final check only after we have settled on a final solution.

When RCTs are impossible to run even for early indicators, solutions can be tested that approximate experimental designs. A more detailed description of these other methods is outside the scope of this article but is available through the academic literature on program evaluation and experimental design.

If the solution is complex, we first test a crude prototype with a small sample of users to refine the design.[9] We can also test components of the design in a lab first, in the way that engineers test wing designs in a wind tunnel. For example, if we are designing a new product and want to refine how we communicate features to potential users, we can test different versions in a lab to measure which one is easiest to understand.

5. Scale

Strictly speaking, innovation could end at testing. However, scaling is often not straightforward, so it is included in the methodology. This step also has parallels with engineering physical products, in that designing how affordably to manufacture a working prototype is, in itself, an invention challenge. Sometimes engineers must design entirely new machines just for large-scale manufacturing.

Scaling could first involve lowering the cost of delivering the solution without compromising its quality. On the surface, this step would be a matter of process optimization and technology, but as behavioral solutions are highly dependent on the details of delivery, we must design such optimization with a knowledge of behavioral principles. For example, some solutions rely on building a trusted relationship between frontline staff and customers, so we would not be able to achieve a cost reduction by digitizing that interface. The second part of scaling is encouraging adoption of an idea among providers and individuals, which itself could benefit from a scientific, experimental process of innovation.

A closer look at the methodology

To be fair, it is sometimes impossible to go through the full, in-depth behavioral design process. But even in these cases, an abridged version drawing on scientific insights rather than creativity alone is always feasible. Notice that the define, diagnose, and design stages of the behavioral design process apply the scientific method in two ways: they draw on insights from the scientific literature to develop hypotheses, and they collect data to refine those hypotheses as much as possible. The first of these steps can be accomplished even in a few hours by a behavioral designer with sufficient expertise. The second component of data collection and analysis takes more time but can be shortened while still preserving a scientific foundation for the diagnosis and design. Field testing with a large sample can be the most time-consuming, but lab tests can be completed within days if time is constrained.

Two sorts of hurdles typically confront the full behavioral design process: lack of time and difficulty measuring outcomes. In our experience, time constraints are rarely generated by the problem being addressed. More often, they have to do with the challenges of complex organizations, such as budget cycles, limited windows to make changes to programs or policies, or impatience among the leadership. If organizations begin to allocate budgets for innovation, these artificial time constraints will disappear.

To better understand working under a time constraint, consider ideas42's work with South Africa's Western Cape to reduce road deaths during the region's alcohol-fueled annual holiday period. The provincial government had a small budget left in the current year for a marketing campaign and only a few weeks until the holiday season began. The ideas42 team had to design a simple solution fast; there was no time to set up an RCT with a region-wide marketing campaign. The team instead used an abridged version of the first three stages to design a solution grounded in behavioral science. Quick diagnosis revealed that people were not thinking about safe driving any more than usual during the holidays, despite the higher risk from drunk driving. To make safe driving more salient, ideas42 designed a lottery in which car owners were automatically registered to win but would lose their chance if they were caught for any traffic violations. That design used two behavioral principles coming out of Prospect Theory, which tells us that people tend to overestimate small probabilities when they have something to gain, and that losses feel about twice as bad as the equivalent gain feels good.[10]

Applying the first principle, we used a lottery, a small chance of winning big, rather than a small incentive given to everyone. Using the second, we gave people a lottery ticket and then threatened to take it away. Since an RCT was not feasible, we measured results by comparing road fatalities in the treatment period with road fatalities in the same month of the previous year; this showed a 40 percent reduction in road fatalities. There were no known changes in enforcement or any other policies. While ideas42 was not able to continue to collect data in subsequent years, because its contract ended, the program saw success in subsequent years as well, according to our contacts in government.

Conclusion: Adopting behavioral design

If you were convinced of behavioral design's value and wanted to take the leap, how would you do it? There are resources available, and many more are still in the works. Behavioral insights are not yet readily available in one place for practitioners to access, but are instead spread out over a vast literature spanning many academic disciplines, including psychology, economics, neuroscience, marketing, political science, and law. Results from applications of behavioral science are even more distributed because many are self-published by institutions such as think tanks, impact evaluation firms, and innovation consultancies.

To mitigate this problem, ideas42, in partnership with major universities and institutions that practice behavioral design in some form, is building an easily searchable Web-based resource as well as a blog that will make it possible to find ready-to-use behavioral insights in one place. In the meantime, some of these organizations, including ideas42, also offer classes that teach elements of behavioral design as well as some key insights from behavioral science that practitioners would need in order to do behavioral design. As the practice of behavioral design is adopted more widely, and its use generates more insights, it will become more powerful. Like technology, it will be able to continue to build on previous discoveries.

Organizations and funders would also do well to adopt the behavioral design approach in their thinking more generally. Whenever someone proposes a new approach for innovation, people scour the methodology for the secret sauce that will transform them into creative geniuses. In this case, the methodology applications of behavioral science, in themselves, do have a lot to offer. But even more potential lies in changing organizational cultures and funding models to support a scientific, evidence-based approach to designing interventions. Here are three suggestions about how organizations can adopt behavior design:

Fund a process (and people good at it), not ideas

Today's model for funding innovation typically begins with a solution, not a problem. Funders look to finance the testing or scaling up of a new big idea, which by definition means there is no room for scientifically analyzing the problem and then, after testing, developing a solution. Funders should reject this approach and instead begin with the problem and finance a process, and people they deem competent, to crack that problem scientifically. To follow this path, funders must also become comfortable with larger investments in innovation. The behavioral design approach costs a lot more than whiteboards, sticky notes, and flip charts – the typical HCD tools – but the investment is worth it.

Embrace failure

In a world where ideas are judged on expert opinion and outcomes are not carefully measured, solutions have no way of failing once they leave the sticky note phase and get implemented. In a new world where ideas must demonstrably work to be successful, failure is built into the process, and the lessons learned from these failures are critical to that process. In fact, the failure rate can serve as a measure of the innovation team's competence and their bona fide progress. To be really innovative, a certain amount of risk and courting failure is necessary. Adopting a process that includes failures can be hard to accept for many organizations, and for the managers within those organizations who do not want their careers to stall; but as in engineering and science, this is the only way to advance.

Rethink competitions

The first XPRIZE for building a reusable spacecraft rekindled the excitement for competitions, which have now become common even outside the technology industry. However, competitions to invent new technology are fundamentally different: with a spacecraft, it is relatively easy to pick the winner by test-flying each entry. In the social sector, by contrast, competitions have judging panels that decide which idea wins. This represents a big-idea approach that fails to motivate people to generate and test ideas until they find one that demonstrably works well, rather than one that impresses judges. Staged competitions could work much better by following a behavioral-design approach. The first round could focus on identifying, or even putting together, the teams with the best mix of experience and knowledge in behavioral design and in the domain of the competition. Subsequent rounds could fund a few teams to develop their ideas iteratively. The teams whose solutions achieved some threshold of impact in a field test would win. Innovation charity Nesta's Challenge Prize Centre has been using a similar approach successfully, as has the Robin Hood Foundation, with the help of ideas42.

Revolutionizing how we innovate presents a huge opportunity for improving existing programs, products, and policies. There is already sufficient scientific research and techniques to begin making the change, and we are learning more about how to better devise things for human interactions every day. The more we use a scientific approach to innovate, and construct platforms to capture findings, the more science we will have to build on. This immense promise of progress depends on changing organizational cultures and funding models. Funders can and must start to bet not on the right 'big ideas' but on the right process for solving challenges and on the people who are experts in that process. They must also not just expect failures, but embrace them as the tried and true means for achieving innovation.

9   Open innovation for impact
Designing prize competitions for outcome

Sara Holoubek

Sara Holoubek is the CEO and founder of Luminary Labs, a strategy and innovation consultancy working with private sector, nonprofit, and government clients to address the thorny problems that matter, including stemming chronic disease, rethinking the future of work, democratizing science, and using data to make smart cities safer. Having spent the first part of her career in venture-backed start-ups, she is particularly passionate about connecting the dots between emerging technology and incumbent industries to the benefit of society. Sara writes and speaks extensively on the intersection of technology, innovation, and humanity and has been recognized by LinkedIn as a Top Voice in Technology, Mashable as a female founder to watch, SmartCEO magazine as a New York Brava award winner, and PepsiCo WIN for her contributions to women in technology. She is also an active angel investor and advisor who has served as national chair of Step Up, a nonprofit that helps teen girls from under-resourced communities fulfill their potential; served as an inaugural member of the RWJF Pioneer Fund Advisory Group; and participated on the Aspen Health Innovation Project Planning Committee. Sara holds a B.A. from the University of Iowa and an M.B.A. from HEC Paris.

★ ★ ★

Following the 2007–2008 American recession, innovation was the name of the game. New job titles were minted, centers of excellence were formed, and corporate garages quickly dotted the landscape. At the time, Luminary Labs was working with Sanofi U.S., a pharmaceutical company, to identify viable 'beyond-the-pill' solutions that utilized emerging technology, including the rapid increase in smartphone ownership, to support people living with diabetes. The 2010 introduction of health care reform in the United States, which encouraged the industry to strive for the 'triple aim' of optimizing the patient experience, health outcomes, and cost, amplified the urgency of this request.

In response, we developed the inaugural Sanofi U.S. Data Design Diabetes Open Innovation Challenge, which called on designers, developers, data scientists, and the world at large to submit solutions to improve the outcome or experience of people living with diabetes. The most innovative and human-centered concepts would be awarded a prize purse of $220,000 with no strings attached; the finalists and winners could take the prize money without any further obligations to the sponsor, who sought to stimulate the marketplace and identify potential partners. In what had historically been a closed industry, this was a fresh and new model: it was good for the patient, the innovator, and the company.

Prize competitions like Data Design Diabetes belong to a field known as open innovation. The term was coined by Henry Chesbrough of The University of California, Berkeley, who describes open innovation as "a distributed innovation process based on purposively managed knowledge flows across organizational boundaries, using pecuniary and nonpecuniary mechanisms in line with the organization's business model."[1]

Traditionally, organizations have created closed environments in which to execute against particular aims. They compete for talent, invest in research and development, create intellectual property, and build a fortress around the entire thing. But what if organizations accepted that the best ideas might not come from within their four walls? Or that the most novel solutions might live at the fringes of an industry's or field's ecosystem? Or that partnership is the path to viability? This is precisely the kind of thinking behind open innovation: when organizations open up, they can both accelerate the identification of novel ideas and create tangible value for themselves, and the world at large.

Open innovation is not just for commercial businesses that aim to do good and do well. Both government and nonprofit organizations have long embraced open innovation to address some of the world's most pressing problems. In the eighteenth century, Britain offered a significant prize purse for advancements in seafaring navigation, and Napoleon's investment in a competition led to innovation in food preservation. More recently, The Defense Advanced Research Projects Agency's 2004 Grand Challenge ignited a decade of progress in autonomous vehicle technology.[2] In 2016, the Robert Wood Johnson Foundation funded The Mood Challenge for ResearchKit™ – a competition designed and produced by Luminary Labs – to further the understanding of mood. And, in 2017, the MacArthur Foundation issued a competition for a $100 million grant to fund a single proposal that promised real and measurable progress in solving a critical problem of our time (this prize went to Sesame Workshop, one of the other contributors in this book, which, in partnership with the International Rescue Committee, created programming for refugee children).

To be sure, open innovation is not the only tool in the social impact toolbox. And when an organization needs to be prescriptive or has a preconceived idea of what its ideal solution looks like, a more traditional procurement method may be preferred. But open innovation is particularly helpful when one is receptive to a wide array of solutions and willing to accept that some will completely miss the mark.

At Luminary Labs, we're focused on the problems that matter – from the future of health and science to the future of work and smart cities. Over the past eight years, we have found that open innovation, and incentive prize competitions in particular (Box 9.1), reap the same benefits for impact as they do for commercial aims: by tapping the power of the crowd, organizations can identify solutions that are both novel and viable. Defining the problem, investing in design, and optimizing for outcome are key to making open innovation work.

Box 9.1 Hackathon or challenge?

Organizations practice open innovation in many ways, and – thanks to big tech – hackathons, sprint-like events that last a day or a weekend, have become standard fare across a number of industries. The first documented hackathon was in 1999, and Facebook has promoted 'epic, all night' hackathons as a key element of its company's culture.

But where hackathons are valued for the ability to stimulate early thinking, identify talent, and produce rough prototypes, open innovation challenges, also known as incentive prize competitions (or simply prizes), unfold over months, or even years, often with the aim of exceeding a threshold or proving real world viability. Multi-stage challenges, also known as down-select challenges, do this by narrowing the pool of entrants at each round of judging, culminating in one or more winners.

Designing for outcome

So what makes for a good impact prize competition? We believe that there are three contributing factors: first, clearly defining the problem to be solved; second, investing in challenge design; and third, providing solvers with the resources required to close the gap between concept and viability.

Defining the problem

In an era in which people are seeking the 'iPhone of health care' or the 'Uber for homelessness,' it is easy to gloss over the *problem* at hand. Rather than putting the spotlight on prescriptive solutions or novel technologies, successful prize competitions commence with a clear and concise definition of the problem to be solved, as well as the piece or pieces of the problem that they aim to address through an open innovation mechanism. Defining a problem too broadly can make it difficult to obtain actionable results. Too narrow a definition can limit innovation within a prescriptive range of approaches. An ideal problem sits somewhere in the middle, where it has the opportunity to stimulate and expand a market.

For example, the U.S. Food and Drug Administration (FDA) Office of Foods and Veterinary Medicine (OFVM) sought to improve food safety through an incentive prize competition produced by Luminary Labs in 2014. While the American food supply is among the safest in the world, the Centers for Disease Control and Prevention (CDC) estimates that one in six Americans are sickened by foodborne illness annually. The overall negative economic impact of foodborne illness in the United States, including medical costs, quality-of-life losses, lost productivity, and lost life expectancy, is estimated to be as much as $77 billion per year.

In our early conversations, the FDA noted that it was already connecting with food safety innovators on a regular basis. The purpose of the competition, therefore, was to identify new approaches beyond the known solver base. We set out to design a 'Goldilocks' call to action – one that wasn't so broad that it would elicit intangible solutions, and yet not so narrow that it would only appeal to insiders. Striking a balance would require us to be clear on which part of the food safety problem to address. Was there a preferred pathogen? In which produce categories would we focus? Where in the food production system were we most interested? Was there a trade-off regarding acceptable thresholds, such as speed or accuracy? And would we consider novel technology – such as spectroscopy or metagenomics – a bonus or a requirement?

Early in the process, we settled on the pathogen *Salmonella* and the speed at which it can be detected. *Salmonella* causes over one million illnesses in the United States every year, with about 23,000 hospitalizations and 450 deaths, and is particularly hard to detect. According to David G. White, PhD, FDA OFVM's chief science officer and research director:

> Detecting low levels of Salmonella in produce can be like finding a needle in a haystack: difficult, expensive and time-consuming. Even a simple tomato might have up to a billion surface bacteria that do not cause harm to humans. Quickly detecting just the few types of bacteria that do cause harm, like Salmonella, is a daunting task.[3]

To further narrow the problem, we focused on produce – which is responsible for nearly half of foodborne illnesses and almost a quarter of foodborne-related deaths – and specifically, leafy greens, with an emphasis on sample preparation and/or enrichment in the testing process. We now had a problem to solve and a call to action.

At this point, we took a step back and asked the FDA what would constitute a 'big win.' They noted that their internal teams were either tracking or researching a number of revolutionary approaches such as metagenomics and quantum

Figure 9.1 The Goldilocks problem statement

detection, as well as new applications of existing technologies, such as spectroscopy. As a thought exercise, we considered a more specific call to action that included this technological focus: "to improve the speed of Salmonella detection in leafy greens through spectroscopy." Ultimately, however, we determined that narrowing the areas of technology would be too prescriptive and would reduce our ability to tap into a broad and diverse solver base. As a result, the challenge criteria noted that FDA was most interested in solutions that made use of revolutionary approaches or new approaches for existing technologies, but did not make this a formal requirement (Figure 9.1).

Investing in challenge design

In addition to the clarity of the problem statement definition, the level of investment in challenge design is a good indicator of how successful the prize competition will be. The market is flooded with platforms that aim to democratize open innovation, and better access to tools and crowds is a good thing. But in the absence of challenge design, even the strongest problem statement is not guaranteed to meet its objectives.

Thoughtful challenge design first addresses why the problem has not yet been solved. Some problems are hard nuts to crack, expensive, or even dangerous to solve. In other cases, the solver base might be unaware of the problem, uninterested in the problem, or unaware that their current work has applicability in other fields. In rare situations, there are simply not enough solvers with the required expertise.

The answers to this question are then balanced with incentives. People enter prize competitions for a variety of reasons. A common framework, inspired by the age of exploration and popularized by the U.S. Prize Authority, is Good, Glory, Guts, and Gold. Good speaks to the intrinsic motivation, glory to external validation, guts to the challenge itself, and gold to resources (both monetary and nonmonetary) offered as an incentive. Any given challenge might have one or more primary motivators, and solvers tend to be rational, weighing the benefits of allocating their time and energy in pursuit of a prize.

The challenge design itself can serve as an additional motivator – or deterrent – to participation. For example, onerous criteria may result in a smaller pool of submissions. This might be acceptable to the sponsor, but if the sponsor is seeking a large number of solutions from a cross-section of solvers, it would be wise to reduce the barriers to entry or reconsider the challenge timeline and incentives in order to attract more solvers. Intellectual property (IP) stance is also a hot button issue for solvers. While many prize competitions allow the innovator to keep the intellectual property, sponsors frequently include protections against future claims or a license to the solution and its derivatives. Solvers weigh these trade-offs against the prize purse. If the purse is too small, an early stage team might feel that it has more to gain by not entering.

Numerous challenge design questions surfaced during the research phase for the U.S. Department of Education EdSim Challenge, which called upon augmented reality (AR), virtual reality (VR), and gaming developers to produce educational simulations that would strengthen academic, technical, and employability skills. In 2012, the gaming industry had overtaken the movie industry, earning $79 billion globally.[4] But despite growth in consumer adoption, especially among youth, there was limited innovation in development of simulations for the K-12 and postsecondary education markets. The growing base of experts in AR, VR, and immersive game technologies either did not recognize the market opportunity or found that the commercial gaming opportunity was far more lucrative.

Simulation development, even at prototype stage, is a very costly endeavor – to the tune of over $1 million. We quickly discovered that to stimulate interest in developing education simulations, we would need to communicate the market opportunity (today students learn from textbooks, but the future will include simulations), the cash prize purse would need to be significant enough to offset the costs of development, and nonmonetary incentives would need to have real value to participants.

While traditional research and intellectual property searches are helpful tools to understand what has been done, engaging with real solvers is the best way to understand the combination of incentives – Good, Glory, Guts, Gold – to inspire participation. Early in the process, we had gained input and buy-in from influential stakeholders, including educators, the game industry, academia, big tech, and hiring organizations, through a formal convening, expert panels, and public feedback. In addition to providing valuable information, these conversations fostered relationships that came to bear later in the program; adding to the government-provided $680,000 prize purse, respected organizations such as IBM, Microsoft, Oculus, and Samsung provided both software and gear, including recently released VR headsets and free cloud services. These resources sent a clear signal to the market that there was an opportunity to transform learning through commercial game-quality simulations.

But what exactly were we asking participants to submit? And what would the parameters be for the winning solution? The design and development of a working simulation has many phases, and while the prize purse was significant, solvers

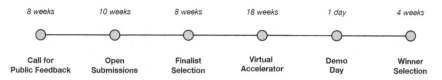

8 weeks	10 weeks	8 weeks	18 weeks	1 day	4 weeks
Call for Public Feedback	Open Submissions	Finalist Selection	Virtual Accelerator	Demo Day	Winner Selection

Figure 9.2 The Edsim Challenge timeline

made it clear that the requirements of the first-round submission would need to be achievable enough to merit the effort.

We designed the flow to include two rounds of judging, each requiring different degrees of fidelity (see Figure 9.2). The open submissions round would seek a detailed concept and design, including a description of the concept, simulation experience, and learning objectives; development plan and technical consideration; early thinking around implementation and scaling; and storyboards or visual mock-ups. During this round, the jury would narrow the pool to five finalists who would each receive $50,000, hardware and software from the sponsors, and access to a virtual accelerator to support development of a playable prototype to be presented at a demo day. The second and final round of judging would require detailed plans, including a description of the learning outcomes and assessment metrics; interoperability considerations and open source elements, and a playable prototype. Following a demo day, the grand prize winner would take home $430,000.

In September of 2017, the jury, which hailed from organizations including Ford, Microsoft, and Girls Who Code, had the chance to immerse themselves in fully functional simulations during a demo and pitch day. From a hands-on visit to the operating room to an exploration of astronomy concepts, the participants explored a wide range of educational experiences that teach career and technical skills. The winner was Osso VR, a surgical training platform that enables users to practice cutting-edge techniques through realistic, hands-on simulations, bridging the gap between career exploration and career preparation. By late 2018, Osso VR's team had raised $2.4 million in capital and launched a partnership with eight American medical residency programs including those at Columbia, UCLA, Harvard, and Vanderbilt.

Challenge design is both an art and a science that requires balancing the interests of the sponsor and the solver through motivation and incentives. When these are in harmony, they inform a suite of highly interrelated elements – including the call to action, criteria, timeline, terms and conditions, intellectual property stance, prize amounts and structure, submission form, jury selection, and judging rubrics – to support the overarching goal and desired outcome.

Closing the gap

Most start-ups fail, and many concepts never make it past paper. This is precisely why venture capitalists place bets on teams with the ability to 'close the gap' between a good idea and a commercializable product or service. The same can be said of open innovation: a frequent complaint is that the solvers' concepts often die on the vine. Challenges that solicit ideas are nice, but making those ideas real is always preferable. This is particularly true for impact challenges. It's one thing to fail to meet a commercial aim. Failure to meet a humanitarian or societal goal can result in entirely different consequences.

Back in 2011, when we launched our first challenge, most prize competitions were simply offering money for ideas. Our client, however, was in search of solutions that could be commercialized in the near term. We developed a multistage challenge methodology that shepherds the strongest solutions through an iterative process, ultimately closing the gap between the concept and real-world viability.

To do this, we borrowed the best practices from two rising trends (at that time) in business and adapted them to fit the open innovation challenge format. We looked to traditional tech accelerators that offered resources in the form of seed money, education, and mentorship, and modified their typical structure so that founders wouldn't be required to move across the country or give up equity. We also drew from design thinking methodologies (which Chris Larkin describes in a previous chapter) to firmly assert that the innovation needed to be human-centered, and we added educational modules that helped turn concepts into tangible and market-viable products and services. Interestingly, these two circles – tech accelerators and design thinking methodologies – did not yet intersect. We combined empathy building, subject matter knowledge, rapid prototyping, and business modeling to support iteration. And it worked; the winning team pivoted its solution mid-challenge after engaging with end-users and participating in rapid prototyping exercises. They have since raised more than $25 million in capital, recruited over 30 enterprise clients, and launched their service nationwide.

When designing the Alexa Diabetes Challenge, a $250,000, multi-stage prize competition sponsored by Merck & Co., Inc., Kenilworth, New Jersey, U.S.A in collaboration with Amazon Web Services (AWS), it occurred to us that nearly every solver would have a significant technical gap, as voice-enabled technology was in its infancy and health applications were few and far between. During this time, U.S. smart speaker sales had doubled and nearly half of all Americans had used a voice assistant.[5] And yet, the majority of early applications were for entertainment purposes. The challenge hypothesized that voice assistant uses would evolve from managing music playlists to managing life, including supporting people newly diagnosed with Type 2 diabetes.

The challenge received nearly 100 submissions from a broad cross-section of solvers – including academic research teams, individuals, start-ups, and even public companies. We needed to ensure that the finalist teams had the skills, especially the ones outside their expertise, to effectively produce *viable* solutions. To do so, each of the five finalist teams received $25,000, promotional credits from Amazon Web Services, and access to the virtual accelerator, which included an in-person boot camp at Amazon's Seattle headquarters. The boot camp featured a deep focus on the patient experience and behavioral economics, with sessions led by experts in diabetes education and health care innovation as well as Type 2 diabetes patients themselves. The finalists also worked directly with the AWS team to explore how they could harness Amazon services for transformative health care solutions. Last but not least, the teams participated in a 'round robin' session, rotating through working meetings with ten experts in diabetes management, health tech, data privacy, AI, voice technology, and voice user experience.

Anne Weiler, CEO of Wellpepper, the Alexa Diabetes Challenge winner, noted that when deciding whether to enter the challenge, she considered the prize purse and presumed publicity as table stakes. It was the learning opportunities, as well as the dedicated space and time to explore the problem, that ultimately enticed her to enter. Our 2018 survey of prize winning teams – semifinalists, finalists, and winners of 14 impact-focused challenges we produced over the past eight years – reiterated this sentiment. While only 10 percent of teams surveyed said learning opportunities – in the form of a virtual accelerator that could include a boot camp, piloting, and/or mentorship – were the primary motivation for entering, after the challenge, nearly half of teams surveyed (47 percent) named learning opportunities as an important benefit of participating.[6]

Measuring outcomes

As competitions, open innovation challenges inherently seek a winner. In this sense, one could measure the success of a prize competition by simply asking if a winner was selected. Some challenges clearly state that an award will only be made if a team meets the criteria. In 2018, the Google Lunar X Prize competition, which offered $30 million to the team that would be the first to send a private spacecraft to the moon before March 31, 2018, went unawarded.[7]

But this does not necessarily mean that the challenge was a flop. While no team made it to the moon in time, both finalists and nonfinalists continue to forge ahead, suggesting that open innovation challenges – and especially those focused on impact – are both a short and long game. In the short term, the objective was not met within the required time frame. However, in the longer run, the competition stimulated the market to do something it otherwise may not have, and it is expected that a commercial team will eventually make it to the moon as a result.

Google, however, may be an outlier. Most organizations value, and oftentimes require, quick wins to make the case for open innovation. Therefore, a more common approach to evaluating the success of a challenge is to assess both the quality and quantity of submissions in relation to the sponsor's objectives. Nearly every challenge will result in submissions that don't meet the criteria, but if the majority are outside of the range, or the winner didn't quite hit the mark, it is an indicator that something was amiss in challenge design.

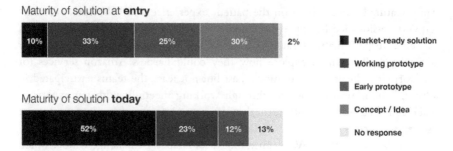

Maturity of solution at **entry**

| 10% | 33% | 25% | 30% | 2% |

Maturity of solution **today**

| 52% | 23% | 12% | 13% |

- ■ Market-ready solution
- ■ Working prototype
- ■ Early prototype
- ▨ Concept / Idea
- ▨ No response

Figure 9.3 Prize winner maturity over time

For sponsors that seek to stimulate a number of solutions, success hinges on what happens after the challenge. Did prize winners continue to develop their solutions? Or did they immediately disband? In our 2018 survey of prize winners, we found that almost all (92 percent) of teams surveyed continued developing their solutions after the challenge; at publication, 10 of 13 were market ready and two were working prototypes (Figure 9.3).

Another indicator of progress is the filing of patents. Eight teams from our survey reported filing at least one patent related to their solution since participating in a challenge. Two of those teams – Diabetty and Sugarpod by Wellpepper – filed patents for their voice technology solutions after participating in the 2017 Alexa Diabetes Challenge. And two others, finalists in the FDA Food Safety Challenge, filed patents after participating in the boot camp, suggesting that learning opportunities can create additional value.

Money talks, and the level of interest from the investment community is often a proxy for a challenge's ability to stimulate or even create a market. While raising money does not guarantee success – venture-backed companies regularly flop – capital is critical to ongoing development, especially for solutions addressing the thorniest problems. Our survey found that two-thirds of teams raised funding after the challenge – in the form of grants, venture capital, seed or angel investments, crowdfunding, and prizes – in amounts ranging from $5,000 to $25 million. Osso VR, the EdSim Challenge winner, raised $2 million in venture capital and has deployed its surgical training solution through partnerships with eight top U.S. medical residency programs.[8] Smart Sparrow, a finalist of the same challenge, received a $7.5 million investment from global education nonprofit ACT. Our survey estimates that prize recipients from our challenges have gone on to cumulatively raise $100 million in capital.

For some challenge sponsors, the pinnacle is the ability to deploy the winning solution. For example, the Purdue University team that was named grand prize winner of the 2014 FDA Food Safety Challenge has developed more advanced prototypes in partnership with other investigators and the challenge runner-up; collectively, they continue to work with scientists at FDA as they create an instrument for field testing.

Conclusion

In the 20th century, organizations prioritized internal excellence, protected intellectual property, and stoked competitive rivalries. In the first decades of the 21st century, we're witnessing the emergence of a new way to win – open innovation is all about partnership and collaboration in pursuit of new solutions to complex problems. Digitalization and globalization make it possible to tap the collective intellect of the Earth's population, and not just those experts whom an organization has hired. And a global body of solvers willingly participates, engaging in the co-creation of new products, solving algorithmic challenges, making use of open data sets, and competing in prize competitions.

We now have an entirely new framework for solving problems, one particularly well-suited to solving the problems that matter. The newness of open innovation brings certain challenges; not unlike the early days of 'digital,' most organizations are experiencing the growing pains of developing the competency. Though the field is well-studied, open innovation is still practiced differently by different sectors, industries, organizations, and even from one individual to the next. There are no established organizational, investment, or reporting models for open innovation, no common vernacular, and its champions are still busy educating and socializing the concept within their organizations. Tapping into the truly transformative power of open innovation will require a seismic shift in the way people think and the way organizations work.

In the interim, we are in a moment of extensive experimentation as private sector, nonprofit, and government organizations create proof points of how opening up can create community, stimulate markets, and surface viable solutions to the benefit of humanity.

10 Technology for impact

Exponential innovation and cautious optimism

Deena Shakir

Deena is a Partner at GV, formerly Google Ventures, where she helps start-ups scale and grow by connecting them to the world's largest organizations. Prior to joining GV, Deena spent five years at Google doing business development for early-stage products in health care, research and machine intelligence, and search. She also spearheaded social impact investments for Google.org. Deena previously led public – private partnerships with Global 2000 companies as a Presidential Management Fellow in the office of Secretary Clinton at the U.S. State Department. At the U.S. Agency for International Development, Deena was a partnerships advisor where she helped launch President Obama's first Global Entrepreneurship Summit in 2010.

Passionate about start-up entrepreneurship, Deena co-founded her first company at age 19 and is an angel investor and advisor to several young companies. Deena was an Aga Khan Fellow at The Aspen Institute's Program on Nonprofit and Social Innovation, where she supported the Global Philanthropy Program. She also covered the White House for BBC News and was the Lead Anchor for a bilingual news show on Al Arabiya. Deena holds a joint BA in Social Studies and Near Eastern Languages and Civilizations from Harvard College and an MA from the Georgetown University School of Foreign Service. She delivered the 2008 Harvard Class Day speech, 'From Baghdad to Boston: Dropping the Global H-Bomb.' Deena serves on the boards of directors of several nonprofits, including AMIDEAST, TechWadi, and Tarjimly. She is also on the Brain Trust of Girls Who Code and a Kauffman Fellow (Class 23).

* * *

I have a fairly untraditional background for a venture capital partner. I've spent the last decade in a variety of disparate roles – as a journalist, a diplomat, a philanthropist, a consultant, and even an academic. While the threads connecting these varied roles may not be self-evident, I have always been optimizing for one thing: the impact I can make on the world.

Though a far cry from my current vocation, I graduated from college planning to pursue a PhD in anthropology. Coming of age as a hyphenated Arab and

Muslim American in post-9/11 America, I believed I could make an impact most poignantly via academia, using my position to interrogate the problematic portrayals of the region and teach students on the subject. But before diving into the PhD commitment, I decided to start with a master's program at Georgetown, which fortuitously landed me in Washington, D.C. around the time of Barack Obama's 2008 presidential inauguration. After nearly a decade of turmoil between the Middle East and the U.S. – from sanctions on Iraq to the War on Terror – this new administration's position on the Middle East evoked in me all the hope for change it promised. And that hope turned into action just a few months into President Obama's tenure when he gave a much-acclaimed speech on New Beginnings with the Muslim world.[1]

In his speech, the former president announced a dedicated program on global entrepreneurship as one of several new ways of engaging and building bridges with the Muslim world. I was interning for the BBC at the time, exploring journalism as a kind of vocational anthropology, and remember being struck by the idea that entrepreneurship and technology (which often go hand in hand) could be such a powerful avenue for realizing the impact I wanted to see in the region I cared so deeply about. I had always been interested in entrepreneurship and technology: I grew up in Silicon Valley and co-founded an e-commerce company in college. But I hadn't really considered these ventures as part of a viable impact-minded career path until that speech. It was a watershed moment for me.

Thus ended my brief foray in academia and journalism and began my advent as a civil servant – first at the U.S. Agency for International Development and eventually at the State Department, where I helped launch the first Global Entrepreneurship Summit. The Global Entrepreneurship Summit was the first time I had the chance to witness in action the power of entrepreneurship to build bridges, drive economic growth, and provide livelihood and dignity to millions.

And then, several years later, the Arab Spring happened.

Beginning in Tunisia in 2010 and subsequently spreading to other North African and Middle Eastern countries, the Arab Spring launched with a series of popular revolts and demonstrations against established autocratic regimes. Over the course of roughly two years, protestors and activists expressed disillusion with their governments and called for more democratic and representative leadership. Having spent two summers living in Egypt in college, I never thought I would see this day – let alone so soon.

Enabling – although by no means responsible for – their efforts was the now more widespread use of smartphones and the more popular use of social media platforms, including Twitter and Facebook. Through these networks, and in conjunction with traditional community organizing, activists bypassed state-sponsored media channels to learn about what was taking place, organize protests, and connect with their peers to mobilize a movement. While these emergent technologies hadn't necessarily been designed to amplify resistance movements, they were trans-forming the interactions between individuals and their communities and, in this case, literally accelerating revolution. Social media platforms were democratiz-ing access to information and people, empowering communities to organize and mobilize online.

And the same has continued to be true in the years since: in the wake of tragedies and seismic political shifts, movements such as Black Lives Matter, the Women's March, and the March for Our Lives have leveraged social media tech-nology both to rapidly mobilize support and to sustain momentum over time. Technological advances have allowed these groups and others like them to amplify their messages at an unprecedented scale, increasing their potential for fast and meaningful impact.

Given this power and potential, it makes sense that there is a lot of optimism today about technology as a tool for impact. I was, and am, one of those optimistic people, and it is this belief in technology's revolutionizing power that ultimately landed me back in Silicon Valley – first at Google.org, then at Google.com, and now as a partner at GV (formerly Google Ventures), a venture capital firm.

But as anyone who has watched HBO's *Silicon Valley* or read TechCrunch will attest, it is often the subject of satire just how many start-ups or tech founders believe their product will 'change the world.' On-demand dry cleaning? Chang-ing the world. Weed delivery on demand? Changing the world. Self-driving cars? Changing the world. While the satire is not lost on me, I genuinely believe that we are living in a remarkable time, where technologies build upon one another to exponentially – not incrementally – improve processes and democratize access. At GV, I am fortunate enough to support some of these companies every day. But I also believe strongly that we need to temper our optimism about technology and impact. We need to be thoughtful and proactive about the tools we make, considering the intended and unintended consequences of our investments and inventions.

Tech for impact: A few examples from GV's portfolio

Claudine, a 20-year-old woman living in rural Rwanda, had serious complications while giving birth to her first child in February 2018. She needed blood urgently. The roads leading in and out of her village were badly in need of repair, and there was no way a medical crew from the nearest hospital could reach her in time. Then, something amazing happened: within 30 minutes of the distress call, essential medi-cal products and blood units dropped to her from out the sky. The delivery saved her life.

Zipline, one of GV's portfolio companies, together with the Rwandan govern-ment, has launched the world's first and now fastest drone delivery system operating at a national scale. Together, the partnership has delivered thousands of units of blood. It's a stunning example of how innovation can be distributed across the world to help those in need. Zipline was started by former professional rock climber and Harvard scientist Keller Rinaudo. Its headquarters are in San Francisco, but its real office is located several thousand acres away in the mountains overlooking Silicon Valley, where they conduct all their drone testing.

Zipline is an example of one way of thinking about technology for impact. But here is another that might seem different at face value. Impossible Foods is a company dedicated to making meat entirely from plants. Since its debut at Chef David Chang's Momofoku Fishi restaurant in New York City in July 2016, Americans have eaten about 6 million Impossible Burgers – the company's first product.

According to CEO and Founder Dr Patrick Brown:

> In eliminating the need for animals in the food system, we will return massive tracts of land to biodiversity, reduce food insecurity, and global conflicts, and let the Earth heal itself. Eliminating the need for animals in the food system is the easiest path to preserve our planet – without compromising quality of life.[2]

This potential for impact comes from the technology behind the burger itself. It uses 75 percent less water, generates 87 percent fewer greenhouse gases, and requires 95 percent less land and 100 percent fewer cows than a cow's meat burger.[3] And it does all this while delivering the same amount of protein and iron as a burger made from a cow – but its protein comes entirely from plants. If Americans were to replace just 50 percent of ground beef from cows with Impossible Foods' plant-based beef, we would conservatively be able to:[4]

- Spare the atmosphere of at least 45 million metric tons of carbon – the equivalent of removing the emissions of at least 11 million drivers in the United States for a full year.
- Save at least 3.2 trillion gallons of water – equivalent to the water used by at least 90 million Americans in one year.
- Release at least 190,000 square kilometers of land now being used for livestock and the crops they consume – a land area the size of New England, which could be restored to healthy wildlife habitat, reducing atmospheric carbon in the process.

The company's goal is to eliminate the need for animals for food production by 2035. At their estimates, this goal could be met before my three-year old daughter graduates college!

The comparison of Zipline and Impossible Foods gets at the heart of the challenge when trying to characterize 'tech for impact.' Unlike other vehicles for or disciplines of change – from design or engineering to media and grassroots mobilization – technology, as a 'field,' is not united by a discernable method or philosophy. In fact, we can think about it more as a 'cross-cutting' discipline since technology has a role to play across many of the other approaches to impact. (You'll see tech, in one form or another, talked about in nearly every chapter of this book.)

So if not characterized by a method, how should we think about technology in the impact space? As I see it, there are three inherent aspects of technology that make it particularly powerful for creating positive social change. The first of these is an instinct for *innovation*. Technology is about striving to do things better and, in the process, making new and better normals for people and the planet. For Zipline, innovation comes in the form of drone technology, and for Impossible Foods, it comes in the form of the science behind a new kind of meat. A second inherent aspect of technology is *access*: through connectivity, technology enables more and new groups of people to receive services, products, and information. Zipline's democratization of health care to even the most rural parts of Rwanda is a great example here. A third aspect of technology that makes it so powerful in impact-minded work is *scalability*. In a world where our biggest problems are systemic ones, we need to be thinking about change at scale. This is how Impossible Foods is thinking about the technology they've created: by changing the way people consume 'meat,' they can influence the system contributing to climate degradation.

Innovation, increased accessibility, and scalability are defining characteristics of many of GV's social-impact-minded portfolio companies. A few more examples follow below.

Andela – tech for inclusive employment

Andela is building a network of technology leaders across Africa to help companies overcome the tech talent shortage and build better products, faster. Not only does Andela instruct people in person, but thanks to growing access to Internet connectivity, 20,000 aspiring programmers across Africa have used its free online learning and training tools. By 2024, Andela hopes to have helped prepare 100,000 software developers in Africa for jobs, including thousands working for Andela.

Element Science – tech for heart health

In the first weeks to months following a heart attack, patients can have a much higher risk of dying suddenly from lethal heart rhythms. Cardiologist and serial entrepreneur Uday Kumar proposed a radical idea to prevent these recovering patients from dying: a user-centric wearable patch defibrillator. The device Element

Science has now developed around this vision will ultimately help many patients at risk of sudden cardiac death live longer lives.

Flatiron Health – tech to cure cancer

Flatiron Health is doing for cancer data what Google did for information on the Internet. Much of the available, real-world clinical data is unstructured and stored across thousands of disconnected clinics, medical centers, and hospitals. By unlocking this data, we can begin to accelerate research and improve cancer treatment. It is worth noting that Roche recently acquired Flatiron for $1.9 billion – an exemplary testament to tech for good that can return to investors. Today, the company has access to over 2.1 million de-identified patient records and counts many of the top life science companies as clients.

These are just a few of the many companies we're betting on to help improve lives today and in the future. Each new innovation stands on the shoulders of the one before it, each generation building on and accelerating the returns of past generations. Ray Kurzweil dubbed this concept 'the law of accelerating returns.'[5] According to Kurzweil, "We won't experience 100 years of progress in the twenty-first century – it will be more like 20,000 years of progress (at today's rate)."[6] This accelerated rate of innovation explains how our personal computing power became millions of times greater than NASA's at the time of man's landing on the moon in less than 50 years.[7] It is why machines can now sequence a human genome for $1,000, whereas the first sequencing cost more than $2.7 billion and took 15 years.[8] Change is not linear or gradual, it is exponential. According to Mary Meeker's 2018 Annual Report on Internet Trends, for the first time in history, roughly 50 percent of the world (or 3.6 billion people) have some sort of access to the Internet.[9] As the remaining 50 percent of the world gets online and innovation continues to accelerate at this exponential pace, just imagine the impact we will see.

The Fourth Industrial Revolution: Exponential innovation

At its core, technology, as I see it, is no longer a disparate field, as it arguably was conceived a decade ago, but actually a way of doing everything differently – from cancer research to burger production to credit financing and everything in between. Just as the Industrial Revolution changed the way we work and live, today's technological advances are fundamentally transforming the way we do everything. Each technological revolution has altered the way we produce and consume – from drawing energy out of water to the harnessing of electricity to digitization. The revolution we are in now, the so called 'Fourth Revolution,' is one catalyzed by the rise of information technologies.[10] These new technologies flatten the temporal and spatial boundaries that separate us from one another, provide us with access to people and perspectives from around the world, and enable us to share our stories and ideas more widely and rapidly. They have fundamentally reshaped how we understand ourselves as a species – who we are and who we can be. Over the last two decades or so, we have been starting to see ourselves more and more as connected agents within larger information systems, environments, and communities.

We are indeed now in the midst of a revolution that is bringing exponential – not incremental – change, as evidenced by some of the aforementioned examples, I'm incredibly optimistic about the potential of these new technologies to make the world a better place.

At the same time, we are right to be wary of technology's pitfalls and unintended consequences. The Arab Spring was met with government crackdowns and violent counterinsurgencies, including the ongoing deadly civil war in Syria and the advent of problematic political turmoil. As evidenced in the last few years, social media can be manipulated to influence elections and other political events. Children are growing up with profound addictive tendencies to screens, the consequences of which remain yet to be observed. We also encounter more subtle consequences of technology's growing presence in our everyday lives, from privacy violations to concerns that in spending more of our time online, we are losing our ability to engage with one another on a human level and as a society.

A recent piece in The Atlantic actually argued that "technology favors tyranny," and that

> together, infotech and biotech will create unprecedented upheavals in human society, eroding human agency and, possibly, subverting human desires. Under such conditions, liberal democracy and free-market economics might become obsolete.[11]

Discussions around the ethical implications of our emergent technology are just in their infancy. The oft-celebrated haste with which we build products, services, or businesses has produced enough examples of overlooked ramifications that companies large and small are beginning to thoughtfully consider the human implications of tech, and in particular AI. Google has recently published updates to its AI principles;[12] the Institute for the Future, in partnership with the Omidyar Network, Pierre Omidyar's philanthropic investment fund, has come up with an 'Ethical OS Toolkit,' – "a guide to anticipating the future impact of today's technology. Or: how not to regret the things you will build."[13]

It is clear we need to keep asking a few critical questions as we progress into this brave new world. Among them are things like: how can we harness technology and ensure that the tech we deploy is helping rather than hurting? What are the ethical implications of technology, and how do they inform the ways in which we develop new tech? And, importantly, how can we predict and militate against the unanticipated consequences of the technologies we build?

Conclusion: The age-old questions about technology, society, and change

Today, we're more enamored by and more wary of technology than ever before. We're thrilled by the prospect of smart assistants, but suspicious of how much they know about us. We can't wait to have self-driving cars, but remain skeptical of how safe they really are. We believe in the power of big data, but want to make sure individual privacy is protected. This tension isn't new – tech's ethos is change, and humanity has long-held reservations about change and how it plays out across society.

One major question that has dogged technology for centuries is whether disruption is positive or negative. Did the advent of social media, for example, positively change the way we connect and engage by building a new community platform, or has it transformed the connective fabric of society? Disruption is about breaking systems. This can be a good thing, because it means that tech can enable us to create real, systemic, and sustainable change. But disruption is inherently risky. Systems are webs, and breaking one system or part of a system can have a ripple effect on others, changing them for better or worse. Disruption is messy and unpredictable (as much as we like to think we're in control) – and often comes with unintended consequences.

Also to be considered, as the examples above allude to, is the nature of the communities and interactions that technology facilitates. Tech is the great connector. It enables people around the world to find one another, and this heightened access to others may spark greater empathy, cooperation, and coordination toward shared global goals. Connection can also mean locating small tribes of people that share – and validate – individual points of view. In the case of Black Lives Matter, activists used tech to mobilize a community around equal rights and social justice. In other cases, actors have deployed the connective power of technology to more malicious ends; consider white supremacist group Unite the Right's use of social media to organize the infamous rally in Charlottesville, Virginia in 2017. By connecting people through tech, we make possible the amplification of all kinds of ideas and worldviews – including ones that go against the very social changes we seek to create.

This question begets another: can technology ever be neutral or apolitical? Is tech a blank platform that individuals populate with political views? Or, in allowing (or suppressing) its usage by certain groups and individuals, is tech inherently political? Most theories around 'groups' and communities of people within society suggests that they are political by their very formation: they share a worldview, an interest, a vision, or ideals that are distinguishing from others. Distinction is at the heart of social politic. Should we think, then, about these technologies as neutral platforms that allow these groups a voice? Or are these platforms instead responsible for the substance of the content, making them part of social politics? In other words, do we hold people or platforms accountable for the content of a post?

Moreover, technology is designed to address problems and challenges, but many argue that those with the most power are typically the ones building the tech and determining which problems to solve. Indeed, more often than not, these leaders have been white cis males. Tech leaders, it can be argued, may solve for 'elite' problems while amassing capital that helps to keep those elites in power. To what extent is tech responsible for solidifying and exacerbating social and economic inequity – rather than truly 'democratizing access' to everything, for everyone, as is so often claimed?

Some of the biggest challenges surrounding technologies (and tech companies) today are bound up in these age-old questions. From social media to transportation, blockchain to 'big data,' we're all worried about whether these revolutions are for the better and what their consequences – good, bad, and ugly – might be.

I wish I had the answers to these questions, but I don't. Even if answers are elusive, we need to bring these questions to the forefront of our work because they probe us to rethink who is creating, investing in, and using our technologies. To truly invest in the future, we need to continue to invest in people and ideas that are as diverse and colorful as the world we live in. We must recommit ourselves to inclusive and impactful innovation, so that Claudine's children – and yours and mine – will live in a world with exponentially more opportunity, better education, less infectious and chronic disease, fewer greenhouse gases, and more access to basic health services.

11 Communities for impact

Harnessing the crowd to create a world we all can live in

Lara Stein

Lara Stein is currently the Executive Director of Women's March Global, the global sister organization of Women's March National. Most recently she was the Chief Engagement Officer at Wondros, where she developed strategy and thought leadership around community engagement, exponential organization, and leveraging the crowd to scale. Lara also recently acted as the Executive Director of MIT ReACT, a new institute-wide organization at MIT dedicated to developing a global educational platform for displaced populations and refugees. Previously Lara was Managing Director, Global Development at Singularity University, where she was responsible for Singularity University's global expansion and implementation vision and strategy. Lara is also the Founder of TEDx, a global movement and platform dedicated to ideas. She currently sits on the board of Lalela, a nonprofit dedicated to education through the arts in South Africa, and Equality Now, an international network of lawyers, activists, and supporters who have held governments responsible for ending legal inequality, sex trafficking, sexual violence, and harmful practices.

★ ★ ★

To understand where I'm coming from when I speak about communities, we have to go back in time.[1]

I was born in South Africa during apartheid. Officially in place from 1948 to 1994, apartheid was a government-mandated system of racial segregation designed to codify the power of the nation's white minority while disempowering its black majority and other nonwhite citizens. The decades-long era saw black South Africans forced out of their homes, their jobs, and the public sphere. When activists protested, the state reacted swiftly and brutally; South African security forces killed hundreds of protesters during the regime's rule.

My family was actively against apartheid (my brother would go on to contribute to South Africa's new constitution), and my perspective on the world was hugely informed by my experience growing up during this moment in South African history. I witnessed firsthand the suffering that systems like apartheid brought to whole segments of society. And yet, in observing the many activist groups that emerged to oppose the regime, I also saw how alternate systems could be designed to bring people together over shared ideals, and, ultimately, create real change. These activist groups were largely grassroots, established around shared goals like ending apartheid and empowering black South Africans. By harnessing powerful relationships and identities, they were able to carry out collaborative actions against the system for years.

Change didn't come fast. But it did come – in no small part because of the ideas and actions that united these internal resistance groups.

Throughout the various chapters of my life, I often come back to what I saw growing up in South Africa. While we hope that political entities will act in their people's best interests, governments are only one part of the solution when it comes to systems change – and, as South Africa's case illustrates, they are sometimes the very forces that push back against crucial reforms.

Though large bureaucracies have their role to play in impact, grassroots communities often constitute the backbone of enduring social change. A community, in the broadest sense, is an organized, collaborative network of people. From prayer groups to get-togethers at the local pub, the value of the community is that it helps people find order. It helps give life meaning because it deals in the currency of connections, ideas, and stories – those things that shape the way we see the world and how we act within it.

Flourishing grassroots communities are fundamental to systems change because their structures allow for the shaping, sharing, and spreading of stories. Systems, after all, are only based on the stories humans create. With apartheid, for example, the story was about the inferiority of a people based on the color of their skin. Grassroots movements dismantled any sense of 'truth' in that story, and as it became fiction, the infrastructures that upheld it had to go, too.

No two communities are truly alike, but if we have to categorize them, I see two that are relevant for social change. The first is a community based on *sharing*. It's the breaking of bread, the coming together of like-minded souls to have a conversation, inspiration, and the understanding that comes through this exchange. This was the premise of the first community I built. TEDx was about bringing diverse people together to hear and engage with ideas arising from local communities. It was a space where people could convene to discover and cultivate connections with one another and be inspired.

This action is the foundation of a second kind of community relevant to social change. This one goes a step further than simply sharing stories – it forms with the ambition of harnessing stories and *mobilizing* its membership to take collective action in order to address shared challenges. The aim is to change the way the world works to reflect the story this group knows to be true. This is a core goal of where I will take the evolution of my work in the future, as well as of the community I am currently working with, Women's March Global. Here, people come together around the shared belief that the rules of the world need to be re-written to provide men and women the same opportunities. This community is centered around the ability of stories to drive grassroots action.

Building communities, of many varieties, has been the focus of my professional work for the last twelve years. I've spent a lot of time contemplating how we can create communities that reconnect people in a profound and actionable way. How can we design communities that foster relationships and spark conversations about the future we want to live in? And, once assembled, how can these networks of like-minded souls take action together on a local, regional, and global level?

The thoughtful, deliberate design of communities that I am talking about is particularly critical today. Our world has seen radical changes: to our technology, our climate, our cultures, and our geopolitical realities. As in any moment of rapid change, people are seeking meaning and turning to communities to find it. But in our modern lives, technology unicorns seem to be the ones increasingly designing our communities. Through their platforms, they promise meaning, order, connection. And yet, most of the data suggests that despite – or, in some cases, because of – these platforms, we feel more alienated, more lost, and less and less connected. And beyond that, these platforms meant to facilitate exchange often peddle 'fake' stories or are designed to produce echo chambers that inhibit the potential for true exchange of ideas. The structures of these platforms have not been designed to serve the critical function of productively inspiring and activating their communities.

This is not to say that online forums do not have value or cannot serve some of the same functions that in-person community gatherings can. In fact, I think there is tremendous potential in online gatherings. (My own work at both TED and Women's March Global would not have been possible without the connective power of the Internet.) But technological advances have made it easier for us to create the bare-bones structures of community without the core elements through which communities truly flourish.

Both online and offline, we need to be more thoughtful and deliberate about the kinds of communities we build, to ensure that they serve us in achieving the future we want.

Connecting to inspire: Lessons from building the TEDx community

My career before TED ran the gamut from documentary filmmaking to children's television programming production, from technology to web strategy. After heading up the flagship office of an Internet strategy rollup, I stopped working for four years to have kids. Navigating my path back into the workforce after that time off, particularly as a woman, was probably the hardest thing I've ever done.

As I tried to figure out my re-entry, I thought long and hard about what truly mattered to me in a career. In the end, it boiled down to this: if I was to leave my twins at home to go back to work, I wanted it to be for a job with purpose. I also wanted to lead an interesting life, and I wanted to give back and make a real impact. Though I had found aspects of these things in various parts of my career up to that point, it was at TED that they converged for the first time.

I joined TED in 2009. At the time, TED consisted of one small annual conference still fairly unknown outside the United States, and TED Talks had just launched online. I was brought on to work for one of the TED Prizes called Pangea Day. The brainchild of a filmmaker who wanted to create a 'Super Bowl of film watching,' Pangea Day asked the question: what if we could get the whole world to watch an inspiring short film together at the same time? My role in bringing the Pangea Day vision to life was to organize the global community of hundreds of thousands of people around the world who would watch this short film together, and to help raise the funding to pull it off. All told, about three thousand unique groups of people convened online to watch Pangea Day, and I came out of the experience profoundly moved by the power of community to connect people around something of shared importance. Others in the TED organization were moved by the Pangea Day success, too. We began to ask what it would take to scale our TED community, bringing a more diverse array of people and perspectives from around the world into its fold.

I set out looking for answers to this question. Creative Commons (an online content- and knowledge-sharing community) and the growing open source movement more generally had always intrigued me, and I started thinking about what an 'open' TED Talk platform might look like. What if we built a format that gave anyone, anywhere, free license to host a TED-like conference? What if we *really* opened up the TED brand to a global community, allowing us to realize our mission of sharing 'ideas worth spreading' on an even greater scale? I spent the summer of 2008 contemplating these questions and developed a framework with rules and guidelines for what these communities could look like. At the same time, I developed a branding hierarchy and principles guiding the global use of the TED identity. At the end of the summer and after much deliberation, I pitched the concept of independently organized TED-like conferences to the executive team at TED.

And with that, an early version of TEDx was born.

We launched it as an experiment in March 2009 with a basic Google Doc application form, and by the end of the year organizers had hosted more than 250 events around the world. About a decade later, TEDx facilitates around 3,000 events each year, and TEDx talks have collectively hit one billion views on YouTube. Of course, the TEDx platform has evolved over the course of its existence. However, its original concept – fostering authentic connection through local idea-sharing and inspiration – has largely remained the same. We are proud to have created one of the largest event-hosting communities on earth.

During my time directing TEDx, and in those early months in particular, I gained invaluable insights into the structures that can help a global community thrive. One important structural question to crack involved regulation. TEDx was a free license, with only minimal guidelines (which would later become harder 'rules') dictating how organizers could host a conference under the TEDx brand. Excited though we were about the creative potential that this openness could unleash, we also recognized the risks that it presented: an unmediated platform could easily be misused and abused in ways that could harm community members and the brand itself. I spent much of that first summer in 2008 exploring the delicate balance between exercising control over the platform and letting go.

In negotiating this tension, we drilled down to the essentials (much as I had done while preparing to re-enter the workforce): which aspects of TED's vision and identity were critical to replicate in TEDx events, and which could we afford to be more flexible with? For example, we decided that to facilitate fresh thinking and connections, TEDx conferences needed to be multidisciplinary: rather than centering on specific topics such as health care or education, each event was to be based around a more abstract theme, inviting exploration by speakers and performers from diverse backgrounds and perspectives. We left it up to the organizer, however, to choose the theme and curate their event with presentations which they felt best reflected the innovation and creativity of their community.

In the end, we delivered the free license with relatively few regulations and a framework based on trust: anyone could start a TEDx conference, and, as long as they adhered to the guidelines, their license would be renewed. Remarkably, we found that in this trust-centered environment, the community policed itself and only rarely did people step outside the agreed-upon guidelines. Trust in our members was one of the most important cornerstones of our community and remains at the heart of TEDx's work today.

Another key structure that we established in designing TEDx was a clear system for gathering feedback from our community, which empowered us to innovate quickly and effectively. We actively solicited – and implemented – ideas from the community for improving the TEDx model.

At one point, for example, I attended an informal three-day meeting between TEDx organizers in Asia. A TEDx advisor who happened to run a professional development center at the base of the Great Wall of China at the time had invited these regional organizers to discuss how they could grow TEDx in Asia. Watching the group brainstorm and run through imaginative scenario-planning exercises under the commanding presence of the Great Wall was a transformative moment for me. I could see that we needed to make our model more responsive to regional groups seeking to self-organize and collaboratively design what TEDx would be to them. The 'self-organized regional workshop model' became the backbone of our community structure, as it was clear that TEDx was not just about lone-ranger events. Ideas like this one emerged from our global community constantly, and we continued to entrench feedback channels to better understand what our communities were feeling, how they were innovating, and how we could nurture their creativity.

A third structural element of TEDx's global community that evolved over time was the collection and leveraging of on-the-ground knowledge through local ambassadors. At first, when problems arose at TEDx conferences around the world, my team in New York would be called and would try to assess and mitigate the issue from afar. We learned that appointed regional ambassadors, who possessed valuable insights into the cultures and self-governance systems of their local communities, were actually much more effective and efficient at dealing with those issues.

These structures and others resulted in a TEDx community that was grounded in certain global core values and yet incredibly responsive to local needs, allowing it to play different roles in different places. In regions where technology overload had left people feeling alienated, for example, TEDx brought people together for inspiring in-person conversations with others in their locale. In places where speech restrictions could make it difficult to disseminate ideas, TEDx provided a nonpartisan and nonpolitical forum for discussing ideas free from animosity: at events in Palestine, Iraq, and Israel, for example, people arrived in jeans for casual, nonthreatening convenings around issues of importance to their communities.

While structures we put in place enabled TEDx to flourish, the most critical ingredient in allowing it to continue to do so is not its structure, but its ability to evolve. As a successful community's needs and ambitions shift and change, its structures will, naturally, need to evolve with it.

TEDx was an experiment in a lot of things, but for me, the most important findings about building community structures that emerged tied back to two questions that are at the heart of every global community building challenge. First, how can we negotiate between global and local to best cultivate and empower communities? Second, how much should we seek to control those communities and how much should we 'let go' in order to enable them to grow and achieve their own visions? The answers to these questions are not static, however. To create a sustainable community, structures must continue to be evolved to serve its members, recognize their investment and expertise, and retain their invaluable leadership and institutional knowledge.

Every community is different: you can't just wholesale adopt and adapt structures that work for one community to another. So, when tapped to help build a structure for the global community for Women's March, I asked myself a lot of the same questions – about global versus local priorities, and about control versus trust as an operating system – but arrived at very different answers.

Connecting to act: Lessons from building the Women's March Global community

Women's March was very different from TEDx from the start. In establishing TEDx, we sought to create an idea-sharing platform from scratch for a community that did not yet exist; with Women's March Global, we wanted to cultivate and harness the power of an organic movement for social change. With TEDx, our ambitions were apolitical; with Women's March Global, our ambitions were inherently political.

The March was born out of a moment of anger and passion. In the lead-up to the 2016 United States Presidential Election, polling had strongly predicted a victory for Hillary Clinton, who would have become the first female president in the country's history. Then, to the horror of women and others across the nation, Donald Trump – a man who had admitted to assaulting women, referred to Mexican immigrants as rapists, called for a ban on Muslims entering the country, and more – had been elected instead. The weeks and months following the election saw numerous rallies, marches, and other actions protesting the election and the new president. On January 21, 2017, the day after Trump's inauguration, millions of people across the United States and around the world peacefully marched in protest.

What most fascinated me about the Women's March – like the related #MeToo and #TimesUp movements that would emerge later – was that it brought together, in a massive and public way, women's groups that hadn't traditionally collaborated. Feminism has a history of division; time and again, women's rights movements have had difficulty adequately addressing the ways in which racism, classism and other discriminatory attitudes intersect with sexism and misogyny. In this moment, however, women's rights advocates of all stripes were united in anger, passion, and a compulsion to act. After the March, there was a palpable desire among its supporters to keep its momentum going. They wanted to continue bringing together disparate groups who shared a stake in women's advancement in order to create more equitable systems.

More equitable systems for women is obviously not just an American issue. In the wake of the original Inauguration Day protest, Women's March chapters began organically self-assembling around the world, acting upon their own local needs and challenges. Originally, there were no guidelines for these chapters; they could dream up and build whatever formats they deemed appropriate for their communities, from public demonstrations to intimate gatherings to political actions. Core areas of focus varied by chapter as well: U.S.-based chapters tended to focus primarily on local political issues and increasing voter turnout, while the many international chapters prioritized different causes that were relevant to their regions.

I was brought on to the Women's March Global team to help design structures that were appropriate for this international network of organic, grassroots communities. Our work is still in progress, but we started by digging into those two overarching tensions I had grappled with at TED: global versus local and control versus trust.

On the first point, we knew we wanted Women's March Global to be a unified platform. As the larger entity overseeing hundreds of Women's March communities, we had a vision for how we wanted to present human rights issues on the global stage and drive them forward. At the same time, we understood that in order to be effective, each chapter had to have the agency to push for the changes its community needed. We were constantly questioning how our global messages and strategies would work when filtered to local chapters. Equally important, we wondered how we could in turn amplify the visions and actions of local chapters, and at what stage we should take that step: was it when those ideas reached a critical mass of support at the local or regional level? Or, was it when we felt that we had sufficient thought leadership in place at the global level to execute those ideas on a larger scale?

The ways in which the Women's March Global community continues to be shaped will ultimately be a combination of local, grassroots inputs, collaboration with partner organizations, and global thought leadership. To help us strike the right balance in this regard, we have sought to listen to the grassroots community while also building an advisory board whose membership represents the diversity of both the community's geography and its priorities. We have also developed an ideological infrastructure that both articulates a unified, global vision and incorporates the perspectives of local chapters: the Health, Economic Security, Representation, and Safety (H.E.R.S.) Framework.[2] The four pillars of this framework, which align with and map onto the United Nations' Sustainable Development Goals, encompass what we found to be the most pressing issues for our diverse, worldwide community. Mirroring the intersectionality of the Women's March movement, each of these pillars is intricately linked to the other three, and none can be divorced from the others.

Our efforts to privilege local autonomy as much as possible within our global community have gone hand in hand with our discussions about control versus trust: we knew that any guidelines or resources we offered needed to come with the understanding that, ultimately, we trusted local chapters to determine what worked best for them to pursue their unique ambitions. This hyper-local, hyper-fractionalized, and hyper-action-oriented community character of Women's March Global is very different from that of TEDx, which, despite the curatorial flexibility, provides its organizers a more strictly enforced identity and overarching approach to follow. Supporting an organic and diverse community such as Women's March Global requires structures that are therefore even more flexible and readily adaptable. How the overarching Women's March Global entity built these trusting structures to empower local communities' self-direction, offer bespoke tools unique to their diverse needs, and help them share knowledge and best practices between themselves are some of the critical questions we continue to think about.

Conclusion: The future of community building for social change

Both TEDx and Women's March Global are worldwide communities comprised of a network of grassroots communities. They harness the power of like-minded people coming together to inspire and to make change – both important catalysts for systems change. But grassroots communities are just one piece of the systems change puzzle.

It is time for us to intentionally design a new kind of community. This kind of community is fundamentally different from those like TEDx and Women's March

Global, which – despite some regional and strategic differences – are both comprised of like-minded volunteers who are united around a shared purpose or values. To fully harness the action-driving power of community in the future, we need to evolve our perception of communities to include bringing together people across different stakeholders who are *not* like-minded. We need people who think differently and represent different vantage points to come together, and we need to design structures that allow them to effectively share ideas and take cooperative action – in a deeply local and global way – across those differences.

Looking forward, if we want to create real, sustainable change across our systems, we need to establish communities based on *diversity* – ones that bring together our corporate entities, our government entities, our nonprofit entities, and our grassroots to create more opportunities for impactful collaboration. Each of these organization types works in different worlds and uses different tools and approaches in its efforts to create positive social change. We need government, corporate, grassroots, academic, and nonprofit stakeholders at the table, because only with cross-sectoral and cross-disciplinary representation and approaches can we tackle real world problems. This book, in assembling voices from different disciplines and sectors who seek to drive systemic change, is a start. Nonetheless, we have a long way to go.

We need to figure out how to integrate all of these pieces into a 'blended ecosystem,' in which each one constitutes a part of the whole and helps shift the world in the directions we need to go. We need to ask ourselves: how can we create an ecosystem in which corporations have a vested interest in generating impact as well as revenue? How can we imaginatively design governments and large public interest organizations to be more agile and innovation-savvy? And, how can we bring these entities together at the local, regional, and global level to solve problems that occur across these scales?

These are some of the questions at the forefront of my mind as I embark on the next phase of my journey as a co-founder of Boma. The roots of the word 'Boma' lie in the languages spoken in the African Great Lakes. The Boma was a circular enclosure for the community and elders to gather, normally built out of branches. It was a sacred space for community gatherings and meaningful discussions to be had, a space where decisions were made and actions were taken. I think this is a beautiful analogy for the kind of powerful change platform we need: a devoted space full of collective energy, creativity, and willingness to cooperate for something bigger. When given the space to work together, we can be vastly more effective in our efforts to create a better world.

Speaking to a nation about to begin its long recovery from apartheid during his Presidential Inauguration, Nelson Mandela proclaimed that "none of us acting alone can achieve success."[3] Those words still ring true today. If we can find better ways to meaningfully act together, there's no telling what we'll achieve.

12 Brands for impact

Harnessing the power of private sector brand-building to empower girls across the globe

Farah Ramzan Golant, CBE

Farah was appointed as the inaugural CEO of kyu EMEA in October 2018. Headquartered in New York, kyu is a collective of creative businesses including IDEO, the global design firm, Kepler Group, a data-driven media company, Sid Lee, the advertising and experiential agency, and SYPartners, the transformation consultancy. In this new role, Farah will drive kyu's international expansion plans, with a specific remit to look for new investment and strategic acquisition opportunities.

Farah is the former CEO of Girl Effect, a creative nonprofit launched by the Nike Foundation to create youth brands and mobile technology to empower girls to change their lives. Farah has 25 years of business experience from the global creative industries. She served as Chief Executive of All3Media, leading the strategic sale of the company for its private equity owners, Permira. Previously she had a 22-year career at Abbott Mead Vickers BBDO, becoming its Chief Executive in 2005 and joining the BBDO worldwide board in 2007. She served on the British Prime Minister's Business Advisory Group from 2013 to 2015. She has been a Trustee of the Royal National Theatre in London, a director of Huntsworth PLC and served on the advisory board of the Cambridge Judge Business School. She currently serves on the advisory board of The ALDO Group and on the boards of The Prince's Trust International and Sadler's Wells. In 2011, she was awarded a Commander of the Most Excellent Order of the British Empire (CBE) and was named Business Woman of the Year in 2010 Asian Women of Achievement Awards.

★ ★ ★

Ours is a story about breaking down boundaries – boundaries between the private sector and development, between gender specialists and data scientists, between siloed issues like 'education' and 'safety,' and between the 'developing' and 'developed' world. Most importantly, it's a story about breaking down boundaries between girls and their agency to create their own futures.

Ours is also a story about building – building visions for the future, building brands, building partnerships, building sustainable models for change, and building a sense of self-worth and value for young girls globally.

Our story begins with the girl. Launched in 2004 by the Nike Foundation and its partners, Girl Effect was founded on a single premise: that the most effective way to break the cycle of global poverty is to improve the situation of adolescent girls. An adolescent girl in poverty is often one with the least ability to realize her personal potential, but at the same time she is uniquely able to break the generational cycle of poverty in her entire community. If she is able to make her own choices about when to marry, her education, her health, and bring new kinds of value to her family, she, alongside millions of girls like her, can determine a new path of growth and prosperity. Change, therefore, starts with the girl. Her ability to break out of poverty for not only herself, but for her family, her community, her country, and the generations that will follow her, is what we called 'the Girl Effect.' The focus on the girl and unleashing her potential is still the concept at the heart of our organizational charter.

From the outset, Girl Effect's work challenged people to think differently about girls. Credit lies with Maria Eitel, the then CEO of the Nike Foundation and now its Co-Chair, for showing the world that girls could be the highest point of leverage to disrupt systems that lock progress. At the 2008 World Economic Forum in Davos, Girl Effect – along with the NoVo Foundation, the United Nations Foundation, and many other brilliant partners – launched 'The Clock is Ticking' campaign, which made the case for why we must put girls on the global agenda and allocate more resources to them. Continuing this work, in 2013 the organization consulted with more than 500 adolescent girls living in poverty in 14 countries across 4 continents to understand their hopes, fears, practical needs, and ideas for solutions to the challenges they face. These insights informed the Girl Declaration – a concrete set of goals, targets and indicators created with over 25 development partners, with the ambition to inspire a deep girl focus within development institutions. The Girl Declaration also helped to put girls at the heart of the post-2015 development agenda and created a rallying cry for world leaders. Backed by UN Secretary General Ban Ki Moon, the Girl Declaration garnered the support of hundreds of signatories, including Malala Yousafzai, Desmond Tutu, and over 20 companies, and brought the international community together around a common agenda for adolescent girls. The Girl Declaration campaign led to girls being placed front and center in the Sustainable Development Goals – a landmark commitment that holds the potential to change the world for girls by 2030.

With this global commitment, the decision was made in 2015 that Girl Effect would become an independent organization. The Nike Foundation, with their farsightedness, had gone beyond advocacy for girls and also incubated a variety of high-potential ideas under the Girl Effect umbrella. Drawing on Nike's brand-building expertise, Girl Effect had begun experimenting with how the tools of a commercial brand – media, mobile, data, and other innovations – could be brought meaningfully into the development sector to address the holistic reality of the girl. Nike Foundation and Girl Effect felt that in order to accelerate the change they set out to achieve, they had to bring in outside eyes to create a strategic focus and scale up the incubations with the biggest potential to impact girls across the globe.

It was at this point that mine and Girl Effect's stories came together. I had worked for 25 years in the private sector. Nearly all of these years were spent at a wonderful agency founded on the power of creative ideas to encourage people to think, feel, and behave differently. I 'grew up' at this agency, starting as a graduate trainee and leaving as a CEO, and learned how to build brands from some of the most wonderful mentors and clients. To generate return on investment, I quickly learned that brands married the power of creativity with both the new potential of mobile and digital innovations and the rigor of data and measurement. After over two decades working in this space, I took what I had learned to television content production and spent two years preparing the company for sale. My career was rooted in creating content (whether long-form or short-form) that was 'sticky,' that made people think and feel differently, and that yielded shareholder return.

I had just led the strategic sale of the company for its private equity owners, Permira, for $930 million and was thinking about my next big challenge when Girl Effect asked me to become its CEO. Joining Girl Effect meant an opportunity to guide and lead an organization creating branded assets – but this time in emerging economies, with new audiences, and with different outcomes and metrics. Rather than engaging audiences to drive sales, Girl Effect was preoccupied with engaging audiences to drive impact. Girl Effect was also an opportunity to serve a new kind of stakeholder: girls in poverty around the world. I saw immediately the ability to transfer my private sector discipline and know-how to this development challenge. Needless to say, I accepted the CEO role at the moment when Girl Effect registered as an independent entity, knowing that I had much to learn in development. Our work since then has been funded through the generosity of private enterprise, including the Nike Foundation, as well as other philanthropic partners and institutions.

The power of brands in development contexts

From day one, our team hit the ground running to deliver on our mandate to focus the organization's strategy and streamline its portfolio. As we narrowed in on our strategy, we wanted to position the organization and its activity to take advantage of the tectonic shifts happening in development contexts. Take Ethiopia, for example. In a country with a population of 100 million, 75 million of those people are under the age of 25. There is a massive, growing youth audience with access to mobile and a hunger for content that young people can leverage to unlock change for themselves. This demographic was unreachable even just five years ago which made any effort to create change at scale a difficult task.

Now that we have growing access to this audience – an access that will only continue to expand as bandwidth and social media presence rise in low-income economies, we have an even greater opportunity to connect with girls who are marginalized and vulnerable, reaching this generation like no other in an effort to shift harmful gender norms.

At Girl Effect, we see youth brands and the power of mobile as an incredible tool to empower girls to change their lives. We are a creative nonprofit and build brands and mobile platforms to better understand girls' lives and the challenges they face. We then design brands that enable girls to get information, to connect with others, and to find a voice so they can build the confidence to create positive change in the lives.

We work with girls and the people in their lives to build brands with the potential to shape the way they and the members of their communities think about gender norms and behave in light of them. But before diving into some favorite examples of our youth brands and how they work to create change, it is important to take a step back and talk about what we mean by 'brand' in the first place, and why it has the power to do the hard work of enabling the girl and her social environment.

The idea of the 'brand' is an ever-changing one that I've seen evolve time and time again over my corporate career. Most recently, though, when working with global organizations like Pepsi, Mercedes, and the BBC, there was an understanding that a brand is far more than the sum of its parts. Let's start with what brands are *not*. Brands aren't a logo or a slogan, nor are they a simple, static, single-minded concept, and they are definitely not an advertising campaign. Think about a very pertinent example – Nike. Nike is bigger than the swoosh or 'just do it,' bigger than a sneaker, and bigger than its last TV advert. As I see it, brands are highly dynamic entities loaded with big ideas and points of view about the world and how it works.

The best brands allow consumers to own these ideas and have a role to play in co-creating them. We can't think of consumers as passive members of a target audience, and must instead see them as active members of a community who want to belong, to influence, and to engage. The set of values and ideas, then, that a brand encapsulates must be shared among this group. Consumer research processes help commercial brands make sure they are listening to their communities and amplifying their values. The way brands activate in the world – the partners they work with, the advertising and media they put out, the events they organize – are also moments to engage the community in co-creative brand-building.

Brands that effectively encapsulate a body of ideas about the world and engage consumers in developing these ideas are elevated from a simple product to a larger *belief system*. To me, this is what brands have the power to be – a belief system.

By belief system I mean a worldview and an ethos, or a vision and values, that are shaped by and shape thought and behavior of a community.

Though we have a different consumer than commercial brands do, at Girl Effect we think that brands are belief systems anchored in a higher purpose, but made dynamic by the participation and ownership of our consumers in the process. Every brand we make sets out to empower girls inside their own realities, to find their voice, develop a strong inner confidence, and connect with those around them to build their own futures together. This is the belief system we invite girls and youth to co-create with us.

How they go about doing this and the exact tenets of that belief system are specific to any given context, since each of our brands are free to chart their own course, anchored deeply in the local culture and drawing on its music, storytelling and traditions to shift the narrative on girls. Our first brand, for example, was built in the Rwandan context and addressed needs specific to the girl living there. Rwanda has made real progress when it comes to gender equality. Women currently hold 64 percent of parliamentary seats, and a similar ratio of boys and girls enroll in primary school. Yet most girls still do the majority of household chores, meaning they have less time to pursue other interests or study, and as a result, they have fewer opportunities to participate in secondary and tertiary education and in the formal workforce.

Audience insight told us that Rwandan girls didn't have an adolescence – they went from being children in their parents' house to wives in their husband's homes. Ni Nyampinga, Girl Effect's youth brand in Rwanda, was based on this deep insight. The brand name is a traditional Kinyarwanda phrase that means 'a beautiful girl inside and out who makes wise decisions.' Ni Nyampinga is about reclaiming adolescence as a time for girls to learn and grow – by overcoming social expectations and fulfilling new ambitions, girls are helping to lift all of Rwanda.

Ni Nyampinga is made up of a magazine, radio drama and talk show, a network of clubs and digital platforms, made by girls for girls. Seven Rwandan girl journalists create all the content, while four researchers piece together insights on the lives of girls in Rwanda. Four times a year, 30 girl ambassadors distribute the magazine across the country.

But Ni Nyampinga speaks to everyone – not just girls but boys, families and community leaders as well – to challenge the perceptions and behaviors that hold girls back. In this way, Ni Nyampinga has sparked a national discussion about what girls can achieve. Ni Nyampinga is truly a nation-wide movement, with eight out of ten Rwandans aware of it and half of all people over the age of ten having read or listened to it in the past year.

Following a very similar model, Girl Effect's second brand was Yegna in Ethiopia. The context in Ethiopia is dramatically different from Rwanda. While Rwanda is a relatively small country, Ethiopia is a hugely diverse, sprawling country where realities for girls can change dramatically. Despite new infrastructure and aid programs to enable girls' progression, prevailing social norms and attitudes mean that many do not complete school and marry too early, while also facing gender-based discrimination and violence.

Our insight-gathering process also revealed an astonishing finding – that one in five Ethiopian girls don't have any friends, meaning they felt isolated and disconnected from the world around them. Yegna, Girl Effect's multi-platform youth brand in Ethiopia, tackles these issues through its radio drama and talk show, TV special, digital channels, and music. It inspires behavior change for girls, boys, their families and communities, by encouraging them to rethink what it means to be a girl in Ethiopia today.

Yegna, which is Amharic for 'Ours,' tells the story of five girls, each an archetype that you can relate to, who start their own band. It shows how a network of friends can make you stronger. Its storylines, which deal with vital issues from education to sexual violence, have been developed with girls, their families, and communities across Ethiopia, to ensure that they accurately reflect their realities. Since launching in 2013, Yegna has reached over nine million people and is provoking positive conversations about the important role girls can play in Ethiopian society.

Our theory of change: Empowering girls to change their own lives

Girl Effect draws equally from brand-building know-how in the private sector and development expertise to inform how change happens. We do this by anchoring our work in our theory of change. Theories of change (or an articulation of an organization's hypothesis for how change happens) are standard in the development sector, and our iterations of this guiding theory have all drawn heavily from development and gender studies with academic rigor. We see the evolution of our theory of change as a positive thing and feel that it's valuable for any organization to revisit and revise their guiding theory of change based on the learning and evidence from practice.

As this book is coming out, we've just finished a revision journey of the theory of change that guides all of our work at Girl Effect. The process took many months and involved review of evidence from our past work as well as deep conversations with our own people and with a panel of experts on behavior change, gender, development, monitoring, and evaluation, among others.

Like all theories, Girl Effect's theory makes a number of assumptions. First, it assumes that change takes time. We aren't looking for a quick fix or flashy results. Since girls are our shareholders, we must deliver lasting, sustainable change and this requires a slow, thoughtful process of transformation. Second, it assumes that change is complex. There is no neat or linear process, and so we have to take an iterative approach based on evidence of where our efforts have and have not been effective. It also assumes a holistic, systemic approach to change-making. Rather than focusing on a single issue, we adopt a bigger picture lens and our investments seek to address a range of thematic issues – like health, safety, education, and economic empowerment – as well as more complex and multifaceted issues – like her sense of self-worth, her ability to freely express herself, and her relationships. In other words, we must acknowledge her interconnected reality and address it as such. We must also acknowledge that we are one grain of sand on the long beach of actors working on gender equality initiatives, and that real change requires many actors working to affect many parts of the systems that shape a girl's world. Collaborations and partnerships are therefore crucial in order to coordinate and scale impact. These partners may be development actors doing similar programming. Likewise, they may be stakeholders from supply-side services who, by working together, can bring about long-lasting change by ensuring issues around demand and supply of the things girls need and want for their lives are holistically addressed. And finally, our theory of change assumes that in order for change to be sustainable and holistic, it has to be girl-led. Girls must be the co-creators of their own change. They therefore take part at every stage of our work – as designers, field researchers, and data collectors – so our insights are unfiltered and authentic as well as actionable.

With the girl at the heart of our theory of change, we hold ourselves ultimately accountable to the sense of *agency* she feels and to the *behaviors* that she adopts as a result of engagement with our work. Changes in these things – agency and behaviors – are the outcomes we seek. Speaking first to the agency piece, we see agency as her capacity to define her own life goals and act upon them. This doesn't necessarily mean that she does act, but it means she has the power and autonomy to think, feel, and voice her opinion. While we want her to exercise her own agency (a focus I feel makes Girl Effect distinctive), like most gender equality efforts another pivotal outcome for us is that girls adopt new behaviors as a result of contact with our work.

We see three components as affecting her sense of agency and her behaviors: the girl herself, her social environment, and her structural environment. These components make up the foundational pillars of our theory of change.

The first pillar is the girl herself. We see her as an individual and we recognize that she has certain needs, rights, and aspirations. When translated into practice, this means that we start any initiative by gathering insights from her and the people in her life to understand the negative gender norms that are influencing her opportunities in life. How do these barriers affect whether she drops out of school? Whether she accesses health care? Whether she is safe from violence? One of the things I've found unique about our approach at Girl Effect is that we also go beyond these typical development questions and seek to understand the larger realities of her world and what opportunities mean to *her*. At the end of the day, we exist to empower adolescent girls and that means enabling her to have the opportunity to generate a world and a life that is fulfilling to her beyond just fulfilling certain needs she has around her education, health, and safety. Recognizing this reality, we also ask questions like, does she have the space and ability to develop friendships? Does she feel confident to talk to her parents about the things that worry her, like her first period? Does she feel she's valuable enough to demand to stay in school, if her parents want to take her out?

We break down the change we want to see in the girl between motivation and ability. 'Motivation' is her desire to adopt certain changes we might be promoting. If we break motivation down, it includes *outcome expectations* ("If I wear a condom,

I won't get pregnant"), *beliefs* ("girls have a right to visit health clinics"), *attitudes*, ("girls who visit health clinics shouldn't be perceived as promiscuous"), and *perceived relevance* ("since I'm a girl living in Malawi where HIV is a real threat, this content on HIV is relevant to me"). All of our brand content must speak to the girl at her level of comprehension and understanding in order to shift her thinking. In addition to motivation, we try to impact her ability to adopt certain actions. This requires the *knowledge* about condoms, for example, as HIV prevention and where to get them, the *social support* from others in her life to affirm condom use is critical, the *confidence* to go to a health clinic and discreetly ask for a condom, and the *perceived control* that she can talk to her partner about condom usage and affect his behavior.

The second pillar is her social environment. This is a particularly complex and complicated one, but it's a critical piece of the puzzle. We recognize that the girl doesn't live in a bubble, and that the world in which she grows up is one where she is regularly reminded that she does not have the power to make her own life decisions. It's the socio-cultural constructs and relationships that she grows up in that dictate the norms she is expected to subscribe to and the behaviors she sees as acceptable (or unacceptable). Her relationships are also nested in this pillar: her relationship with boys, her family, and her community. These relationships with the stakeholders in her life are so important because they are the ones that dictate expectations and reinforce certain behaviors. To make this more concrete, adolescent girls are eight times more likely than boys to contract HIV in Malawi. Part of the reason for this is that platonic relationships between boys and girls are discouraged – leading to lack of communication between them, and a greater risk of unsafe sexual relations that spread HIV/AIDS (more on this shortly).

At Girl Effect, the two pillars of the girl and her social environment are the focus of our work. We build brands that shape knowledge, motivations, ability, norms, and relationships because literature and practice show the importance of these elements to the development and gender outcomes we want to make. However, to make our work worthwhile and effective, there is a third pillar that is equally critical within our theory of change: the girl's structural environment. This includes things like gender-friendly policies, financing and availability of services, the quality (actual and perceived) of her access points, and the institutions available to her as resources (churches, clinics, school, etc.). Girl Effect doesn't directly work in service provision for this third pillar, but we work with incredible global partners for whom this is a primary focus. Our partnership with Gavi, the vaccine alliance, is a great example here. Cervical cancer kills more than 260,000 women around the world every year and is thus a major threat to girls in the developing world. In a $10 million collaboration, Girl Effect and Gavi are working together in Rwanda, Malawi, and Ethiopia to build girls' demand for the HPV vaccine Gavi makes available, and encourage girls to use health services at critical times in their lives.

Everything we do considers these three individual yet interdependent pillars. Part of this consideration must also be the invisible current that runs underneath them all: gender norms. Gender is fundamentally all about power and values. For example, a girl is attending middle school. Despite the fact that she's performing better than her brothers, her family can only afford to send two of their children to school and they believe boys are a better investment because they can provide for their parents in later life. At the same time, the girl's paternal grandmother is putting a lot of pressure on her and her parents to get married as the time is right to find a husband, and she'll need to quit school in order to do this. In this very simple example, you can see a number of societal forces at play to take the girl out of school.

If we want gender equality we need to shift power and values. But certain people have something to lose in this scenario. When talking about the girl's ability to have the power and autonomy in life to decide what she thinks is best for her future, this has a cost to someone else who currently controls these decisions. To be successful in their impact aims, our brands must be cognizant of these delicate, gendered power and value dynamics that underpin a girl's world. However, we also feel that brands are a tool uniquely able to start to shift these intangibles of power and value. Through a multi-product, digitally led and locally attuned model, we are uniting diverse audiences and creating change in girls' agency. Our unique branded approach goes beyond just content, encouraging conversations and compounding with experiences, to drive our agency-centered approach to behaviour change across multiple thematics.

Building brands and driving behavior change: The case story of Zathu

Malawi is a culturally diverse and beautiful country. It's also a country of deep inequalities and entrenched gender divides. Social norms separate girls and boys at puberty and platonic friendships are discouraged, since culture dictates that the only relationship girls and boys have is a sexual one. Girls in Malawi are taught to 'avoid boys,' and if she becomes pregnant she will face pressure to drop out of school and marry the father. Additionally, girls are expected to take on nearly all household chores, leaving her less time for studying, hobbies, or socializing. These deeply entrenched social norms have led to early marriage, teenage pregnancy, pervasive gender-based discrimination, and soaring rates of HIV: the UN estimates that one in ten of all Malawians carry the virus, with women disproportionately affected, and that girls between the ages of 15 and 17 are eight times more likely to be living with HIV in Malawi than boys the same age.

We wanted to do something about these statistics. To do this, we leveraged our participation in DREAMS (Determined, Resilient, Empowered, AIDS-free, Mentored, and Safe) – an ambitious partnership spearheaded by the U.S. President's U.S.-based Emergency Plan for AIDS Relief (PEPFAR), supported by the Bill & Melinda Gates Foundation, Johnson & Johnson, Gilead Sciences, and ViiV Healthcare. The partnership was designed to address the global HIV/AIDS epidemic and help save the lives of those suffering from the disease, primarily in Africa.

To drive these positive health outcomes in Malawi specifically, we began our engagement as we always do with formative research. We spent months trying to understand the complexity of the situation in Malawi where we wanted to build our brand and products. What's the situation for girls? What is the context of the country like? What are the environment and challenges we need to address to create meaningful improvement in girls' lives? What is the best medium to reach our intended audiences? To answer these questions we conducted literature reviews and months of desk research before talking in-person with girls, boys, and youth community leaders to understand the context more deeply.

We are far from the first to work on this issue in Malawi – the statistics have driven considerable investment by NGOs and governments which targets girls specifically. But we were somewhat surprised to learn in our desk research and see reflected in our ethnographies that decades of international focus on girls had actually alienated boys, further widening the gender gap and leaving boys feeling resentful of the support and resources provided to their female counterparts. Our foundational insight coming out of this formative research phase was therefore that the brand had to bring boys along too – it had to be something shared, something considered 'ours' and not just 'hers.' Capturing this core insight, we named our brand *Zathu*, which means 'Ours' in Chichewa, and it became the anchor for the Zathu brand belief system.

The question then becomes how to creatively bring that belief system to life. So, in order to build a brand and products that could unite boys and girls, create positive behavior change, and drive positive health outcomes, we needed to go back into the field and better understand young Malawians. We studied a range of things, from the issues that affected girls and boys at an individual, societal, and environmental level, to their media consumption habits. Armed with this cultural insight, we then co-created our brand with boys and girls throughout the country, conducting focus groups, in-depth interviews, creative exercises, and product testing. We are also working closely with youth groups, teachers, parents, and religious and community leaders to ensure these stakeholders would be supportive of our approach and champion the Zathu brand.

After months of research and co-creation, Girl Effect, in partnership with PEP-FAR's DREAMS initiative, launched Zathu with the vision of creating a more equal and prosperous Malawi by tackling the structural and social drivers that reinforce gender inequality. Using the power and influence of music, radio, and drama so deeply held in Malawian culture, Zathu follows a fictional music band made up of three boys and three girls that come together to create the 'new sound of Malawi.' Drawing on research learnings, the characters challenge stereotypical gender roles and model progressive, positive relationships between boys and girls. Through a weekly radio show, narrative music videos, and live events, we follow them as they form friendships and navigate the weight of traditions, of family and community expectations, and of their own dreams. To bring the radio show to life (and increase reach and deepen connection with Zathu's audience), Zathu held 25 roadshows in its first year – visiting schools, youth centers, and community grounds across all regions of Malawi (Figures 12.1 and 12.2). There are often crowds of kids chanting when the Zathu bus rolls into town!

To ensure that our brand and products are attracting and engaging the right audiences, we continually monitor and evaluate. Zathu is still a relatively new brand

Figure 12.1 Zathu roadshows (1)

Figure 12.2 Zathu roadshows (2)

so we are still collecting this kind of data, but the results to date have been remarkable. Just six months after Zathu's launch, it reached two-thirds of Malawi's population, gaining 2.6 million regular consumers through its various platforms: 4.4 million young people had listened to Zathu's music, 2.3 million had listened on the radio, and the brand's digital platforms have been accessed more than 1.2 million times. The Zathu band performed to 30,000 young people across Malawi and brand ambassadors have reached 300 youth clubs (7,500 young people) and more than 200 village leaders. Alongside these audience reach statistics, we also used our bespoke mobile research technology TEGA to monitor in a more qualitative way how our brands are performing with our various target audiences.

TEGA is a network of 18–24-year-old girls in the communities in which we work who are employed and trained in mobile data collection via a proprietary app to become Market Research Society (MRS) qualified researchers and Technology Enabled Girl Ambassadors (TEGAs).

So, girls are not just our content creators, our audience, and our brand ambassadors; they also support our brand monitoring, uncovering how we can better respond to the needs of their peer communities. This data helps us design better, more targeted programs and interventions that really impact girls' lives.

Using data like this to monitor and improve our audience reach and resonance is important, and takes a page from the corporate-branding world's book. But unlike most of the corporate world, we also have impact outcomes, or 'return on impact' as I like to call it, that we need to deliver on. Our evaluative work ensures that the brand and its various products we've designed actually create their intended change. Given each brand's unique outcomes, our gender, evidence, and brand teams create unique frameworks to evaluate impact. In the case of Zathu, the desired outcomes were girls' intention to go for HIV screening and their intention to take up the HPV vaccine.

As we celebrated Zathu's first birthday, we were able to begin the evaluation of this impact: 93 percent of girls and 89 percent of boys say Zathu has improved their friendships with the opposite sex; 93 percent of listeners say that Zathu has taught them that girls and boys should be treated equally; and 66 percent of girls aged ten through 24 tell us that Zathu has given them more control over their life choices. By unlocking the power of friendship, Zathu is also having an impact on positive health outcomes: whilst it is still early days we will continue to track this data; the latest PEPFAR metrics shows significant declines in new HIV diagnoses among adolescent girls and women in Malawi.

Linking improved agency, knowledge, and boy – girl friendships created by our brand to HIV reduction is no easy task. Among other approaches, an important piece of analysis here is Structural Equation Modeling (SEM). SEM is a method of understanding pathways to change. Drawing on our theory of change, it takes the theoretical pathways to particular outcomes – in Zathu's case, for example, intention to screen for HIV – and tests them in the real world. So, if our theory of change suggests that if we increase a girl's agency, improve her knowledge, and strengthen her connections with boys, then we will see behavioral outcomes, through SEM we can test that theory. So far, it's confirmed that our theory of change is relevant for girls in Malawi and SEM continues to assist us in shaping our design of Zathu to best drive girls towards HIV screening.

Our next step is to conduct a deeper evaluation of Zathu so we can truly understand the impact that it has made. We will feed back learnings on how it can most effectively create change, allowing us to shape content, messaging and the brand to be as effective as possible but also to identify which paths are most strongly linked to the behavior change we want to encourage. This helps us understand exactly what levers within our messaging and product portfolio are most powerful, allowing us to shape content, channel selection, audience participation and club curricula, and the brand to improve impact.

Conclusion: The next chapter of Girl Effect's story

I hope I have painted a picture of Girl Effect as an organization characterized by the combination of diverse skills that you wouldn't normally find in one place. On the one hand, we leverage brands, media, data, mobile, and innovation and their ability to build belief systems that shape the way people think and behave. On the other hand, we leverage deep development expertise and a rigorous theory of change. Neither of these skill sets is unique on its own, but in combination they are powerful – especially as technology is shifting the tectonic plates of our world. A new generation of youth is rising, with access to mobile devices and social media connecting them to the larger world around them – making them quite unlike any generation that has preceded them.

I couldn't be prouder to have been one part of the Girl Effect story and to have had the opportunity to work every day with a brilliant team, wonderful partners, and inspiring girls around the world. One of the things I admire most about this organization is its learning philosophy. Girl Effect is constantly experimenting with how to bring new and different perspectives into the development context; it's constantly challenging its own theory of change; it's constantly evaluating its own work; it's constantly experimenting with brand-building; and it's constantly listening and adapting to the needs of girls and their communities. Though my time as Girl Effect's CEO has come to a close, I know this organization – founded on a deep insight, powered by ambition and optimism, and guided by its learning philosophy – will continue to bring perspectives together to champion girls, create brands with the power to shift gendered norms and behaviors, and work towards creating sustainable change in the world.

13 Media for impact
The power of media and Muppets around the world

Sherrie Rollins Westin and Shari Rosenfeld

Sherrie Westin is President of Global Impact and Philanthropy for Sesame Workshop, the nonprofit educational organization behind Sesame Street. She leads the Workshop's efforts to serve vulnerable children through mass media and targeted initiatives in the United States and around the world. Westin serves as Sesame Workshop's chief mission ambassador, raising awareness, developing strategic partnerships, and cultivating philanthropic support to further the Workshop's mission to help children everywhere grow smarter, stronger, and kinder. Westin spearheaded a partnership to create the largest early childhood intervention in the history of humanitarian response, bringing critical education and nurturing care to refugee children in the Syrian response region. Working with the International Rescue Committee, she led Sesame Workshop's efforts to compete for and win a historic $100 million grant from the MacArthur Foundation to fund this work. She also championed the development of Julia, the first autistic Sesame Street Muppet, and oversaw the launch of Sesame Street in Communities, Sesame's comprehensive initiative designed to give children the tools they need to overcome traumatic experiences. Westin was named a 'Leading Global Thinker' by Foreign Policy *magazine, and one of Fast Company's '100 Most Creative People in Business.'*

Shari Rosenfeld is Senior Vice President of International Social Impact at Sesame Workshop, overseeing the development and execution of high impact transmedia educational initiatives that help young children, especially those from disadvantaged backgrounds, grow smarter, stronger, and kinder. Rosenfeld manages Sesame Workshop's international offices and expansion efforts in South Asia and sub-Saharan Africa, harnessing the power of media and Muppets to deliver impact on areas such as early education, gender equity, resilience, and WASH (water, sanitation, and hygiene). Over her 25 years at Sesame, Rosenfeld has been instrumental in developing groundbreaking programs in Israel, Jordan, Palestine, Kosovo, and Northern Ireland that promote mutual respect and understanding. She launched Sesame's first international subsidiary office in India, and has since established offices in Bangladesh and South Africa. Currently, she is overseeing Sesame Workshop's partnership with the IRC to address the needs of children affected by the Syrian conflict.

★ ★ ★

One day, Lloyd Morrisett noticed his three-year-old daughter sitting with her eyes glued to the family television screen as it played nothing but a signal pattern. Lloyd, an experimental psychologist focused on education, wondered why television, with its powerful hold on children's attention, was empty of meaningful, educational content. His friend and television documentary producer, Joan Ganz Cooney, found herself wondering the same thing.

It was 1966 and the height of President Johnson's 'War on Poverty.' Given the systemic inequality facing Americans, Lloyd and Joan asked two questions that would have a transformative and far-reaching effect: could television be used to teach young children? And, if so, could it provide children living in poverty the same educational foundation as their more advantaged peers and better prepare them for school?

To answer these questions, the pair took stock of what American children were watching on television. With the generous assistance of the Carnegie Corporation of New York, Joan interviewed hundreds of experts in child development and education across the United States and Canada. Her resulting report, 'The Potential Uses of Television in Pre-School Education,' became the genesis of the nonprofit organization called Children's Television Workshop, later renamed Sesame Workshop, which she co-founded with Lloyd.[1] Backed by the Carnegie Corporation, as well as the Ford Foundation and the U.S. Department of Education, they launched what would become the most impactful children's media and education organization in history.

Joan and Lloyd used the latest research to develop a television show that could give children living in poverty a strong educational foundation. They envisioned a show that would promote equality and acceptance of differences in its young audience at a time when America was divided. The theory of change was simple: if access to education determines our children's futures, then media that delivers educational content to a broad audience can also spread opportunity.

Their show was *Sesame Street*.

The power of Muppets, at home and abroad

The first episode of *Sesame Street* aired in November 1969 as an experiment, and it immediately broke the mold. The new show's 'whole child' curriculum went beyond academic basics to provide the social skills (like empathy, kindness, compassion, and inclusion) that a child needs to flourish. By speaking to its young audience *and* their parents with respect, directness, and honesty, the show could address even the most difficult subjects. Those qualities, plus its groundbreaking racially integrated cast of engaging characters, allowed *Sesame Street* to win wide appeal. Within months, nearly one-third of American children aged two to five were tuning in. Ten years after it first aired, some nine million American children under the age of six watched the show regularly.

American children were initially the only audience that *Sesame Street*'s creators had in mind. Joan considered it a "quintessentially American television show," underestimating the worldwide impact it would have. But as early as 1972, *Sesame Street*'s global appeal became clear. Countries like Brazil, Germany, and Mexico wanted this quintessential American show for their own children. The Muppets had the power to cross languages and borders because a colorful furry monster doesn't look American – or Brazilian, German, or Mexican. *Sesame Street*'s creators realized they could expand their model to young audiences in some of the most under-resourced regions of the world.

Wherever *Sesame Street* went, its theory of change held. No matter the country or media environment, storytelling, popular culture, and relatable Muppets are powerful tools to educate and open minds. *Sesame Street* co-productions around the world teach early learning basics like literacy and numeracy. In countries where girls face barriers to education, Sesame models gender parity to change attitudes and behaviors around traditional gender roles and responsibilities. In places where preventable ailments like pneumonia and diarrhea are leading causes of death for young children, Sesame teaches life-saving behaviors like handwashing. Sesame combats harmful stereotypes and advances conflict resolution. Each international version of *Sesame Street* combines the spirit of the original show with local culture, adapting characters and storylines to be locally relevant and relatable.

And we know this approach works. Over a thousand studies on the efficacy of *Sesame Street* can attest to its impact. A 15-country meta-analysis spanning from South Africa to Bangladesh found that watching local versions of *Sesame Street* consistently produced higher cognitive and social learning outcomes – comparable to that of a traditional preschool, at a fraction of the cost.[2] The results become more pronounced for the most disadvantaged children.

Fifty years after it began, Sesame Workshop reaches over 190 million children around the world through mass media and community outreach programs. Our continued success proves the power of Joan and Lloyd's initial concept: that media and Muppets can connect with children wherever they live, and help them grow smarter, stronger, and kinder. Looking back, Joan Ganz Cooney reflected, "It never occurred to us that we couldn't change the world."

The Sesame approach: Our method for impact-driven media

Today, we are still guided by those core questions that launched Sesame Workshop in 1966. What do children need? How do children learn best? What are the best platforms to reach them?

Knowing that every geography brings different answers, we always approach these questions with a rigorous, research-driven process. We begin each project by assessing the unique needs of the children we're trying to reach. Then we consult with local experts to lay a foundation for curriculum-driven, culturally relevant programming. Formative research determines our content creation and distribution channels, and we work closely with local producers and partners to bring our content to life. Once a program is off the ground, we conduct summative research and impact evaluations so we know what works and what doesn't. We continuously iterate to improve.

As we move through the various phases of this process, everything we do is guided by five underlying principles: a focus on a child's earliest years where we can have the greatest impact; a deliberate appeal to the grown-ups watching alongside children; an ability to tackle the most difficult issues from a child's perspective; a localized approach that tailors content to realities on the ground; and a commitment to meeting children where they are regardless of the platform. These principles are at the heart of Sesame's impact.

Focusing on a child's early years

Before the age of five, a child's brain forms as many as 700 neural connections per second, laying the foundation for all of the learning, behavior, and physical and mental health that will follow. If we can reach children at this highly impressionable stage with quality education, we can affect their long-term well-being and the way they see the world.

Take *Baghch-e-Simsim*, the local version of *Sesame Street* in Afghanistan, as an example. The lead Muppet is a six-year-old girl named Zari who loves school and wears her uniform proudly. In a country where roughly 60 percent of girls are not in school, Zari is a role model with the power to change perceptions (Figure 13.1). In one episode, Zari asks a doctor how she can become a doctor herself someday. In another, she encourages her younger brother to think about what he might become when he grows up. Just as we feature women as doctors and pilots, we model how boys can help around the house. *Baghch-e-Simsim* breaks down gender stereotypes often formed at an early age. Our show spreads the message that girls and boys should have equal rights and responsibilities – and that their achievements are equally valuable.

Our intention is not just to expand the worldviews of individual children, but to affect the prosperity and well-being of entire communities. Both boys and girls who watch *Baghch-e-Simsim* test 29 percent higher on gender equity attitudes.[3] Frequent viewers of the show are less likely to say girls and boys cannot play games together, more likely to say that it's important for both girls and boys to go to school, and more likely to say boys and girls can be doctors and engineers when they grow up.[4] By focusing on young children, our programs have the power to open minds, influence attitudes, and plant the seeds for lasting societal change.

Figure 13.1 Zari, the lead Muppet on the local version of *Sesame Street* in Afghanistan

Speaking to both parents and children

Sesame Street's creators believed that learning would be deeper if adults watched with children. That's why Joan Ganz Cooney enlisted Jim Henson in the show's early days to create engaging characters. It's also why we've always featured humor, celebrities, and parodies accessible to adults. Since James Earl Jones made the first celebrity guest appearance in 1969, more than 600 celebrities have visited *Sesame Street*, using their star power to amplify important content. Guest appearances include everyone from Michelle Obama who explained healthy eating habits, to Christopher Reeve who demonstrated how his wheelchair worked, to Whoopi Goldberg who spoke about differences among all of us, including skin (or fur!) color. Likewise on *Galli Galli Sim Sim*, the local version of *Sesame Street* in India, we feature Bollywood music, and on *Baghch-e-Simsim* in Afghanistan (where more than 70 percent of parents watch the program alongside their children) we've welcomed many Afghan Premier League soccer stars onto the show. Along with our characters, these celebrities serve as trusted friends and messengers for children and adults alike. By holding the attention of adult viewers, we encourage adult-child interactions that are critical to a child's development.

Our approach has the added benefit of changing attitudes among adults. We know, for example, that *Sesame Street* programs have changed fathers' minds about allowing their daughters to attend school. One father from a remote Indian village said, "According to what I hear from the *Sesame Street* radio program, my girls need to continue their education. For them to be able to study, this can help the country." Qualitative research from Afghanistan shows a similar shift in fathers' willingness to send their daughters to school.

Tackling the most difficult issues from a child's perspective

Our show has a long history of tackling tough issues that children face, always through the lens of a child. Here in the U.S., we've helped children cope with divorce, the incarceration of a parent, and the loss of a loved one, among other challenges – topics that adults often find difficult to discuss with children.

We also deal frequently with stigma. In South Africa in the 1990s, for example, one in four children were affected by HIV and AIDS but widespread stigma hindered understanding. To normalize the face of HIV/AIDS, we created an HIV+ Muppet named Kami for *Takalani Sesame*, the local South African version of *Sesame Street*. A vibrant five-year-old Muppet, Kami spoke about the disease and modeled ways to cope with grief and loss. In one segment, she created a 'memory box' filled with photos and mementos of her mom, who died of AIDS. In another, Kami and her Muppet friends played the 'train game,' where Kami's friends must touch her so they can all chug along together – showing young viewers that HIV isn't transmitted through touch.

Takalani Sesame gave children and adults a lexicon for HIV. South African parents and caregivers who watched 'Talk to Me' (a *Takalani Sesame* prime time television special on HIV and AIDS targeting adults), were twice as likely to talk with their children about the illness than those who hadn't. Likewise, educators who watched were four times as likely to talk to their classes about HIV and AIDS as those who hadn't. Children exposed to Kami showed substantial gains in knowledge about how HIV is and isn't spread and had substantially more positive attitudes toward interacting with those affected. In Nigeria, where *Takalani*'s curriculum was adapted, one study showed that after meeting Kami, 93 percent of children thought it was all right to play with a person who had HIV/AIDS, compared with only 38 percent before meeting her.[5] By breaking down the culture of silence around HIV/AIDS, *Takalani Sesame* provided a powerful antidote to stigma and fear.

Tailoring content to local realities

Our *Sesame Street* co-productions have the power to change attitudes around the world, because they reflect the cultures and communities they serve. We know children learn best when they see themselves in characters, storylines, and shared cultural experiences. By reflecting our audience's world, our characters become trusted friends and powerful role models.

Creating a *Sesame Street* co-production in a new region requires extensive engagement with local educators, experts, government ministries, artists, and media producers. These partners identify the most pressing issues facing their communities and help us create local characters and storylines that children can relate to. With their help, we avoid stereotypes or preconceived notions held by adult gatekeepers. Only then can we create engaging content that moves the needle on issues like gender or inclusion, while still maintaining credibility.

Content sensitivity is at the forefront of our work around conflict resolution. In settings like Israel, Palestine, Kosovo, and Northern Ireland, our initiatives use the most disarming ambassadors of open-mindedness – our Muppets – to promote mutual respect and understanding. We call it 'Muppet Diplomacy.'

After the Kosovo War, the region was characterized by patchy access to education and an atmosphere of distrust between ethnic groups. In 2004, after months of consulting with local advisors and conducting research, we launched a new co-production. It was the first educational media ever produced locally in Kosovo. Produced in two languages, *Rruga Sesam* in Albanian and *Ulica Sezam* in Serbian, the show spoke across the language gap of its audience.

Alongside early education, the shows carried the *Sesame Street* message: to see each other's similarities rather than be blinded by our differences. Guided by local partners, our programming depicted children from different ethnicities overcoming social and language divisions. Just seeing that *other* children did similar things and enjoyed similar activities (like playing with siblings and spending time with their grandmothers) had an impact. Four years after the first episode of *Rruga Sesam/Ulica Sezam* aired, research showed that children who watched were 74 percent more likely to demonstrate positive attitudes towards children from different ethnic backgrounds than those who didn't.[6] Our show helped young Kosovars understand – and begin to unlearn – the stereotypes that long and bitter histories had given them.

Likewise, our local production in Northern Ireland offered children a foundation of open-mindedness, empathy, and appreciation of diversity. With help from local experts, we created *Sesame Tree* as the country emerged from a civil conflict marked by cultural and religious divisions. Inspired by a centuries old 'fairy tree' that, in Irish folklore, is inhabited by magical forces, the show featured Hilda the Irish Hare and Potto, a purple monster, who live together in a tree. When the two characters become frustrated sharing their space, they divide it in half with a table. Soon, each wants something from the other side, so both must cross the boundary to reach it. On one trip across the room, Hilda tells Potto some news that she's heard, and they both realize how good it feels to share. Leaders from opposite sides of the divide attended the series launch event. Ian Paisley, a loyalist politician and Protestant religious leader, and Martin McGuiness, a Sinn Fein leader and former IRA commander, acknowledged the important model this episode provided. It offered a powerful metaphor for a region moving toward a shared future.

As seen in Kosovo, studies showed that children who watched *Sesame Tree* as preschoolers were more willing to include others. A body of research affirms that this work has had a measurable impact on children's pro-social skills and behaviors. In both countries, the nonthreatening nature of our content and our deliberate efforts to understand the cultural and political nuances amplified our impact.

Reaching children where they are in order to teach

While local relevance is hugely important to our success, equally important is our ability to reach our audience. The media landscape has evolved since *Sesame Street* began as a television series, requiring us to adapt our distribution methods. We now provide content via radio, print, digital media, mobile phones, handheld battery-operated projectors, and even television sets mounted on rickshaws. To choose the most effective platform, we continually assess mass-media distribution methods and pair them with on-the-ground services through partner organizations.

In densely populated slum areas of Delhi, Mumbai, and Kolkata, we tried a new distribution 'technology' – a repurposed vegetable cart equipped with a TV, car battery, and DVD player (Figure 13.2). Overseen by local teachers, mobile community viewings include episode screenings and interactive games and activities that engage children, their siblings, and caregivers. The mobile viewing program has already reached thousands of children and caregivers. Research shows increased awareness and viewership of the show, as well as shifting attitudes about early childhood education.

No two distribution models look the same. To deliver our tailored content, we often partner with direct service providers who have infrastructure and deep

Figure 13.2 A repurposed vegetable cart brings early learning to children in India

networks within communities. We continuously learn from our experiences wherever we go, and to reach the most vulnerable children, we rely on philanthropic support. For example, USAID alone has helped us launch local versions of *Sesame Street* in more than half a dozen countries around the globe.

The power of partnerships: Combining media with other platforms to scale impact

The plight of Syrian refugees is one of the greatest humanitarian crises today, requiring coordinated efforts by the global community. As the war rages on, millions of Syrian children have grown up amid violence, insecurity, and displacement. Few have opportunities to learn and play, and many are at risk of 'toxic stress' – a biological response to prolonged adversity that disrupts a child's brain development. And despite all we know about the value of investing in a child's early years, displaced children have little access to early education and the support they need to overcome the trauma of war.

With a landmark $100 million grant from the MacArthur Foundation, Sesame Workshop is partnering with the International Rescue Committee (IRC) to create the largest early childhood intervention in the history of humanitarian response. Through a new local version of *Sesame Street* and direct, in-person services for the most vulnerable children, we will reach millions of children and their families in Iraq, Jordan, Lebanon, and Syria. Our aim is to harness the power of media to bring our proven educational content to both refugee families and their new neighbors in host communities. Beyond its impact on the young audiences, the program is designed to serve as a scalable model for future crises.

Our partnership will combine Sesame Workshop's experience in diverse, conflict-ridden areas with the IRC's deep engagement in the refugee community – including its established network of community workers and local partners. Working together, our direct services will reach the most vulnerable displaced children and families (Figure 13.3). Home visitation and caregiving support sessions will help parents provide the nurturing care and stimulation young children need to overcome the trauma of displacement – all while providing caregivers with practical techniques for managing their own stress.

We will also transform community sites, formal and informal schools, and other points of aid into nurturing care and learning centers. We will provide frontline staff with training and high-quality educational materials to enhance their instruction. These sites will feature storybooks, video clips on preloaded pico projectors, activities, and training guides designed for formal and informal preschool settings – all with the familiar Sesame characters from the new series.

We know the importance of reaching children wherever they are: in their homes and communities, in health centers and preschools, on their mobile phones and on televisions. Because the majority of refugee families don't live in formal camps, but

Figure 13.3 Elmo visits displaced children in Jordan as part of Sesame's partnership with the International Rescue Committee

in neighborhoods and host communities, the new television series is designed to reach refugee children side by side with their new neighbors.

By reaching children at multiple points in daily life – at home, at school, on television or mobile phones – we reinforce our high-quality content, emphasizing the tools that children will need to rebuild their society. Speaking through the Muppets of *Sesame Street*, we can bring hope and joy to families who so desperately need it.

Conclusion

Sesame Workshop's mission is to help children everywhere grow smarter, stronger, and kinder. Our work is made possible by philanthropic support and by the partner organizations that share our mission. We once asked, "Can television be used to teach young children; and, if so, can it help disadvantaged children start school on an equal footing with their peers?" Fifty years later, we know that the answer to both questions and to so many more is a resounding "Yes!" Around the world, our programs have proven media's ability to inspire change and bring opportunities to children in need.

In 1969, *Sesame Street* harnessed children's television to address the inequalities of that time in America. Though today's children face new challenges and encounter different media platforms, they are just as receptive as our original young audience. Using multiple platforms on multiple continents, we reach more disadvantaged children today than ever before. We look forward to the future of *Sesame Street*, built on 50 years of success, bolstered by innovation as the world changes, and with a broader reach than ever before. As always, young children are the greatest hope for our future. The most impactful investment we can make is helping them to learn, grow, and reach their full potential.

14 Advertising for impact

How Christmas lights helped end a war

Jose Miguel Sokoloff

Jose Miguel Sokoloff is one of the most internationally awarded and respected advertising creatives and peace proponents in the world. Jose Miguel's philosophy of employing soft power over force for effective behavior change manifests in the communications he has designed throughout his career to address cultural and societal issues in ways that transcend borders and challenge norms. Native to Colombia, Jose Miguel's most recognized work for the Colombian Ministry of National Defense has propelled him from advertising creative to cultural figure, having spoken and appeared across a variety of widely recognized platforms with mass audiences such as TED Global, NPR's This American Life and WIRED, in addition to the ad industry's most renowned forums such as the Cannes Lions International Festival of Creativity. In December 2016, Emmy award-winning journalist Lara Logan interviewed Sokoloff for a feature profile entitled 'The New Colombia' for CBS News' '60 Minutes,' one of the most successful broadcasts in the history of American television, which resulted in a 2017 Emmy nomination for 'Outstanding Feature Story in a News Magazine.' Jose Miguel's responsibilities as Global President of MullenLowe Group's Creative Council involve leading the networks' top creative talent to continued success for clients' brands in addition to enhancing network integration, collaboration, and growth. Under Jose Miguel's creative leadership MullenLowe Group has been named a Cannes Top 10, a Gunn Report Top 10 Global Creative Network, Number One Creative Agency by WARC 100, and Unilever's Agency of the Year.

★ ★ ★

Just as much as guns, helicopters, radios, and boats, advertising is a tool – and, like all tools, it can be used to build, repair, create, and improve – or to destroy.[1] This is the story of how we used it to help end a war.

But first let me backtrack. By 2007, Colombia's civil war against the FARC had been running for about 50 years, making it one of the longest civil wars in history. And the fighting had taken a brutal toll. Over six million people had been displaced from their homes and farms, 200,000 had died over the past decade, and Colombians were tired of feeling afraid, threatened, and unsafe.

Although my country had been afflicted by war for nearly every day of my life, living in Bogotá, I (like most city dwellers) went about my day-to-day life just about as far from its realities as you could imagine. After graduating from college, I went to business school and then into advertising where I started out as a copywriter. However, I did not start in advertising to change the world. I was never a very hard worker and I figured advertising was easier relative to most other professions, and a lot less boring. I could learn about a lot of things that were part of our daily lives and try to have 'conversations' with people through the creative work to change their minds about things; either to switch brands, to begin using a product, or simply to use more of it. It was the introvert's dream; I could talk to the world out there and hide behind the creative. It turned out to be hard work, but it has never been boring. Most of all, the challenge of finding the right thing to say, saying it at the most relevant moment, and getting the desired results is still the biggest thrill I can think of.

While a war that had dragged on for half a century raged in the jungle, I was busy making calls and rushing to meetings, helping clients sell toothpaste, polish the image of their bank, or track sales data for the underwear they made. As the government churned out new strategies to bring the war to a close, I advanced in my career and started my own advertising agency. This was an important moment in my professional life. When I had previously worked at the big agency Leo Burnett, the impact of our advertising work for huge clients could not be measured precisely because they pumped money into so many other channels that influence sales – like distribution, pricing, and years of brand-building. We knew we *were* an important part of that equation, but just how important we were to the success of our clients we had no way of knowing. This is the tragedy of our business.

But when we opened up our own little shop, we felt the impact of our work very directly. We initially had hardly any clients, and most of them were very small. One particular entrepreneur who had not engaged professional advertisers before asked us if we wanted to 'go into business' with him. He needed to sell a fixed amount of units to cover his costs, and we calculated how many he needed to sell to cover our costs. We agreed that after all costs were paid for we would split the earnings, and if they were not covered we would take the hit proportionally. The entrepreneur gave us full control over the advertising creative and the media mix. We aired one spot, which was very different from anything else out there at the time, on national TV for about a week. His product sales exceeded even our most optimistic calculations. We had learnt the power our tools. After this experience we decided we would also use our expertise to help causes we thought were worthy. We therefore added charities and good causes to our client portfolio, fundraising for veterans and even politics and elections.

As an agency, we were doing well enough. But when the phone rang in the spring of 2007, the direction of our business changed dramatically.

The power of storytelling

In early 2007, the government was closer than it had ever come to winning the civil war. Their armed forces were strong, the guerrillas were in retreat, and for the first time in most people's memory a military victory seemed within reach. In an armed conflict there are essentially three ways to weaken your enemy's 'army.' The first and most obvious is to kill them – but they can also be captured or, better still, convinced to leave their ranks. This last is arguably the most difficult to achieve, but at this point in the war, the government's strategy for winning depended on it.

Long before we picked up the phone, the government had already developed a comprehensive system that they hoped would entice the guerrillas to leave their posts and rejoin civil life. The government's demobilization program supported ex-guerrillas with medical and psychological help, along with training for new jobs and security if their lives were in danger. After demobilization, the former guerrillas would enter a separate program (called the 're-insertion program'), which worked with the communities and the demobilized guerrillas to help them reintegrate themselves into civil life. The only twist was how to reach them and convince them to take the first step.

Vice Minister of Defense Sergio Jaramillo had called us that day to ask if we could help. We listened as he explained where we fit into his strategy. The government had every conceivable plan in place to end the conflict – military, political, legal, foreign affairs, economic – except one: a strategic and organized communications plan.

Before reaching out to us, the national army had been running a series of TV commercials that showed a smiling guerrilla being surrounded by soldiers and walking calmly. The voiceover said that he had demobilized and would start a new life. But if you looked at the spot without the benefit of the audio, you were left wondering whether he had been captured. Any why he was smiling. The strategy was very literal – simply spelling out the benefits of demobilizing and joining the reintegration program. In my opinion, to say is not to *communicate*, and these ads said all the right things but I'm not sure they were communicating anything that struck at the guerillas' core enough to encourage the desired behavior.

So it was clear where we could offer our help – by saying less and communicating more precisely. As Jaramillo emphasized to us, he didn't need the actual advertisements (or 'assets,' as we call them in our lingo). All he needed was a strategic approach for the next few years so he could organize his communication efforts and make them more coherent and effective.

Though we knew how to create coherent and effective communications, nothing we had worked on – not with the banks or the underwear companies or even the political campaigns – had remotely prepared us for this. But we said yes and began to approach the problem in the way we knew best. Although we knew nothing at all about getting through to armies, we knew a lot about getting through to individual human beings. And because successful advertising is built on understanding the individuals that comprise your audience, we realized we would have to talk to as many demobilized guerillas as possible. We requested access, and the military granted it.

So we began our interviews, one demobilized guerilla at a time. We tried to understand their motivation to join, their hopes and dreams for the guerrilla movement, and – most crucially of all – why they had risked their lives to escape it. Over the course of these conversations, we heard stories that didn't match the image of the shadowy jungle fighters whose menace had stalked our entire conscious lives. Instead, we heard stories of disillusionment, injustice, and hardship endured during years of guerilla fighting – the soldiers who were forbidden from falling in love; the teenagers forced to shoot young recruits for crimes they had not committed; the women who were compelled, multiple times, to undergo abortions and then decided that, this time, their child would live. We were amazed at the resilience of the young people we spoke with, and their deep sense of right and wrong.

Here's one of the stories that has stayed with me. Jovanny Andrés (not his real name) had been recruited against his will at the age of 13 when the guerillas had arrived in his neighborhood. They rounded up all of the young people who were old enough to fight, and informed the parents that their 'contribution' to the war effort that day would be to give one child to the guerilla forces. As the eldest son of his family, Jovanny had no choice but to go.

Becoming an adult in the jungle meant growing up in violence and with deprivation that encompassed not only the literal scarcity of food and water, but also the denial of the ordinary human experiences that teach us critical thinking, empathy, and optimism. Instead of school, his education encompassed only regular political indoctrination – he knew who Marx had been and could talk a little about his writings, but had never heard the name Gabriel Garcia Marquez. He lived in camps, leaving only occasionally to run some errands in small towns, for which he was grudgingly trusted to come and go.

When he was 22, a new recruit arrived. He thought the young woman looked scared and beautiful, and he helped her adapt. They became friends, and quickly fell in love. When they were sent out to combat, they looked out for each other. When they volunteered for night watch, they patrolled together. One way or another, they managed to spend their time in each other's company. As Jovanny recalls it, they would talk about what their life would be like when they finally got out, how many children they would have, where they would live, and how they would make a living.

But soon they were discovered. Although the ranking officers in the guerilla units frequently kept wives and lovers with them, relationships were strictly forbidden for foot soldiers. Their squadron decided to make an example of them and sent the girl to a far-away part of the country, from which no communication would be possible between them. Jovanny stayed behind, heartbroken.

From countless stories like these, the guerillas, we realized, were just as much prisoners of the organization as the hostages they took. This was our big insight.

It also turned out this was old news to the government. Jaramillo and his team had heard these same stories over and over again for years, and they knew firsthand the rawness and power of these human struggles. They believed, as we did, that these human experiences could persuade many guerrillas to leave, and quickly accepted the strategy we proposed to them. It was simple: we would broadcast these individuals' stories on the radio. We strongly suspected these experiences were not isolated cases, but rather emblematic of a deeper disenchantment with the guerilla group's ideals and methods. By changing the army's communications approach from a threatening one to a more personal one, we could show many guerillas that there was the possibility of another, better life – a life they had known before joining and could come back to. We hoped that with enough stories aired for a long enough time – a couple years, at least – the guerillas' tolerance for the injustice and cruelty that seemed endemic within their organization would lower, and they would leave. We had to validate their experiences, and make them understand that they weren't alone. The game wasn't about making them too scared to stay. It was about giving them the courage to leave.

Jovanny still hadn't found that courage. In the months following the transfer of the girl he loved, he wondered if she was alive. In fact, she had found a way to escape. And we know this because she was one of the first stories we recorded when the government gave us access to former guerillas. Her story claimed one of the 100-plus radio spots we made during the first three years of our program. The new post she had been sent to turned out to be in territory she knew very well, and as soon as she saw a chance she left, turning herself and her weapons in to a passing military convoy. The army immediately sent her out of the combat zone, and she began the demobilization program.

Meanwhile, Jovanny had continued fighting with the guerillas. He probably would have continued if he hadn't patrolled one night with his transistor radio and heard the voice of his loved one. He learned that not only was she alive, but she had escaped. She was somewhere in a city far away, safe from harm, and ready to start a new life. Hearing her story gave him the courage to escape, too. He demobilized soon after by handing himself in to the Red Cross in a nearby town.

I can't say for sure if this story has a happy ending. Although he did everything in his power to find her, we could not facilitate a meeting. In the guerilla organization, every soldier who abandons the cause is considered a military target. This means there was no way for her to know if Jovanny wanted to find her only in order to kill her.

Over time, stories like this began to have the impact we had hoped for. It was emerging that the guerillas maintained their ranks through a system that was brutal and inhumane, and more and more guerillas started to demobilize. Notably, the waves of demobilizations began to include commanders – a development that we were particularly eager to encourage. Demobilized guerillas are good, but demobilized commanders (especially those with over five years in that position) are better. Because commanders are harder to replace than the rank and file recruits and because they could offer information critical to the army's success in the field – not to mention the symbolic gravitas of a leader leaving the cause – their loss weakens the guerilla organization in a much more long-term way. On top of that, the information they could offer was often critical to the army's successes in the field. We began trying to record and broadcast their stories, too.

But the strategy backfired, and with it, the entire plan we had designed. The remaining guerilla leaders started to tell their people that it was impossible that their dedicated leaders would ever think or say such lies – they had obviously been forced to say these things at gunpoint. Suddenly we found ourselves without a blueprint. All we knew was that demobilizations were dropping and we had nothing new to say.

Bringing Christmas to the jungle

Around Christmas 2010, three young members of our team – Juan Pablo Garcia, Sergio León, and Carlos Andrés Rodriguez – bought a set of Christmas lights with their own money. They had noticed that at Christmas, no matter how well or poorly the guerillas were faring in the war, the number of demobilizations normally increased. And they had an idea. As one of them put it: "We were looking for symbols of Christmas, and the most universal one is the Christmas tree, and the jungle is full of trees. So we decided to make a few Christmas trees in the jungle."

And they did. With the full support of the army and Ministry of Defense, our team – a collection of advertising agents – entered the combat zone to find nine large trees along paths that the guerillas were known to take. While the soldiers provided cover, the team rushed to string up Christmas lights, and finished with a sign: "If Christmas can come to the jungle, you can come home. Demobilize. At Christmas, everything is possible."

The results shattered our expectations. We saw a 30 percent increase in Christmas-time demobilizations from the previous year. To give context, the demobilizations recorded during December of that year alone represented about 5 percent of the total guerila fighting force at the time.

But perhaps even more valuable than these results were the lessons we learned. One: focus on that which unites us, not what divides us. As long as we spoke to the human being in the guerrilla and not to the soldier, we could be more personal, and therefore more effective. Two: you can't argue against emotion. This time, it was impossible for the guerrilla leaders to attack our approach because we were only stating the obvious: it is better to spend Christmas at home with your loved ones that in the jungle in combat. Three: do not judge. We never questioned the guerrilla and their motives or ideals. We just showed them what they were missing.

It was these lessons that allowed us to adapt our communications strategies to the changing and dynamic nature of the war. The demobilized guerilas we were talking to raised a new problem for us to confront: fewer people were traveling on foot. By the next Christmas, the frontline of the war had been pushed back to the deepest part of the jungle, forcing the guerillas to make use of the waterways. We had also noticed heavier recruiting by the guerilla forces in river villages, confirming that at this stage of the war there was more movement by water than by land. We needed to come up with something just as beautiful and evocative as the Christmas trees, but adapted to water and easy to deploy.

So in 2011, our team pitched the idea of placing sentimental messages from guerilla's families in small, floating globes that would drift down the rivers and could easily be collected if they were not picked up. We had these globes engineered to be sturdy enough to withstand the journey down the river, and to light up at night. We visited villages along the guerilla's river routes to collect Christmas-inspired messages (knowing that these were likely from actual acquaintances or even the family members of the guerillas). Any doubts we had about how these people felt about our idea evaporated when we received not only personal messages, but also religious objects, jewelry, and even some childhood toys. Again, the army carried our team up the river, deep into the combat zone, and covered us as we deposited more than 7,000 of these globes into the water (Figure 14.1).

We waited. And again, the results surpassed our hopes. That Christmas, families reunited, with an average rate of one guerilla demobilizing every six hours.

Figure 14.1 Operation River Lights

A 2011 campaign that collected sentimental trinkets and messages from families of guerilla members and floated them down the river in glowing plastic balls. Here, army soldiers are helping the advertising team deposit the orbs.

One team

In 2013, the tenor of the conflict shifted again. Peace talks had begun in Havana, and at this point, the question on the table was not so much whether – or even how – the war would end, but when. With no more war to fight, the guerillas knew they would have to come home to their villages, their families, their communities. They also knew they would probably face a cold, if not hostile, reception – after 50 years of a brutal conflict, public opinion remained strongly against them. We wanted to make sure their fear of rejection or retaliation didn't keep them from demobilizing sooner rather than later. But that was easier said than done. The remaining fighters included those who had stayed on despite the stories we broadcast on the radio, the Christmas trees, and the messages we sent down the river. As we spoke to more demobilized guerillas, however, we learned one important thing: most would see their mothers before they saw anybody else, and they feared how their mothers would respond to their return.

So we asked their mothers to invite them home. They gave us pictures of their children when they were small – pictures that only their children would recognize. We used these pictures to make them into posters with a message from their mothers: "Before you were a guerilla, you were my child. Come home." (Figures 14.2, 14.3). These few pictures produced an impact far out of proportion to their number. Although we collected only 27 pictures for the posters, more than 120 mothers welcomed their children home in time for Christmas that year.

Figure 14.2 Mothers' Voices

A 2013 campaign displayed childhood photographs of fighters in villages that the FARC would pass through.

Figure 14.3 Army soldiers holding 'Mothers' Voices' posters

But we knew we couldn't stop there. We still had to address everyone else whose lives would be affected by the guerillas coming home. This time, though, we had something going for us that had absolutely nothing to do with the war: the FIFA World Cup of 2014. In a soccer-crazed country – whose team was doing exceptionally well that year – it would be difficult to find a better common denominator between the guerillas and the people who had lived in fear of them for 50 years. And for all the fighting and political indoctrination, we knew the guerillas weren't immune to the soccer bug. We had learned in our interviews that they followed their local teams all tournament long. But because the military pressure on them had been steadily increasing, they had by now been driven to places where it would be virtually impossible for them to see the games or even hear them on the radio. We decided to capitalize on this.

Our plan was to invite them to come back and watch the World Cup with all of us. We contacted major sports commentators, past footballers from the national team, and ordinary people on the street to gesture to an empty seat beside them while watching the tournament. It didn't need a caption. Everyone knew it meant "Come sit here beside me." What was nominally an invitation to watch soccer was also an invitation to normalcy – to a life without constant fighting, where you could do everyday things like go to a bar with friends and watch a game; to a life where you wouldn't feel alone. We circulated these on television shows, commercials, and, crucially, through the army's own radio broadcasts that we knew reached the remote locations where the guerillas made their camps.

This time, we didn't need statistics to measure our success. Soon after the World Cup campaign started, the guerilla leaders attending the peace talks in Havana demanded that all advertising efforts designed to diminish their forces cease completely.

The government agreed. But our work was already done. We had helped demobilize more than 18,000 guerrillas over a ten-year period. And days later, a peace deal was signed.

Conclusion

Advertising is almost a bad word these days. It's something everyone hates until they have to sell their house. At its best, it's considered part of a corporate sales pitch – something that convinces consumers they want something they might not actually. At its worst, it's seen as a kind of modern propaganda machine.

But I think advertising is probably one of the biggest forces of change for good that humanity has ever possessed. It speaks to the most human element of people. It is short, easy to understand, and direct. When done well, it says what it has to say in a charming and convincing way, and it can influence the way we think and act for generations. I'm not saying it can't be misused: much like the computer I'm typing on which can be used to write poetry or to bully someone via social media, the power of advertising can be used to less virtuous ends. It's a function of how you decide to use it.

But there's a lot of change to be made out there. The tools of advertising can turbocharge it.

15 Public policy for impact

Building programs and partnerships for the common good

George Kronnisanyon Werner

George Kronnisanyon Werner is a public sector leader and innovator who has spearheaded successful national and government-wide reform programs across a range of areas including education, workforce reform, and health. He served as Liberia's Minister of Education from 2015 to 2018, taking the helm following the deadly Ebola outbreak and leading a series of bold reforms aimed at overhauling the education system to give all Liberian children access to free, quality education. Werner previously served as Director General of the Civil Service Agency, playing an instrumental role in implementing the Public Sector Modernization Project with $11.5 million funding from the World Bank, SIDA, and USAID. Werner also has significant experience in the health sector, having served as co-chair of Liberia's Health Workforce Development Taskforce, which had a mandate of addressing the country's shortage of skilled health care staff. In recognition of his expertise in this area, he was later appointed by UN Secretary-General Ban Ki-moon to the UN High-Level Commission on Health Employment and Economic Growth, which crafted recommendations to ensure the equitable recruitment, training, and deployment of the estimated 40 million new health professionals needed globally by 2030. Werner now uses his firsthand knowledge to help Big Win Philanthropy assist other African leaders to implement transformative reform agendas aimed at developing human capital and maximizing demographic dividends for long-term economic growth.

★ ★ ★

When I was in elementary school, I remember gathering in the auditorium with my classmates. We were in rural Liberia, and a group of politicians was coming to our school. The town chief and paramount chief, along with some parents, also joined the assembly to listen. Many of the politicians who spoke that day were sons and daughters of the town who had spent all their professional lives in faraway Monrovia, Liberia's capital city. One speech after the other, they spoke of how bad things were in the country and how electing them would bring much-needed relief. We applauded them.

When they were done speaking, the town chief stood up. "We've been clapping for far too long a time," he said. He went on:

> Our ancestors did so too before us. Our hands are sore, swollen, and tired. You come around when it is time for elections. But once you get elected, we don't see you. We don't get the benefits you promise. Why should we believe you now? Our ancestors taught us how to rely on providence, hard work, and respect for ourselves and for nature. We rely on fishing and farming to feed our families and send our children to school, and we want them to grow up to be like you someday. But our hands are tired of clapping, and our children see that too.

For some reason, the chief's comments have never left me, and they resounded even more loudly as I took on public service myself many years later.

I grew up in Grand Kru County, situated within a region completely cut off from the rest of Liberia due to poor roads and decades of neglect by successive governments. Years of instability made conditions worse for the people of southeastern Liberia. In 1980, when I was barely eight years old, a coup d'état set off over two decades of instability, including a series of disputed elections, failed attempts to overthrow elected presidents, executions of political rivals, tribal tensions, and a protracted civil war (1989–2003). These successive crises decimated Liberia's economy and human capital and left an estimated quarter of a million people dead. I grew up under repressive and self-serving governments, and I joined government determined to reform it for the common good.

In the aftermath of the civil war, my first roles in the government focused on developing policy blueprints that would create legal frameworks for a working, participatory government and review the mandates and functions of public sector institutions to make them fit for purpose. We could not rebuild Liberia, within the context of decades of decay and death, without investing in its people and rethinking public sector institutions. We needed to enable environments for civil servants to deliver critical public services and for the private sector to thrive.

When I joined President Ellen Johnson Sirleaf's administration in 2011, I knew I was being given an incredible opportunity to be a change agent in postwar Liberia. Even eight years after the formal end of the civil war, Liberia was paralyzed and in need of urgent rehabilitation. Water and electricity were hard to come by. In many government buildings there were no desks or chairs. People were showing up for work, but many were just there with no assignments or job descriptions. Civil servants were being paid very little, and it was difficult to access pay and benefits. There were no banks in many parts of the country, and mobile technology was not yet accessible for most Liberians. The challenge to get Liberia moving in the right direction was monumental. The costs of violence and hunger were visible everywhere – in the faces of children and mothers, in the streets and broken buildings. It seemed like a nightmare at the time, but hope still lived in Liberia.

I, personally, dreamed of a Liberia with a clear pathway to shared prosperity and integral human development. To me, that meant stability and policy consistency. It meant using Liberia's strength in agriculture and biodiversity as a driving force for economic growth. It meant increasing fiscal space by working to strategically shift our role from predominantly importer to predominantly exporter. And it meant a well-considered prioritization of productive education, investing in training and innovations that promoted equal access to quality and relevant learning. I wanted to be in a position that enabled me to facilitate a discussion around rethinking the entire government architecture, from agriculture and the economy to education.

To do this, it was vital to formulate public policies for the common good.

The art of making sausage

Although there is no universally accepted definition of public policy, it can generally be described as the overall framework within which government actions are taken (or not taken – there is a policy where there is no policy) to achieve public goals. In other words, proactive public policies originate to solve a perceived problem. In academic circles, some models of public policy emphasize policy as the legislative *outcome*, while others elevate the *process* of policymaking (Box 15.1). I want to focus on the process: the art of crafting and implementing reform-minded policy.

Generally speaking, the government develops, adopts, and implements policy through its formal legal and administrative channels. In the Liberian example, our democratic government has three branches: executive, legislative, and judiciary. Bills generally originate from the executive via the governance commission in Liberia. The executive transmits these bills or policy frameworks for legislative consent. Lest you think this legislative consent process is as neat and simple as it sounds, let me assure you it is not. It is contentious, filled with loud disagreements and compromises, and, often, what is originally thought and presented is not what emerges as law in the end. The sentiment (mis)attributed to Otto von Bismarck, Chancellor of Germany at the end of the nineteenth century, captures this well: "Laws are like sausages, you better not be there when they are made."[2] The process is messy, grueling, difficult, and you take what you can get. Though tedious at times, it is nonetheless an essential part of the balance of power in a democracy, a necessary accountability checkpoint.

Let me give you a glimpse into this sausage-making, but in an administrative rather than legislative channel. When the Ebola outbreak hit Liberia in 2014, my job was supervising all government personnel. As the outbreak worsened, the cabinet agreed that we needed to decongest all government institutions for public

Box 15.1   Basic models of public policy[1]

Institutional model: Focuses on policy as the *output* of government, the ultimate decision-making authority. This model emphasizes constitutional provisions, judicial decisions, and common law obligations. The policy process must be adopted, implemented, and enforced by some governmental institution, which provides crucial legitimacy to policy.

Incremental model: Focuses on the *process* of policymaking. This model suggests that public policy is primarily a continuation of past government activities with only incremental changes. It holds that the current policy and programs possess a certain legitimacy as they already exist and that new policy focuses on increases, decreases, or modifications of current programs. This model does not require the establishment of clear goals; instead it tinkers with current programs with the hope that goals and alternatives will become clearer over time.

Group theory/pluralism: Focuses on the *process* of policymaking, but specifically on the struggle among groups to influence public policy. This model sees policy as the equilibrium reached through group struggles, and the role of government is primarily to establish the legal and regulatory rules for politicians and groups engaging in necessary bargaining and negotiating. The power of each group is checked by the power of competing groups, resulting in a marketplace of policymaking.

Elite model: Focuses on the *output* of government, but specifically sees passed policy as reflecting the preferences and values of the power elite. The model claims that society is divided between the elites who have power and the nonelites who do not. In democratic nations, policies adopted and implemented are decided by elite representatives of nonelites. But since elites influence the nonelites through mass campaigns, this model sees changes in public policy as small and incremental reflections of the changes in elite values.

health reasons. We introduced a policy that classified many government employees as 'nonessential' workers, allowing these employees to stay home for the duration of the epidemic. We called the policy of decongesting public institutions the Non-Essential Worker Policy. Government institutions painstakingly went through their personnel listings, with the support of the Civil Service Agency, and determined which employees should stay home.

However, the timing of the policy raised suspicion and existential anxiety. Some, including the legislature and opposition politicians, felt it was the government's way of taking advantage of a crisis to make good on its desire for a small government, better services reform agenda. I was branded 'the worst person in the world' for developing the policy. Although all branches of government followed the de-congestion protocol, calling the policy 'Non-Essential Worker' laid bare a truth that there were many people on government payroll doing nothing.

We can see here the sausage-making process laid bare: I would develop public policy, with the consent of the executive, without regard for legislative considerations. I did not like the composition of the Liberian legislature. To be frank, I did not think of them as having the best interests of the country at heart. They made too much money (at least $15,000 monthly) and, on some occasions, demanded too much to fulfill their legislative responsibilities. When called by the legislature to engage them on any policy initiative that seemed too radical to them, I would stand before them like a teacher with a lesson plan. The legislature saw through my actions, and I became a lightning rod (a controversial reformer some would call me) and arguably the most cited cabinet minister before the plenary of the legislature during the second term of the Sirleaf administration. On one or two occasions, I was found in contempt when I implied, before the full plenary, that they were not being sensible in understanding the benefits of decongesting government institutions during Ebola.

Reform-minded policymaking is hard anywhere. It can be personal and political, tedious and taxing. But it is particularly challenging in a place like Liberia due to changes in power dynamics and resource-strapped settings. In a development context, multilateral and bilateral agreements have a significant influence on the development of policies and the removal of previously existing policies. The addition of these other powerful stakeholders changes the government's power to persuade its public, other government officials, and interest groups. Additionally, the resource-constrained settings create a challenge for the government to implement the public policy after its development. Thus, this suggests that in a development context the success of a public policy is not equally weighted between its adoption into law and its implementation. Rather, the value of the public policy comes from its successful *implementation*.

Implementing partnership schools for Liberia

I was appointed as Liberia's Minister of Education as the Ebola outbreak was beginning to wane. Even apart from this terrible epidemic, I inherited an education system plagued with persistent, significant challenges. Years of conflict had caused debilitating delays and interruptions in education. Many children were already parents themselves, struggling to raise and provide for families. We needed to act fast to protect the gains we had made for peace by reducing the crushing burden of youth idleness, dependency, and disillusionment. For those young people who did attend school, educational outcomes reflected a low-quality system. Three studies of Grade 3 oral reading fluency found mean scores of 18.9–25 correct words per minute, a mark far below international benchmarks of 45–65 correct words per minute, which are associated with literacy and comprehension at that age.[3]

The situation for teachers was equally dire. Just over 50 percent of the teacher workforce had the minimum qualification required to teach their respective grade.[4] Moreover, even as the Ministry had nearly 20,000 staff on payroll – which accounted for 80 to 85 percent of our spending each year – we observed high levels of teacher absenteeism and teachers who abandoned their posts entirely.[5] Even among teachers who showed up to their classrooms consistently, the school day typically lasted only two or three hours, rather than the contractually required eight hours. Hence, a significant number of teachers were receiving compensation without doing the expected work.

Furthermore, we discovered critical barriers to improving administrative and managerial quality. We learned that there were gaps in teacher support and supervision, with hundreds of schools having only one or two teachers to cover all grades (and usually with one assuming the duties of the principal). Schools' student-to-teacher ratios ranged from 33:1 to 90:1 across the system, and the schools were consistently under-resourced, lacking desks, chairs, textbooks, and other learning materials.[6] Although the Ministry employed a range of decentralized staff to monitor schools, most were not receiving regular visits from the District Education Officers.

Considering these issues and the highly scrutinized nature of the education sector – Liberia had four education ministers over the course of 12 years – I had my work cut out for me. The public clearly had appetite for a quick recovery and so any public policies we initiated needed to accelerate progress rapidly.

Over my tenure, we implemented several policies. A crucial one early on included the vetting and testing of nearly 19,500 teachers in Liberia and the identification of more than 2,000 'ghost' workers – who were found to be deceased, nonexistent, or utterly absent – from the payroll. After successfully removing 83 percent of the 'ghosts' identified, we earned $2.3 million in annual savings that could be reinvested in training existing teachers or hiring new and qualified graduates as replacements.

The other significant policy we devised and launched was a public – private partnership we branded Partnership Schools for Liberia (PSL), which saw the government partnering with eight education providers to manage a small group of public schools (Box 15.2). The program aimed to test new ways to deliver quality education within a resource-constrained environment. After the first year, an independent evaluation found evidence that students in PSL schools were learning 60 percent more on average than their peers in other public schools. Teachers were also 20 percent more likely to be in school and more likely to be engaged in instruction during class time. But these gains were not assured from the start.[7] Simply getting the program off the ground was a battle, which drew international headlines.

Box 15.2   Partnership Schools for Liberia (PSL)[8]

Partnership Schools for Liberia (PSL) is a public – private partnership aimed at testing new models for improving Liberia's public schools. Through PSL, the Liberian Ministry of Education partnered with seven educational providers: some local, some international; some for-profit, some nonprofit. These providers have assumed responsibility for the day-to-day operation of the schools within the program, with oversight from the Ministry of Education. The schools remain public and free for all students, and the teachers remain on government payroll.

Key facts (2017–2018 school year)

Number of schools: 194
Number of students: 50,000+
Number of teachers: 1,500+
Number of providers: 7

Results from independent evaluation

- Students in PSL schools are learning 60 percent more than their peers in other public schools.
- Students in PSL schools spent roughly twice as long learning each week.
- Teachers in PSL schools were 20 percent more likely to be in school during a random spot check, and 16 percent more likely to be engaged in instruction during class time.

As mentioned, policy lives and dies by successful implementation. As I see it, there are four central aspects to effectively implement policy: first, designing a policy that is based on comprehensive data; second, communicating policy and its implementation to the public; third, building cross-sectoral collaboration; and fourth, determining proper measurement mechanisms for a policy's impact.

Design a policy that is based on comprehensive quantitative and qualitative data

When I took the helm at the Ministry of Education, I already understood some of the challenges that I would face trying to implement any kind of education reform. I had read all the studies and knew all the stats. And, as a former teacher, I had seen it for myself. But before I started designing and implementing policies, I knew I needed to hear from teachers, parents, and students firsthand.

We therefore started our campaign with a listening tour during which we visited all 15 Liberian counties. We made sure to interact with teachers, students, and parents at the grassroots level, to hear their concerns and priorities. The students we met showed a healthy appetite for learning, but they simply didn't have the support they needed. Many didn't have textbooks, desks, or chairs, let alone qualified teachers. These observations and others informed our sense of urgency.

However, anecdotal evidence is not sufficient when planning a nationwide reform program. To design an education reform program, you need robust, credible data.

Concurrent with the listening tour, we carried out an in-depth, comprehensive analysis to secure reliable data on the strengths and weaknesses of the entire education sector, from early childhood to higher education. We partnered with international experts, supported by the Global Partnership for Education (GPE) and the World Bank, but wanted to keep government at the forefront of gathering, analyzing, and storing the data. This Education Sector Analysis (ESA) enabled us to ensure robust research drove our policies and reform agenda. It also gave potential funding partners and the public confidence in our vision.

From the ESA, we built our 'Getting to Best' Education Sector Plan. It proposed an overhaul of our education system through the introduction of a set of interventions, including vetting and placing of qualified teachers, improving performance management across the school system, implementing a School Quality Assessment framework, and launching the PSL pilot. Because it was based on robust data and analysis, we were able to generate significant international support for the reform plan, including securing an $11.9 million grant from the GPE to dramatically improve access to quality education in disadvantaged communities.

Communicate your policy and its implementation to the public

In hindsight, we did not invest enough time in communicating our reforms and bringing the public along. This was partly because of the accelerated timeline for the reforms. Given that we started out just two years before the end of President Ellen Johnson Sirleaf's final term, we understood that we had limited time to make an impact. But this haste meant we learned the hard way that, when operating in a democratic and transparent society, two-way communication is vital to rolling out new policies to the public. Democracy is a complex trust-based system, and communications is an essential element of trust-building. The trust gap widens when citizens do not have adequate information to buy into any public policy initiative.

While we had engaged stakeholders throughout the process of designing our reforms, we could have done more to bring the broader public along and communicate the positive impact the reforms were designed to have in their communities and for their children's futures. Soliciting more input and ideas from the communities we intended to serve, and the education staff who would be involved in the

182 George Kronnisanyon Werner

program, could also have helped shape the program to achieve even greater success. Instead, because we didn't prioritize communications enough when we launched the partnership, we spent a lot of time trying to change the narrative after others, including international activist organizations, had already defined the program.

We faced a similar challenge during the undertaking of the reform to vet and test all teachers, when some teachers initially thought the program was just a ruse to kick them off the payroll. Rumors spread quickly, and teachers were reluctant to participate. However, once we communicated that the exercise was a way to improve the quality of our education by assessing whether teachers could benefit from additional training, they were more willing to embrace the process.

Even though PSL was far from the only initiative we launched, it sucked up a lot of the oxygen and overshadowed the rest of our agenda in part because communication was an afterthought rather than an integrated part of our process from the beginning.

Communication is equally critical for engaging nonstate actors. Clearly defining roles and responsibilities for all parties involved helps clear up any ambiguity that can result in delays or a lack of delivery. To help in this, anyone seeking to implement a similar public – private partnership should implement a transparent, competitive procurement process from the outset and ensure consistent contracting and distribution of responsibilities across all providers.

Building cross-sector collaboration with partners from both the public and private sectors

When implementing policies, partners from the public and private sector, including civil society organizations, are essential in helping drive the necessary change. Getting buy-in from these various organizations can uncover a variety of resources that may be necessary for achieving the policy objectives. For us, partnering with the GPE and the World Bank ensured that we had the education experts who were equipped to assist us in compiling our comprehensive Education Sector Analysis, along with building our 'Getting to Best' Education Sector Plan.

Still on the international front, with the fiscal constraints we faced we needed to seek outside donors who provided the millions of dollars required for the innovative PSL program. The Ministry of Education's entire annual operating budget is $45 million. This means across all public schools, Liberia spends a meager $50 per pupil per year, most of which goes toward paying teachers' salaries. So, there was a need to find more resources and disrupt a failing system. Apart from the funding needed to run PSL, organizations such as Big Win Philanthropy and USAID helped us with vetting and testing our teacher workforce.

Locally, we needed to get the support of the teachers' association, parent – teacher associations, and civil society groups focused on education. We included leaders from these organizations in all significant decisions we made regarding our policies. Even the president herself presided over some stakeholder negotiations.

There were also times when the government disagreed with partners in terms of what it saw as being in the best interest of Liberian children. For example, we forged ahead with the public – private partnership initiative even when some partners disagreed with us.

Furthermore, it was essential to build collaborative relationships with our colleagues in other ministries as they were vital stakeholders in the reform delivery process. Most importantly, I benefited from working for an enlightened president, Ellen Johnson Sirleaf, who understood the importance of education for rebuilding Liberia after years of conflict and the Ebola crisis. It is crucial to get political commitment and will for implementing reforms, particularly those that may spark controversy or pushback.

Determine proper monitoring and evaluation mechanisms for policy's impact

Evidence-based policymaking is essential, especially in the context of a developing nation where there are limited resources and a particular need to seek maximum benefit from every investment. Committing to the collection and use of evidence in decision-making also strengthens accountability and shares it across all stakeholders involved in crafting and delivering policies.

When evaluating a policy's impact, it is essential to carefully select a measurement and evaluation framework, ensuring that it is designed to provide all the insights needed to make informed decisions.

We commissioned a Randomized Control Trial (RCT), an independent evaluation of the PSL program, to measure whether the program was successful in improving learning outcomes. We selected this framework because we were advised that it represented the gold standard, and we wanted to ensure that the results would be accurate and credible. Though it had some limitations (such as a lack of qualitative insights), the RCT did provide valuable insight into the program and enabled us to see what was working and what needed to be strengthened. With elections and a change of administration imminent in Liberia, it also gave the new administration data on which to base any decisions about the future of the program.

In the 2017–2018 school year, more than 50,000 children were enrolled in PSL schools, taught by reinvigorated and retrained government teachers, supported by energized parents and resilient communities. They had the full backing of the Ministry of Education and I am proud of what has been achieved so far. But while I believe this policy holds great potential, there is no magic bullet to fix any problem, and certainly not one as complex as education in Liberia – or indeed anywhere. PSL is just one of a range of reforms we undertook to improve our education system. These included plans to reach out-of-school children; the deepening and strengthening of school accountability mechanisms; and an aggressive payroll cleaning program. Individual policies are powerful, but a series of synergistic policies can change a system.

Conclusion: Make public policy great again

At the beginning of my public service, I looked upon myself as a technocrat. I did not consider myself a politician. Being a politician seemed a dirty career in my mind. But I was naïve and mistaken. The institutions I headed were created through political dialogue, from the executive to the legislative and judiciary. Though never neutral and frustratingly bureaucratic at times, I found eventually that public policymaking is a beautiful mess which advances the common good.

Change takes time and concerted effort to achieve desired impact. For the public sector, change often moves at a snail's pace, and this can be frustrating. The systems that must be fixed to make service delivery more efficient and effective are resistant to change. Democracy engenders debates, messy exchanges, compromises, and sometimes does not appear suited to countries that require swift government action to make life better for people. Just watch a typical representative legislature to see how much time is spent debating an issue, and you will see why some countries, with less appetite for pure democracy, are making greater headway.

Patience is a luxury that many citizens in poor countries cannot afford, and the jaw dropping contrast in lifestyle between career politicians and the constituents is such that there is a growing gap in trust and confidence. There is a cost attached to conditions that hold ordinary citizens back. There is a sense that corruption and old-school systems make government-led change ineffective and hard, especially compared to businesses and other institutions that may seem more efficient at scaling 'impact.' However, we must continue to believe in public policy as foundational to change-making and collective decision-making. The complex ecosystem of good policymaking, which incorporates diverse stakeholders, should not be a reason to circumvent a key step as fundamental as public policy formulation.

Without policy, we have no binding guidance on the way forward. Without policy, we have no agreement on personnel issues. Without policy, we have no way of holding ourselves or being held accountable for being public servants. Public policy, as it were, is a compass for how we deliver public services in a free, open, and fair manner. The public policymaking process itself is at its best when it is able to gather, and solicit from, multiple stakeholders various ideas that aim at resolving outstanding, seemingly intractable challenges and leveraging meaningful partnerships.

The future of policymaking holds a promise embedded in collaboration, within and outside of governments. We are connected, one to the other, always interacting. We think through issues together. We act collectively to resolve societal challenges, from the grassroots to the helm of society. We do so by listening to one another, by defining the issue together, and by figuring out together the best approach and the amount of resources needed for action. The complex and intractable problems we face are more nuanced than a black and white analysis. Public policy should not be about the exercise of power, as if to impose on citizens from above, but rather an exercise of negotiation and collaboration among all with a stake in the outcome. We need courageous and committed political leadership to support change agents in both the public and private sectors, and to champion policies that serve the common interest.

We call *all* to action for the common good. There can be no future for human progress without meaningful partnerships between governments and the private sector. We need increased dialogue between governments and the private sector for the common good. There are some things that government can do well, such as regulations and the creation of enabling environments. There are other things that the private sector does very well, such as efficient management of systems and monitoring and evaluation for results and mutual accountability. Together, progress can be accelerated for all.

16 Investment for impact

A simple primer on how money can serve values

Eric Maltzer

Eric Maltzer is the Director of Impact Investing at Medora Ventures and Adjunct Professor of Entrepreneurship, Lloyd Greif Center for Entrepreneurial Studies, USC Marshall School of Business. At Medora, Eric helps family offices and foundations start impact capital funds, drawing on his experience as a private investor (Valmiki Capital and Clean Energy Venture Group), a public equities analyst (Sage Asset Management), and a public sector finance expert (U.S. State Department). At the State Department, he managed a multi-billion dollar U.S. – China public – private partnership, which leveraged more than $40 for every $1 of government investment. Eric has founded two companies, and advised many others in the clean energy, education, and technology sectors. Eric has an MBA and a Certificate in Finance from MIT's Sloan School of Management and a Master's in Public Policy from Harvard's John F. Kennedy School of Government. He has a B.A. from Yale University in Ethics, Politics, and Economics. He hails from Tampa, Florida and was the Florida Deputy Policy Director for Barack Obama's 2008 presidential campaign.

★ ★ ★

What comes to your mind when you picture an 'investment?'

Do you imagine a safe, boring line graph that shows the performance of your 401(k)?

Do you think instead of a worthy nonprofit that helps thousands of people gain access to clean water?

Perhaps you think of a university, and student loans that still dictate your life choices?

Or do you equate 'investment' with bewilderment, summoning a nightmare in which you are approached by a banker who speaks only in jargon and brandishes an Excel spreadsheet that might as well be written in Aramaic?

Whatever dream or nightmare you conjured, it is a shame the English language doesn't have more words for 'investment'; when it comes to this word, we are – more often than not – talking past each other. Spending your time and exhausting your patience to raise a child is one kind of 'investment'; buying a ten-year treasury note or giving a million dollars to a start-up is quite a different one. Often, when a friend wants us to take his or her financial decisions seriously, we hear, "it's an investment." Sadly, when translated, the phrase usually means, "I *love* this thing . . . and I will never, ever make money on it."

In the vernacular, the word 'investing' is closely associated with 'inputting' your time or money. But professional investors know that investment is a long and sensitive process; the moment of 'input' in investing is like the moment the key turns the ignition of a car: a spark has ignited, but the journey is yet to be driven.

Elsewhere in this book, you can see how design, social enterprise, media, and other disciplines have impact. By analyzing and understanding those various disciplines, you will be better able to drive systemic change. But there is another discipline you ought to understand, a discipline that interacts with all of the other fields described in this book. A discipline that, arguably, makes the others possible: investing.

In this chapter, we will explore if, when, and how investment has impact. We will define what investment means to capital providers in the civic, public, and private sectors. We will consider a model for evaluating any kind of investment, and then we will discuss a couple case studies. Lastly, we will talk about the relatively new field of 'impact investing,' and you can decide for yourself if you think the field will take off like a rocket or fizzle out like a sparkler. By the end of the chapter, you will be able to talk about a wide range of investments in the native language of investors; more importantly, you should be able to talk in plain English about investing for impact.

The great mobilizer

Before going further, I should tell you how I got into this corner of the investing universe, and why this topic is so important to me.

It started, like most things in finance and economics, with a word I didn't understand at the time and which, I would find out later, makes no sense to anybody in the context it was used. In the fall of 2009, I was working in the State Department's Office of Global Change, a small 20-person group whose mission was to formulate the U.S. position on climate change and to negotiate a global compact to address it. The extraordinary team included climate scientists, lawyers, professors-on-leave, and dedicated civil servants. What that team did *not* include was anyone with an advanced degree in finance or economics. Thus, that October, about two months before the biggest climate summit in a dozen years, one of my colleagues started to use a word that would change my life. That word was 'mobilize.' It was not used as a jocular synonym for "let's go, fellas." It was not used to describe the movements of a panzer division into Belgium or the locomotion of a horseless carriage. The overheard phrase that launched my career in finance was, "We will mobilize

100 billion dollars a year by 2020." Just imagine that. One hundred billion dollars a year. Just mobilizing down the street, without even a horse to guide them.

To be fair, the person who created this phrase – let's call him Jack – meant well. The U.S. team was under a lot of pressure from developing countries to come up with money to help poorer countries produce clean energy and address the effects of climate change on their crops, infrastructure, etc. At the time, we were less than a year removed from the largest recession since the Great Depression, and Jack knew the U.S. government did not have the appetite for sending tens of billions of dollars in direct aid. So Jack did what a lot of people would do in that situation – he fudged. Or rather, he mobilized.

I remember asking Jack (and everyone else in the office), "What does that mean, 'mobilize'?" It doesn't sound like an economic term. Is it real? Is this a thing? I never got a straight answer, though it seemed to mean, "By the power of our moral leadership, we will get others to come forward and donate this money." It surprised me to see that this word was so popular in the international community; it made it into paragraphs 6 and 8 of the Copenhagen Accord.[1] But to the banks, governments, and private investors who were to give out this money, there was never a clear investment case presented, no economic rationale laid out, no return promised. 'Mobilize' was a nonstarter in the investment world.

Even though subsequent years proved that we dramatically increased the United States' investment in climate research and clean energy from the 2005 baseline, I was (and still am) bothered by the failure of our team to come up with a sustainable solution for financing clean energy and climate adaptation around the world. The problem was that we didn't know finance. We knew Jack.

I have a career in finance now, but that episode always feels close at hand. When I hire and when I teach, I keep Jack in mind. I make sure my team knows that – especially in finance – it's never good enough to nod along to the jargon.

And finance folks *love* their jargon. Rare is the modern banker or trader who will admit that part (or all!) of his or her job is to speculate. Instead, swarms of overpaid financiers "build football field valuation models based on analysis of comparables, precedents, and DCFs of the companies' TTM earnings, etc." Oh really? So you're making your best guess of what the companies are worth using some assumptions and an Excel spreadsheet?

Throughout this chapter we will use proper finance terms whenever necessary. After all, it's hard to have impact through investing if you don't speak the language of investors. But let's be honest: there is a lot of nonsense, misdirection, and willful abuse of the English language among finance professionals. Such nonsense is unnecessary. Jargon for jargon's sake is a cloak used by cartels and charlatans to mask the truth.

The best minds in the worlds of finance and investing understand the flows of money so well that they could explain to a sixth grader where the money comes from, where it's going, and why it's happening. Those without that ability would be better off mobilizing themselves into a new line of work.

Obverse and reverse: Investment and impact

This chapter will start with a simple definition of impact, one similar to that offered at the outset of this book. Impact is the achievement of a predetermined social or environmental objective. This definition is contentious in investing (many mainstream investors lower the bar to include any predetermined objective or, in some cases, any objective), but it is pithy, specific, and widely accepted, so we will use it for now.

Picking one definition for 'investment' is not simple, but this chapter will stipulate that a financial investment is the transfer of money (at some risk to the investor) with an expectation of return. Parenting and charity – while valuable and important – are not included in this definition of 'investment.' Likewise, most sneaker purchases and great sushi meals do not make the cut.

Given these definitions, can investments have impact?

How can they not? Perhaps it is possible for an investment to have no social or environmental effect. But choosing to buy a share of Halliburton instead of a share of CVS makes it slightly cheaper for Halliburton to borrow money and grow, and that means a brighter future for the oil field services company. Buying Bitcoin increases the amount of (fossil fuel – fired) electricity needed to mine that asset.

Every building that gets built, every start-up that gets funded, every credit card that gets issued, and every IPO that gets backed relies on investment. To ask if investment has impact is to ask if money has power. Investment and impact are the obverse and the reverse of the same coin. Perhaps there is a better question to ask: can (or should) investment have *positive* impact?

This is a much harder question to answer. To have any shot at answering this question intelligently, we need to understand more about how investors speak and how professional investing works.

Fundamentals of investing

How exactly does investing work? The answer to that question is the same as the answer to many of life's best questions: "It depends."

Like art or poetry, not all investing is created equal. The job of a 'professional investor' does not exist any more than the job of 'professional athlete' exists. Just as gymnasts and basketball players are capable in different ways, venture capitalists don't know much about the bond markets; equity researchers know very little about private debt swaps. Yet every kind of investor is familiar with certain common terms and tools. And every investor has a process to sift and evaluate new opportunities. Before they invest, capital owners have to believe that *this* building, or *this* start-up, or *this* person is the best use of their limited resources. On what criteria do they make those decisions?

Investors in distinct asset classes (e.g., stocks, bonds, real estate) have different backgrounds, skill sets, and temperaments, but, by and large, investors make

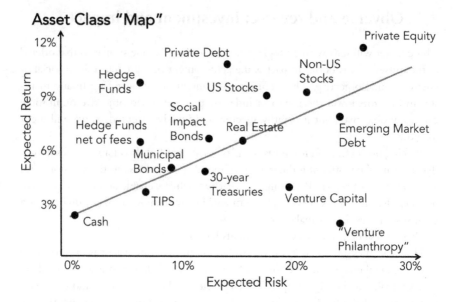

Figure 16.1 Asset class 'map'

decisions based on one common end goal: delivering the highest possible risk-adjusted returns. Holding risk constant, they want to get as high a return as they can; when risk ratchets up, the return demanded by the investor should ratchet up as well.[2] As you can see in Figure 16.1, some asset classes, *on average*, do a better job than others at delivering high risk-adjusted returns.

In the public sector or in civil society, capital owners (e.g., federal agencies like the Department of Defense or nonprofits like Save the Children) are allowed (or even encouraged) to devote their resources to projects or companies that deliver political returns or social returns. But capital in the private sector has to achieve the highest possible risk-adjusted *financial* return, or else the 'bosses' of that capital (aka 'shareholders' or 'bondholders' in public instruments or 'limited partners' in private ones) will put their money elsewhere. As such, private sector investment is not an allocation, nor an allowance, nor a grant, nor an act of kindness. Financial investment is an act of self-interest. Healthy returns safeguard the investor's survival. Investors live or die by their returns.

With stakes so high, how do investors – in their various asset classes – operate?

The table below shows what investors in various asset classes seek to do. To demonstrate how investors are connected, I've used the example of when and how each kind of investor would (have) want(ed) to give money to Google (no, the answer is not 'anytime Google wants it').

Different investors made vastly different returns on their investment in Google because they took very different kinds of risk. The seed and venture investors made a return of hundreds or even thousands of percentage points on their investments;

Table 16.1 Asset classes

Asset class	What	Why	How	When
Private credit (also known as private debt)	A credit card company allows Sergey Brin to buy the domain name 'Google.com' from ICANN	Sergey needs immediate capital and doesn't mind paying a huge interest rate	A credit card company or a bank issues a card to an individual, allowing him to make purchases up to his credit limit	Google is in its embryonic stages
Angel investment	A wealthy individual gives Sergey $100,000 to buy the servers that will host the new website: Google.com. In exchange, he gets the right to buy stock in the company in the future	Sergey and Larry Page need money to build the infrastructure of Google.com, but don't want to pay the high interest rates of credit card companies, or give away as much of the company as required by venture capital	A wealthy individual writes a personal check to the entrepreneurs	Google is in its infant stage
Seed investment	A group of wealthy individuals gives Sergey $1 million to hire engineers to build out the search engine that will power Google.com	Sergey and Larry want to rent space in Menlo Park, California, buy letterhead, purchase a ping pong table, and hire some lawyers and accountants; they need more money than angels can provide, but don't want to give away as much of the company as required by venture capital. Also, seed investors rarely ask for as much control of the company as later-stage investors will.	Family, friends, and acquaintances (perhaps introduced by the angel investor) give the founders of a company $1–2 million; each investor writes a check to the new company	Google is in its toddler stage

(Continued)

Table 16.1 (Continued)

Asset class	What	Why	How	When
Venture capital	A venture capital firm gives Google, Inc. $25 million to grow its staff and infrastructure as quickly as possible	Sergey and Larry want to become the dominant search engine in the world 'to organize the world's information.' They know they will need a lot of money to grow quickly, and are ready to give away pieces of the company	Venture capital (VC) firms write checks to the new company, usually in exchange for 'equity' – a percentage of the company. Sometimes the VCs can issue a 'convertible note', which is a loan that needs to be paid back . . . unless the company does very well, in which case the loan magically 'converts' into equity	Google is in its early childhood stage
Private equity	A private equity (PE) firm gives Google, Inc. $100 million to build new server farms and new corporate offices around the world	Sergey and Larry want to grow the company and need more money than ever. They also want corporate expertise, which often accompanies PE investment	A PE firm writes a very large check in exchange for equity in the company. The firm may also borrow money to purchase even *more* of the company (and then, through the miracle of financial engineering, assign those loans to the company, so the company has to pay back the money the PE firm borrowed) *Note: Google did not actually go through a round of PE financing; if they had, this is when that round would have taken place*	Google is in its teenage years

Real estate (also known as real assets)	Google, Inc. itself invests $100 million in Bay Area real estate, on which it plans to build its campus and server farms	Sergey and Larry want to make an investment of their own, betting that the real estate will not only be needed for the company, but will appreciate in value over time	A company, bank, private equity firm, or other investment firm buys property of some kind in the hope that such property will appreciate	Google is getting an apartment and putting the utilities in its own name
Public equity	Large institutional investors such as banks, pension funds, and extremely high net worth individuals buy $1.66 billion worth of shares in Google, Inc. when it debuts on the NASDAQ. These shares are later sold to the general public	Sergey and Larry are ready to raise money from the 'public' (aka stock) markets. They raise more money than ever before, but this raise means they now have to abide by a mountain of rules and regulations put out by the U.S. Securities and Exchange Commission (SEC)	A company enlists an investment bank (in Google's case, no bankers were needed) to 'pitch' the company to prospective investors and determine a price for the company's initial public offering (and, by extension, its market value). The very first shares sold – to an array of institutional investors – bring in millions (and sometimes billions) of dollars in cash for the company. Those initial sales constitute the initial public offering (IPO) of the company	Google has graduated from college and is facing the 'real world'
Corporate debt	Very large banks lend $3 billion to Google, Inc. so that the company can repay creditors who lent it money at higher interest rates when the company was younger	Sergey and Larry have come full circle. Now they – as Google, Inc. – can borrow money from the biggest banks in the world at rates of 2–8% instead of the 20–30% they used to pay on their credit cards	A large investment bank surveys ratings agencies to determine a company's credit worthiness and then approaches other large banks to buy pieces of Google's new debt issue. These pieces are called 'bonds' and can be sold on to the general public	Google is mature and established enough that large organizations will lend it large amounts of money

they invested in Google when it seemed that the company could easily have been outpaced by a larger rival like Yahoo! or Microsoft. These 'early stage' investors need to make '5×' or '10×' returns on their productive investments because most of their investments (80–90 percent in the case of many venture capitalists) fail!

In contrast, the public debt lenders might make 5 percent on their money invested in Google, a rate one-one hundredth the size of the return produced by the early stage investors' money. Why would anyone agree to make so little from Google? Low returns are proper when one assumes little risk. An investment in a Google bond is very unlikely to default. Because the investment is considered so safe, investors are willing to accept a lower return.

To everything there is a season:
Return, return, return

What does it mean to deliver a 'return' on an investment? Until recently, the concept of 'return' was straightforward: the amount of money that came back to the investor over and above what was put in. But since the advent of mainstream socially responsible investing (SRI) in the 1980s and 1990s, some private sector investors have pursued a social return in addition to a financial return. A flood of research by Robert Eccles, George Serafeim, and others has shown that the stocks of companies that rate highest in their care of environmental, social, and governance (ESG) concerns outperform their more traditional peers.[3] With the launch of public equity funds like Generation Investment Management (2004) and venture capital funds like Double Bottom Line (DBL) Partners (2004), it became clear that talented investors did not have to sacrifice one type of return for the other.[4]

Yet still, many investors, academics, and professionals insist that merely considering social returns alongside financial returns – investing for (positive) impact – is adorable at best, and criminal at worst.[5] "How do you expect to maximize returns," they probe, "when you are trying to save the world?"

Any honest stockpicker will admit that you cannot pick every stock in the market and outperform; but as soon as you realize that fund managers are picking *different subsets* of the market, you realize that no one is truly 'maximizing returns'; each actor in the market is just picking a few stocks and hoping for the best. In truth, 'maximizing returns' is just jargon for "Leave me alone; I want no rules or restrictions during my selection process. I am certain that my no-holds-barred process will yield the optimal result." It is as if a very self-assured friend said to you, "Listen, I can pick the ingredients for the best meal or the ingredients for a healthy meal. Which do you want?" "Both!" you say. "Nononono, no can do," says your friend. "I can only pick the ingredients of the best meal if I am allowed unfettered access to anything in the supermarket! Doritos, caviar, discount lard, everything!" I hope you will agree with me that that friend, I am sad to say, is a crazy person.

Why do so many financial professionals labor under the easily disproved belief that social and financial returns are mutually exclusive?

There are at least three possible explanations. First, many investors define 'impact' as 'the achievement of any objective,' whether that is 'bringing jobs to a community' or 'supporting my family,' if not necessarily 'addressing climate change.' Setting the bar this low (on the ground, you might say) ensures that *every* investment is 'impactful,' though perhaps not 'impactful in a positive way.' To investors anchored by this conviction, the notion that there is a higher level of impact or a 'positive impact' is either baffling or suspect. Second, many cold-eyed investors believe that positive impact is either irrelevant or actively counter to the principal objective of investment: financial return. Increasingly large mountains of evidence to the contrary do not seem to sway their views. Finally, those who wish to have a positive impact with their investments have not been able to agree on a way to measure that positive impact. Without common, consistent measurement, investors have had – and continue to have – a hard time proving that their investments are better than any others.

The first two objections to the viability of impact investing are rooted in dogma. The third obstacle to the mainstream acceptance of impact investing is significant, but only in the way that the lack of universal standards for *financial* disclosure 'prevented' investment before the SEC was created in 1934. (NB: a lot of investment happened before the advent of the SEC.)

Now that we know a bit more about how investing works, how can we tell a good investment from a poor one?

The sexy stuff: Models and measurements (for investing)

At the beginning of this chapter, we spoke of what unites investors across asset classes – their pursuit of risk-adjusted return. But how exactly can investors predict what will yield the best risk-adjusted return? Well, they can't, at least not all the time! The best investors can do is approach investment decisions with sharpened critical reasoning skills and a consistent process. That 'consistent process' usually involves one or more reductive 'models' – simplified approximations of the world faced by real-life companies and entrepreneurs. How do these models work? Why are there so many?

Investors in different asset classes often claim that their flavor of investing cannot possibly be compared to any other flavor of investing, and several key players in the investing universe have a vested interest in propagating this idea amidst a farrago of ridiculous jargon. To alleviate these issues, I created a simple framework you can use to evaluate the purpose and effectiveness of any investment, no matter the industry or asset class. It's called the SIMPLE framework. Here's how it works.

Elsewhere in this book, you learned that the process of systems change starts with an input, has an output, and ends with an outcome. Similarly, every target of investment must have an input, an output, and an outcome. You can create a fleshed-out SIMPLE framework for any investment by asking the following questions:

1   What is the **S**park? Why would we invest in this person/organization/idea in the first place? Why will this be popular or valuable or useful in the future?
2   What sort of **I**nvestment is required, i.e., what is the input? Why do the funders think this is a good use of capital? How do the funders plan to be paid back?
3   What is the **M**ain Event? What will the financing be used for? How exactly does the financing get transmitted to the recipient person/organization/idea? What strings are attached to that financing?
4   What is the **P**roduction that results from the financing?, i.e., what is the output? What gets produced because of this financing that otherwise would not have been produced?
5   What does the production **L**ead to? What are the outcomes of financing the person/organization/idea?
6   What are the **E**nds of the financing? What, at the end of the day, are the impacts of the financing? Is this process scalable and/or repeatable?

Where can this framework be useful? Let's try the framework in two case studies to find out. The following cases are based on historical events, but are illustrative in nature; all dialogue, descriptions, and use of our SIMPLE model are taken from secondhand sources or imagined by the author and should not be cited as fact.

Case study #1: Ben & Jerry's, 2000

In late 1999, Antony Burgmans, the co-Chairman of the Dutch company Unilever, one of the largest consumer packaged goods companies in the world, must have been standing on the top floor of the cantilevered soapbox he called headquarters, gazing out the window at the dark chocolatey Rotterdam canals below, thinking of Phish food. Unilever was considering making a bid for Ben & Jerry's Home-made, the quirky ice cream company that had made social consciousness central to its strategy – a concept it called 'Linked Prosperity.' But would Ben and Jerry be receptive to a buyout offer from a multinational conglomerate like Unilever? More importantly, would Ben & Jerry's Homemade make financial sense for the Dutch? Antony had already asked his co-Chairman, Niall Fitzgerald, to start the charm offensive by flying to Vermont and conspicuously carrying his own back-pack everywhere during the visit. Now Antony needed to huddle with his army of consultants and bankers to see whether this investment made sense. Before he called that meeting, he started to doodle on his notepad.

"Well," thought Antony, furrowing his brow at the 'Production' row of his SIM-PLE framework, "look at that. They don't need us as much as we need them. This might get expensive. Time to call in the bankers and see what we can afford." He spot-checked each of the other rows. "This is going to be really good for us. This

Table 16.2 Ben and Jerry's SIMPLE framework

Spark	Why will this be popular or valuable or useful in the future?	Ben and Jerry's has a nationally revered brand name in the United States, the most creative flavor team in the ice cream industry, and an intense following among younger people, who will be demanding Ben and Jerry's for the next 50 years.
Investment	What do we have to put in?	More than money. Because competitors like Dreyer's will be bidding against us, we will have to put in more than the current $17 a share. Maybe we'll have to put in double that? (NB: the final share price at deal closing was a bit more than $43). We'll also have to guarantee Ben & Jerry's corporate culture.
Main event	What will the financing be used for?	Ben & Jerry's, deliciously, is a cash-flow-positive business. It is not in distress and does not need to sell itself. Unilever would be purchasing the business to help Unilever grow more quickly and contribute to the corporation's bottom line for years to come.
Production	What gets produced because of this financing that otherwise would not have been produced?	Nothing, immediately. Unilever isn't changing the nature of Ben & Jerry's. It's just installing an ice cream business inside of a big Dutch box.
Leads to	What are the outcomes of financing the person/organization/idea?	Ben & Jerry's will give Unilever quite a bit of cachet in the United States. Also, thanks to Ben & Jerry's 'Linked Prosperity' model, the acquisition may position Unilever at the cutting edge of sustainability and social business practices.
Ends	Is this process scalable and/or repeatable?	Yes. This gives Unilever an entrée into the specialty ice cream market, a new sector for the company.

investment makes a lot of sense." He felt a low rumble in his belly. "I shouldn't have skipped lunch. I'd pay almost anything for some Cherry Garcia ice cream right now!"

Note: Ben & Jerry's Homemade agreed to be acquired by Unilever, for about $326 million, or $43.60 a share, in cash in April of 2000. In announcing the deal, both companies said that Ben & Jerry's would continue as it always had and that

Unilever, which is based in the Netherlands, would commit 7.5 percent of Ben & Jerry's profits to a foundation and agree not to reduce jobs or alter the way the ice cream is made. Unilever also created a $5 million fund to help minority-owned businesses and others in poor neighborhoods and distributed $5 million in bonuses to employees in the six months after the acquisition. Ben & Jerry's CEO, Perry D. Odak, described Niall Fitzgerald, the Unilever co-Chairman, as arriving for a meeting with a knapsack on his back, an appearance that went over very well with Ben & Jerry's management. "He talked for three hours about all the sustainable-agriculture programs they have," Mr. Odak said. "We were very, very impressed."[6]

Case study #2: Enhancing Capacity for Low Emission Development Strategies (EC LEDS), 2010

In early 2010, the United States team negotiating the global climate change treaty needed some good news. Battered by bad press after the 2009 Copenhagen Summit, the 20-person team was searching for a program that would deliver outsize results for a minimum investment. On a muggy Monday morning, Jack trudged straight in to the director's office and arched his eyebrow. "I have an idea to mobilize $20 million dollars." "Let's hear it," said the boss.

"We're going to help other countries develop strategies to reduce their own emissions! You know . . . teaching them to fish instead of telling them what to eat. We'll call the strategies 'Low Emission Development Strategies,' and since we're helping them figure out how to build those strategies, we'll call our role 'Enhancing Capacity.' What do you think?"

"Jack, I love it! Write it up and let's go get approval for this!"

A young analyst overheard the exchange, got out a notepad, and started writing.

The analyst furrowed his brow. He was torn. Honestly, it was a noble idea with a lot of merit. The 'Spark' and 'Ends' rows showed clearly why Jack's idea had caught fire in the office. But the 'Main event' row showed fundamental uncertainty about what the money would actually be used for. The 'Production' row exposed the essentially speculative nature of pouring money into helping other countries create their own policies. The 'Leads to' row laid bare that there was no direct link between performance and funding.

Note: EC LEDS absorbed tens of millions of dollars of funding from 2010–2017, resulting in LEDS for 25 countries. 'Enhancing Capacity' turned out to be 'money spent on U.S. civil servants' flights, meals, hotels, per diem reimbursement, conference space, coffee, snacks, and plastic name tags for attendees from host countries.' Countries with U.S.-backed LEDS did, in fact, almost always attempt to implement those LEDS in whole or in part. However, without trusted metrics, it was hard to prove that the program was cost-effective and the program was unable to attract

Table 16.3 EC LED's SIMPLE framework

Spark	Why will this be popular or valuable or useful in the future?	Developing countries need to figure out how best to reduce their own emissions. They are much more likely to follow low-emissions development paths if they create those paths themselves.
Investment	What do we have to put in?	$5 million per year to start, eventually $20–25 million per year
Main event	What will the financing be used for?	'Enhancing Capacity?' What is that? Is that a thing? Is that like 'mobilize?' Are we mobilizing enhanced capacity?
Production	What gets produced because of this financing that otherwise would not have been produced?	Ideally, the countries will produce low-emissions development plans. What happens after the production of that plan?
Leads to:	What are the outcomes of financing the person/organization/idea?	Ideally, the LEDS will lead to cost-effectively lowering global emissions, a key foreign policy goal of the United States at the time. What happens to the cost-effectiveness if costs run high? Is there any metric in place to tie money spent to emissions reduced? Who will be held accountable if that doesn't happen?
Ends	Is this process scalable and/or repeatable?	Yes. If it works, this process is repeatable around the world.

long-term co-investors to the project. EC LEDS was shut down in 2017. Its website now claims that the program's work "has completed."

Impact investing is mostly just investing

Impact investments are "[i]nvestments made into companies, organizations, and funds with the intention to generate measurable social and environmental impact alongside a financial return."[7] Impact investing is not an asset class. It is not a niche play. It does not automatically mean that you are accepting a lower return on your investments in order to feel good about them. Impact investing is mostly just investing. Capital owners find funds or investment targets they think will grow in value.

They take an ownership stake. They hope to sell later at a large profit. It just so happens that those funds or investment targets have been additionally vetted by their likely impact on society and the environment.

Although the term 'impact investing' is relatively new (it was officially coined at The Rockefeller Foundation's Bellagio Center in 2007), the investing philosophy has existed in various forms for centuries. In the 1700s, Quakers and Methodists were admonished to avoid investments and businesses that harmed others, like the slave trade, guns, and tobacco.

Later, companies such as Ben & Jerry's and TOMS wove a social mission into their businesses from the beginning. Ben & Jerry's sold for $326 million in 2000; TOMS was bought in 2014 by Bain Capital for $625 million.

Today, impact investments such as these are increasingly popular. These investments can be made in either emerging or developed markets, and investors may target a range of returns from below market to market rate. Currently, nine out of the top ten largest U.S. asset managers are active in impact investing. Impact investing stretches across every asset class, every geography, and almost every industry. Why? Because impact investing is mostly just investing.

Impact investments have four core characteristics that mark them as *impact* investments.

- *Intentionality:* an investor's intention to have a positive social or environmental impact through investments is essential to impact investing.
- *Investment with return expectations:* impact investments are expected to generate a financial return on capital or, at minimum, a return of capital. Investments that lose capital are not investments. They are charity, write-offs, and/or great stories.
- *Return expectations are relevant to the investment's asset class:* impact investments target a wide range of financial returns; expectations of return will vary according to the investment's asset class.
- *Impact measurement:* the investor is committed to measure and report the social and environmental performance and progress of underlying investments.

What's next for impact investing?

Impact investing is approaching its fulcrum moment.

In the coming years, the notion that investments should try to maximize returns *and* positively impact society could become a norm in the investment world. There is ample evidence for this. BlackRock CEO Larry Fink, whose firm is the world's largest asset manager, issued a now-famous January 2018 letter saying, in part, that "To prosper over time, every company must not only deliver financial performance, but also show how it makes a positive contribution to society."[8]

However, impact investing could just as easily fade into the recesses of our collective memories as yet another investing fad.

What happens next is dependent on two things. First, easy-to-use, standardized metrics upon which investors can rely need to be developed and disseminated. 'Impact' needs to mean the same thing around the world, in the same way '20 percent increase in gross margin' means the same thing around the world. Secondly, and critically, readers like you, who have the aptitude and the know-how to become the next generation of investors, need to change the false, unidimensional notion of how to 'maximize returns.' When investment committees stop parroting the dogma that only access to the entire market can yield maximum returns, who knows what's possible?

Conclusion

At the start of this chapter, we said we would explore if, when, and how investment has impact. We said we would be clear and specific about what investment means in the civic, public, and private sectors. I promised a model that could help you evaluate any kind of investment, and I foretold a discussion of the field of impact investing.

Now it is your turn to begin a real exploration of finance and investing. We live on a planet being torn apart by crises and deepening political mistrust. Yet in one powerful way, our globe is more united than ever. For better and for worse, we are meshed together by a market economy with no clear voice and no guiding morality. Investment and power move in picoseconds before us, supplying the wildest demands, each transaction sealed with an invisible handshake. Investment always has impact.

More importantly, what I hope you get from this chapter is that impact *requires* investment.

Ideas can scale in the short run with enthusiasm but they only repeat in the long run with investment. Ideas that generate returns will return. Ideas that cannot generate returns will, sooner or later, become memories. There are few things more powerful than properly conceived, properly directed investment. To learn finance and investing is to learn the most powerful tool for change in the world.

No matter what your path – whether you make your mark in design, in technology, in law, in medicine, in art, or in anything else – I hope you'll take time to study and demystify the world of finance. Like a clockmaker or a chip designer, you'll never regret knowing exactly how the inner workings of the system fit together, and you'll never again put up with anyone telling you that finance is too complicated, too baffling, or too rigid to be directed to serve your values.

17 Social enterprise for impact
Rethinking old models of charity and business

Leila Janah

Leila Janah is an award-winning social entrepreneur and Founder and CEO of Samasource, the largest data services company in East Africa, and LXMI, a fair-trade luxury brand. Her work focuses on bringing living-wage jobs to poor women and youth to reduce poverty and build better communities, which she discusses in her book Give Work: Reversing Poverty One Job at a Time. *Leila is a Young Global Leader of the World Economic Forum, a former Director of CARE USA, a 2012 TechFellow, recipient of the inaugural Club de Madrid Young Leadership Award, and in 2014 was the youngest person to win a Heinz Award. She received a BA from Harvard and lives in San Francisco.*

★ ★ ★

When my brother and I were young and we'd ask my father for an allowance or spending money,[1] he would raise his voice to oratorical heights and recite a line by the Roman poet Juvenal: "My children, 'luxury is more ruthless than war.'" It was his way of teaching us the concept of *jugaad*, which is a Hindi word that means 'resourcefulness.' He wanted us to be strong and scrappy. It might also have been his way of avoiding having to spell out the truth, which was that he probably had little money to give.

Although we were never poor by most standards, my family was incredibly money-conscious. Living in Buffalo and then Southern California, we shopped exclusively at discount and thrift stores, we rarely ate out, and our tightly budgeted vacations took place in campgrounds and national parks. As little as we had, we made do. My only inkling of what true poverty might look like came from an anecdote my mother shared when her children didn't finish their plates – the one about the time she threw a piece of bread onto her Kolkata street for the local stray dog, and a street kid rushed over, pushed the animal away, and gobbled it up.

This story often made me wonder why I was so lucky when there were so many children in the world who were not. The answer, in part, is that generations of people in my family defied the constraints of their circumstances. I'm the great-granddaughter of a man who defied the limits of his low caste to become one of the top trial lawyers in Kolkata; I'm the granddaughter of a woman who spent her youth travelling the world spreading a postwar message of peace, and who did not settle into typical domestic married life after moving to a foreign Kolkata to start an art ceramics studio; I'm the daughter of a mother who never gave up on the hopeless, and devoted her life to healing what had been left to die, and of a father willing to sacrifice everything for a better future.

Three months after my 17th birthday in January 2000, I didn't realize how much this legacy of three generations had shaped (and would continue to shape) my life trajectory. I had just left suburban Los Angeles and moved to Apirede, a small village in rural Ghana. Supported by a community service scholarship I had won, I was going to teach English through the American Field Service (AFS). My friends' parents were horrified that I'd been allowed to leave home at such a young age to live in what surely had to be a dangerous country. But my parents gave me their blessing. They were sure I would be fine and understood that freedom was a powerful teacher. As it turned out, rural Africa is probably a hundred times safer than most big American cities, provided you avoid mosquito bites and have access to healthy food.

Like many Americans volunteering abroad, I assumed my destitute charges at the West African School for the Blind, where I was assigned, would speak terrible English and depend on me to get them through the basics. A small part of me assumed something else: that I'd help my students – and, by extension, their families – become less poor by teaching them to value education and giving them the confidence to work hard. Somewhere along the way, despite my involvement with poor and marginalized communities in California, even I had internalized the somewhat racist myth I'd commonly heard in the media – and would continue to hear, even in the halls of Harvard – that people without means might be in their predicament because they were not willing to work hard enough or had not developed the right personal or family values. Or that certain regions had become poor because they were not 'culturally oriented' toward working hard and creating wealth.

These explanations are fundamentally untrue. What I had discovered in Ghana was that where there is opportunity there is the potential for every human being to do as my family members did – and as most immigrants and marginalized people dream of doing: to rise, and to decide for themselves what is possible. The actual problem is access to opportunity – and the often deeply entrenched, systemic barriers that deny hard-working people the chance to build a future. There is often an underlying problem fueling most injustices in the world, a root cause that needs to be fixed. Identifying and addressing this root cause is a much harder, longer, and multi-faceted endeavor than efforts to 'make things better' in the short term, but it's the only way real, sustainable change can happen. Fortunately, I come from a long line of passionate, determined people who showed me through example that every individual has the power to instigate change. If any of my ancestors hadn't believed in this power, that street child in my mother's dinner-table tale could easily have been me.

Rethinking the charity model

On the whole, we are a less violent, more prosperous, longer-living society than we've been in all of human history. With the exception of climate change, we are living in a world that's unquestionably better than at any time since the dawn of agriculture. But there's one major problem we have yet to solve – global poverty. *Two billion* people live on less than a few dollars a day, adjusted by economists for purchasing power – an income that is equivalent to $2 in an average American city in 2011.

Imagine that.

Poverty at this level is the root cause of most of the social problems, from violence and trauma to disease and famine, that we try to fix through philanthropy and international aid. It's the reason why 300,000 women still die in childbirth each year, when 99 percent of these deaths are preventable. It's the reason why 780 million people live without clean water. And it's the reason why 2.5 billion people don't have toilets.

Let me humanize these numbers. Three years ago, I met a young man named Ken Kihara, who at the time was living in Mathare, a slum in Nairobi, Kenya. In this area, kids play alongside open sewers and people make a living by scooping up bits of scrap plastic and metal for recycling. Ten years ago, one of those people was Ken. He was an orphan. His mother was a victim of tuberculosis, which also killed six of her siblings, because living in a slum due to poverty turns out to be a major risk factor for TB. In spite of all of this, Ken managed to get a scholarship to a boarding school in Nairobi. He was so poor he almost got kicked out for stealing toothpaste and toilet paper. Luckily, the principal let him go and Ken managed to graduate. You'd think that would be the happily ever after moment. But for so many young people around the world, graduating from high school is where the real struggle begins. In Kenya, youth unemployment can reach 70 percent in poor communities. There are no jobs for slum kids, even those who speak good English and finish high school. This left Ken, despite his education, picking up bits of plastic and metal to sell to the local recycler, while also brewing a kind of moonshine called Changa to supplement his income.

Our typical approach to helping someone like Ken involves charity. We see his situation as awful. We see him as a victim of a great injustice and of an economic system that doesn't properly value human life. And so we donate to organizations that build Ken's community a well or a school, or maybe we buy something that provides him a free pair of shoes or a mosquito net. We invest in aid.

The problem is that our system of giving overseas aid wasn't designed to address the root causes of poverty. Our current era of international aid started with America's work to rebuild Europe after the Second World War. Our 'care packages' were intended to be a quick fix that could get Europe back on its feet. But after the relief effort subsided, the organizations that managed and delivered aid, now wealthy with allocations from Congress, began expanding their programs to other regions, including postcolonial Africa and Asia. And that's where the multi-billion-dollar aid industry got its start. Over the past 60 years, at least $1 trillion of development-related aid has been transferred from rich countries to Africa alone. Yet real per-capita income in Africa today is lower than it was in the 1970s, and more than 50 percent of the African population – over 350 million people like Ken – still live on less than $1 a day. The system we have in place has created dependency while too often failing to improve the lives of the people it purports to help.

My experience in Ghana and my early, frustrated work for large development agencies led me to believe that there must be a better way than aid and charity. I studied economic development in an attempt to understand why it was that countries so rich in human capital – where people were incredibly articulate, entrepreneurial, and passionate – had a majority of their population living on less than $2 a day in household income. I started digging deeper to understand why what we had done in the past hadn't worked. In this process I first learned about and became obsessed with the idea of social enterprise.

Social enterprise, or social business, is a concept pioneered by Muhammad Yunus, the founder of Grameen Bank and the winner of the 2006 Nobel Peace Prize for his proof-of-concept work in microfinance.[2] As an experiment in the late 1970s, Yunus decided to make a small loan to a group of very poor women in Bangladesh who had minimal access to capital and could not get a loan from the bank because the loan increments were too high. He tried to give them a tiny loan to see if they would pay it back. And they did. Not only did they pay it back, they had higher repayment rates than many traditional recipients of bank loans. Through this experiment and his other work, microfinance as a model was proved viable and it's made a dramatic difference in the lives of hundreds of millions of people.

Alongside this model of microfinance, Yunus also developed a concept that I think is even more world-changing and powerful: the idea of a company that has a social mission first and foremost. It's a company that operates as a non-loss and also non-dividend enterprise. In the United States we don't really have a category for such a company. You can operate a nonprofit in this way, but Yunus' 'company with a social mission' idea is not perfectly enabled by the nonprofit organizational structure. Instead, social enterprise is best when thought about as a business that makes a profit, puts the profit back into the business, and has a social or environmental objective. There are a range of different flavors of social enterprise. You can make modest amounts of profit or you can make lots more profit, and people have differing opinions about what 'counts' as social enterprise. But personally, I define social enterprise as any enterprise in which people and planet are put at least alongside profit and probably above it.

I was and still am convinced that social enterprise is a uniquely powerful approach to systemic, holistic social change and its model is the backbone of all my social ventures, from Samasource to SamaSchool and LXMI.

Giving work

The premise of social enterprise is that we need to move away from things that make us feel good but don't have lasting impact, and move toward efforts that sustainably empower people at the bottom of the pyramid. Traditional aid has created dependency and deprived millions of people of a sense of self-determination. The only real way to end global poverty is by giving work, and by redirecting aid to social enterprises that hire and train low-income people or teach them how to start and run enterprises that measurably boost their incomes.

Work is beneficial for so many reasons. When people earn a living wage and have dignified, stable employment, research proves they invest in their own infrastructure, health care, community development, and education. This is especially true in the case of women, who are shown to reinvest 90 percent of their income in the health, education, and well-being of their families and communities. Work also builds more stable economies. When people earn wages, these wages are taxed by governments who become accountable to the people they represent, rather than to wealthy donors and nations that provide aid. This lays the foundation for a healthy social contract between people and government. Work, in short, is important at the individual level, at the family level, and, as we are now increasingly seeing, at the societal level.

And now, for the first time in human history, we have a powerful new way to give work to those who need it most. In the last decade, three fiber optic cables have come to Africa and dramatically improved the infrastructure and connectivity across the continent. Getting online is now much cheaper and more widely accessible, and this new connectivity is a big deal for people like Ken. In the industrial era, capital could move freely across borders, but labor could not. The digital economy circumvents this, allowing people who live in poor areas to transcend the geography of their origin and do work from computer centers all over the world. This means that the birth lottery no longer has to dictate the fates of billions of people.

This revolution has made an entirely new kind of job possible, one that is not dependent on big infrastructure like ports or warehouses needed to support traditional jobs. If you have high-speed Internet, you can employ people to do all kinds of work in the digital economy that didn't exist ten or 20 years ago.

Much of this work is not only easy to train people for, but also necessary for developing relatively new industries. One of those types of work is image tagging. There is a massive need for precise image tagging to train computer algorithms to do what humans used to do – to recognize objects and images. This sector, expected to reach $33 billion by 2019, requires accurate, high-quality data to train the algorithms behind so many popular applications, and it needs *a lot* of this type of data – 100,000 to 1 million images to train just one deep learning neural network. The artificial intelligence behind self-driving cars, for example, depends on this kind of image tagging. As we continue to build smart hardware in virtually every category of industry, there is a massive need for these image tags – which can only be done with precision by people – to train computers. This is exactly the kind of work that we can train someone like Ken to do in very little time.

Building Samasource

Sama means 'equal' in Sanskrit. I wanted to build a social business that would measure itself based on how many people we moved out of poverty each year and at what cost to donors. The business model is to employ people like Ken living in extreme poverty to do work in the digital economy for big companies.

Though I knew I wanted to create Samasource to operate as a sustainable business, I actually started it as a nonprofit. When we launched in 2008 we pitched to dozens of Silicon Valley venture capitalists who, despite being fairly risk-tolerant, thought what we wanted to do as a profit-generating business was kind of crazy. Back then the idea of building a sustainable Internet-based business in a country like Kenya where there was no fiber optic Internet (most Internet was satellite-based which is often slower and unreliable) seemed improbable. And perhaps more 'risky,' everyone at the outset thought talent would be our biggest issue. Again and again our idea was met with the sentiment that 'there is no way you're going to get poor people from a slum in Kenya to do computer work when what they need is mosquito nets.'

Having been turned down by all the for-profit funders I could find, I decided to launch Samasource as a nonprofit instead. This made finding funders easier (though certainly not easy), since there were mission-driven philanthropists who wanted to make donations and be able to see those donations used to support a sustainable business model. So even though we've technically been classified as a nonprofit, we've had the ethos of a social enterprise since our start.

With our first funds, we launched in Kenya. It began when I met a guy named Steve Muthee who was running an Internet café with four seats, each with a desk and a computer available for hourly rent. Like many Internet café owners in developing countries he wasn't making much money from his business because most people couldn't afford to spend the dollar per hour that his costs were running. I told Steve I had an idea. What if instead of renting your computers to people who wanted to use the Internet, we used them to hire people from the slums and do tasks for Silicon Valley companies? I could go out and win contracts, I proposed to him, and he could run the business in Kenya.

That Internet café became our first delivery center. What started as four computers in Kenya has now grown into a global network of close to 2,000 full-time workers paid living wages for their work in the digital economy. Most of our work happens in large computer centers located in urban cities like Nairobi. What we've been excited about most recently is building centers in more rural regions where access to the traditional economy is extraordinarily limited.

Gulu, for example, is located in the Northern region of Uganda that is mostly known around the world for its recent devastating civil war (made 'famous' to the world through the 2006 documentary *Invisible Children*). In this town you will see many more NGOs than businesses, but we hoped to change that when we got a grant a few years ago to build the first data center in Northern Uganda. We spent the money on shipping containers. We welded them together and put solar panels on the roof. This became our data center, and we've now employed over 400 people in the region to do image tasks. But what's particularly exciting about this is that the Gulu center has proven our model can operate profitably in one of the most rural and poor regions in the world. Provided that we have the capital to make long-term loans, we can hypothetically set up a center like this anywhere with fiber access. This potential will only grow as new technologies like 5G become increasingly available and enable digital jobs that circumvent the traditional mechanisms by which people find work. I think this is a powerful way to liberate people from the confines of their geographies and the exclusivity of today's capitalism.

I am proud that last year Samasource became profitable off of our earned revenue from client work for hundreds of major tech and automotive companies, including Microsoft and Google. We're now the largest data services provider in East Africa and are operating centers in Kenya, Southern Uganda, Northern Uganda, and India. We mostly focus on creating training data – detailed image and video annotations – for artificial intelligence applications. It's been an incredible journey and one I could not have imagined at that moment in the Internet café where we had our humble beginnings.

But our growth is also exciting because of the changes it brings to workers' lives. We've moved 45,000 people out of poverty in the last ten years and they've stayed out of poverty – the latter being one of the most important metrics of our success. To better understand what life is like before and after Samasource for someone like Ken, we carefully study every aspect of our impact. We conduct household surveys to understand what our workers eat, how they live, and what they spend money on. We find that before Samasource, our workers were eating sugarcane as a primary source of calories, living in unsafe housing, and at risk of health emergencies with no way to pay. During and after Samasource, our workers on average quadruple their incomes, staying out of poverty permanently. They improve their diets, send their kids and themselves to school, and get health insurance and safe housing. We literally see them come to life.

We've been able to replicate our impact sourcing model for about 10,000 workers and their families – that's 46,000 people who have moved and stayed out of poverty and gained valuable skills in the digital economy. These people have invested over $10 million in their own communities, providing what I call a 'trickle up' economic effect from the bottom of the economic pyramid.

The give work model, many ways

A couple of years ago while in Uganda, I started wondering whether there was a way to apply the B2B Samasource model to a different industry. I had come across this amazing ingredient called Nilotica, a rare type of shea butter that only grows wild at the source of the Nile River. Nilotica is farmed or collected by rural women in the same position as Ken, and it's used as a skin moisturizer by the locals who buy it. When I first tried it, I was blown away by what an amazing product it was. I started thinking, why are we spending $200 on luxury skin creams at duty free that are toxic for our bodies, not good for the environment, and don't benefit any women in the supply chain or any women as owners of these companies? Why are we doing all of that when we could be buying a great product made from a fair-trade, sustainable supply chain that elevates women in the same position as someone like Ken, but in a place like Northern Uganda?

So I went to my board, and they gave me permission to start another company. I set it up so that Samasource actually owns a third of the founding equity in the B2C, for-profit social business we founded called LXMI (pronounced 'lux-me').

We launched last year as the first fair-trade and organic skincare brand at Sephora nationwide. Each product has a number on the box that you can type into our website and meet the women across our supply chain who touched the production of your product. This B2C application of the give work concept is tapping into what I see as the beginning of a real revolution in beauty. Similar to the revolution we saw in food, luxury consumers today are looking for products that are not only natural rather than toxin-based, but that are also ethical in their supply chains.

In both the Samasource and LXMI case, we focused our efforts on giving work to people living in conditions of extreme poverty. But the give work model also has potential to make a real difference in more 'developed' economies. To meet the new work needs in my home country of the United States, we adapted our business model to create a program that connects low-income Americans to the independent economy. We call this program Samaschool. Over the last decade, 94 percent of net employment growth in the United States occurred in what are called 'alternative work arrangements,' or independent 'freelance' work outside the traditional nine to five job confines. And yet we are not preparing low-income people for these kinds of jobs. If you go to a training program in east Palo Alto, for example, no one is teaching you about how to take your skills to the gig economy. Our mission is to do just that. We aim to equip people to earn a living wage through independent work. Our trainees are earning between $20 and $40 per hour, which is a huge increase over traditional minimum or very low-wage hourly jobs. After a few months, we see them earning around $1,900 in supplemental income, which is a big deal if you are one in six Americans living below the poverty line (which in the U.S. is defined as a family of four earning $22,500 a year). We've now partnered with the California Community College system and many city-based programs to help roll this training out across many cities around the company.

Where do we go from here? The future of social enterprise

Perhaps one of the most hopeful things to me has been that the Silicon Valley venture capitalists' concerns that our work at Samasource was 'risky business' – in large part because of the talent required – have been proven wrong. In fact, the least of our problems has been talent. I think we still have a lot of paternalistic views about poor people that quickly get dispelled if you spend time in a Kenyan slum where people, just to survive, have to be ten times more entrepreneurial than we do. If you made it to the point where you are a high school graduate in a place like Mathare, you have the most robust set of entrepreneurial skills anyone can imagine.

This is not to say that we don't face challenges every day when building a social business. In fact, we face two sets of challenges – those that entrepreneurs face when starting and scaling a business *and* those that impact-minded nonprofits face. Like any scaling business, for example, we've had to overcome – and will continue to overcome – difficulties in terms of infrastructure and logistics in environments that are not always built for large-scale enterprise. We've also had to think about long-term viability questions: how do we think about automation and what happens when we don't need image tagging anymore? How will we evolve with the industry? Like any business, we want to listen to the needs of our workforce, where we see people quickly graduating from image sourcing and seeking opportunities for 'upward' career trajectory. This has led us to the question of how we can meet demand for higher-value work within our organization. In addition to these business questions, like any nonprofit, we are constantly in fundraising mode. Where this money comes from matters, and we adhere to certain principles for accepting capital from corporate and private investors. We also face the classic problem of impact work: you can't help everyone. The supply to fill our jobs grossly exceeds the demand we create, and we have to think about things like whether we should force people to find employment elsewhere once trained up at Samasource to make room for someone else.

But our biggest challenge is scalable financing. We have a ten-year track record and documentation from an independent third party confirming our financial and impact data; we've moved 10,000 households from an income of $2 a day to over ten dollars a day, which is a 500 percent improvement; and we've done this with a self-sustaining model that can be replicated all over the world. In a strictly for-profit world, Samasource should be a great investment by all metrics; likewise, in a strictly not-for-profit world, there should be no better deal for a foundation looking to reduce poverty. And yet, getting capital from these folks is hard. If anything, impact investors find fair-trade commodities businesses like LXMI more attractive because of its resemblance to a traditional business.

My greatest challenge has therefore been a lacking investor pool for the kind of impact Samasource is trying to make, and this is the same one faced by many true social enterprises. If committed to real impact, I would encourage investment portfolios of all shapes and sizes to devote a percentage of their investment to social enterprises with documented social and environmental return, with credible data, and with the ambition to be a profitable social business. This will be a true game-changer for scalable impact – and not just for poverty reduction, but for all kinds of social change.

Alongside this need to change the way we formally invest in impact, I see the future of social enterprise also finding sustainable revenue sources from another space. When researching my own book, *Give Work*, I came across this statistic: the 2,000 biggest companies in the world spend $12 trillion on goods and services annually. Twelve trillion. By comparison, the GDP of all of sub-Saharan Africa is $1.8 trillion. This is money spent on everything from the rugs in the conference room to the coffee in the lunchroom and the raw materials in our cell phone batteries. If we could tap into just a little bit of this spending and have it go to social enterprises – which actually elevate people out of poverty and measure their success at doing that – how much better would the world be? Even just 1 percent of this $12 trillion spend could potentially lift 40 million people out of poverty based on living wage levels, and that's a conservative estimate.

We are already doing this at Samasource, where we take money that our clients are already spending in their supply chains and direct it to people living in poverty. This means that money from Microsoft and Google is directly fighting not just poverty, but all of its downstream problems, like lack of clean water and sanitation, that we usually try to solve with a charity model. I think the potential – especially with B2B organizations like Samasource which serve these large enterprises – is really huge. Most of the ethical consumption market to date has focused on consumers, which is great, but B2B is where the real money is and it's where I think we will see real transformation happen over the next decades.

To help businesses rethink the way they do business, Samasource is now building a guide of thousands of vendors for companies that want to impact source but don't know how. Our guide will list everything from garment manufacturers to restaurants, with the aim of encouraging businesses to choose vendors that source from the poorest communities and pay living wages. My hope is that one day there will be subsidies for companies and small businesses that choose suppliers that solve a social problem. In the United States, for example, we struggle with an enormous prison population where mostly nonviolent drug offenders are locked behind bars. Imagine if employers received a tax credit for hiring someone coming out of prison who would otherwise be likely to recommit crimes. This would save taxpayers millions of dollars and incarcerate fewer people for crimes of economics – someone needs a job, so they sell drugs – in the long run. We're currently working with one of the largest corporate procurement engines to make this happen at scale.

Conclusion

The last time I saw Ken was in Beirut. It was his first international trip and he was running a pilot we had set up with the World Food Programme to train Syrian refugees in digital work very similar to what Ken had been doing in Kenya. He has now trained over 500 people in Mathare, Kibara, and the Middle East to do digital work. He has moved out of the slum and his daughter is going to one of the best schools in Nairobi. I think Ken is going to become a pioneer social entrepreneur and political leader in Kenya going forward. This is the transformation that can happen when we give work over charity, when we empower people through social enterprise, and when we see people living in extreme poverty as talented producers rather than passive consumers of aid.

As for Samasource, our future will focus on expanding our work of giving work. However, rather than expanding our own digital services offering and setting up Samasource facilities in new countries next year, our plan is to work with and teach partners who want to leverage our model locally. In fact, the refugee program Ken was helping lead trainings for is an example of how we are working with other organizations to create digital work. This approach is what Muhammad Yunus did really successfully with microfinance. He realized he had made a successful bank with many borrowers, but he didn't want to expand Grameen Banks into 50 countries. Instead, he decided to consult with other organizations and entrepreneurs who wanted to set up their own microfinance organizations. He created an industry out of what started as one enterprise.

We want to make impact sourcing an industry. Unlike regular business, social enterprise is not a zero-sum game. New entrants to our industry make the model we share more viable and our impact more far-reaching in the long run. Social enterprise operates under the mindset that the rising tide raises all boats. We are proud to be part of this tide and to help it continue to surge.

Conclusion

Beyond success: Four lessons in building character

Jacqueline Novogratz

Jacqueline Novogratz is the Founder and CEO of Acumen, a nonprofit global venture fund that invests philanthropic capital in sustainable businesses tackling the toughest problems of poverty. Under her leadership, Acumen has invested $115 million in 113 companies providing critical goods and services to the poor across Africa, Latin America, South Asia and the United States. These companies have impacted over 270 million lives to date. In 2017, Forbes listed Jacqueline as one of the World's 100 Greatest Living Business Minds. Prior to Acumen, Jacqueline founded The Philanthropy Workshop and The Next Generation Leadership programs at the Rockefeller Foundation. She also co-founded Rwanda's first microfinance institution, Duterimbere. Jacqueline sits on the boards of the Aspen Institute and IDEO.org. Her best-selling memoir The Blue Sweater *chronicles her quest to understand poverty and bring dignity to the poor.*

★ ★ ★

Dear friend,

I started my career on Wall Street in the early 1980s, working mostly in Latin America.[1] Though I loved the tools of finance, it made no sense to me that low-income people were excluded from banking. I hailed from an immigrant family with a strong work ethic and had already concluded that poverty tells you nothing about people's character, just their income levels.

I knew I had to do something about this. After doing some research on banking for the poor but without a proper plan fully in place, I left my job and headed to West Africa. A course of missteps landed me in Rwanda, a country I knew little about. There, I met a small group of women interested in women's economic development. Together, we co-founded the country's first microfinance bank.

The work was difficult; at times it felt like a series of taking two steps forward, one step back. This is a common theme in a life committed to creating change. You shouldn't sign up if you are looking for something easy. But I also saw how a small group of people bound by a common idea could change at least a corner of history.

That experience gave me a new level of courage. When I first decided to move to Africa, friends and family called me crazy. When we started building the bank in Kigali, the community called me crazy again. I've since learned that being 'crazy' is usually a good sign you're onto something.

So, get in the habit of doing something you fear. Remember that each time you practice courage, you gain courage. Think of it is as a muscle you build for when you most need it.

In time, I learned that my successes and failures usually had less to do with ideas or structures, and more with character, my own and that of each person around me. It was only when I learned to listen not with the intent to convince others of my solutions but with the intent to change myself that I succeeded. It was only when I found the courage to fail and try again that I built the resilience needed to walk the long road to change.

After I left Rwanda, I spent the next decade continuing my apprenticeship, if you will, picking up tools for my toolbox in business school and starting other endeavors. I followed leaders whose actions showed me the kind of person I wanted to become. I continued to be obsessed with both markets and philanthropy and thought I wanted to revolutionize the latter. But in time, I came to understand that my real goal was to create the conditions that would make philanthropy unnecessary. This I'm still learning.

We started Acumen in 2001 to invest patient capital in entrepreneurs defined by their character, men and women willing to go where both markets and aid had failed the poor to solve our toughest problems of poverty: health care and education, agriculture and education. We've invested in more than 100 companies and supported nearly 450 young leaders around the world. I can't imagine a better education. I've learned how markets and government work – and where they fail. I've learned about sectors I didn't even know I wanted to understand: artificial insemination in the dairy industry, chickens in Ethiopia, rice gasification processes, and solar mini-grids. But those are lessons for another time.

Because what separates the solutions that work from those that fail has less to do with the idea or the context in which we invest, be it a stable country or one in post-conflict. It has everything to do with character. Conversely, our failures are too often correlated with betting on entrepreneurs who choose to do what is easy, not right; or they lack moral imagination and curiosity about others; or they lose their resilience and don't stay the course.

The kind of character that leads to success can be summed up in two words: moral leadership. Moral because we need leaders who care about the world, and not just themselves. Leadership to navigate our complex times. We can no longer depend only on profit as a motive without considering other stakeholders, nor can we sit with easy ideology or the arrogance of certainty.

Our problems demand more than that.

Because there is no road map, developing moral leadership requires a compass, one whose 'North Star' points to the flourishing of all humans and a sustainable earth. And we shouldn't settle for anything less.

There are many points to this compass, but let me share just a few today.

First, moral leaders redefine success. The zero-sum model of 'I win, you lose' cannot sustain in an interdependent world in which we rise and fall together. Instead, we need brave individuals driven by a metric based not on how the rich fare but how the poor and vulnerable are treated.

One of Acumen's entrepreneurs, Sam Goldman, was working as a Peace Corps volunteer in Benin when his neighbor's kerosene lantern tipped over and burned down his house, nearly killing the eldest child. Sam woke up to the insanity of a world in which 1.5 billion of us still live in darkness, and decided to do something.

Though he lacked an engineering degree, he found a partner in Ned Tozun at business school. Together, they ventured out with a $30 solar light they'd designed and a mission to eradicate kerosene. Acumen invested in their company, d.light, though none of us fully understood that we were creating a new market altogether.

It took more than a decade of experiments and failures, countless hours spent listening to customers and changing products to meet their needs. Sam and Ned spent many years earning little money, struggling to raise investment capital and grants, experimenting with financing solutions.

There were years when they thought they'd fail. But they never gave up.

To be honest, I also sometimes wondered whether they would succeed. But we were on board because we had bet on these guys to take on the difficult. We bet on the guys' character, on their resilience.

Change takes time. When people ask me how patient Acumen's own investment capital is, I sometimes show them a picture of Sam and Ned when they started d.light in 2007 – young and eager with full heads of hair. And then I show them a picture of them today – smiling, strong, still youthful but with a lot less hair. It's been more than ten years, and Sam and Ned have brought affordable, clean light and electricity to more than 82 million low-income people around the world.

This is success: it doesn't matter how much money they have earned. Through d.light, Sam and Ned are lighting the world.

Second, moral leadership requires building muscles of moral imagination – or having the audacity to imagine the world that can be, and the humility to see the world that is. Emily Stone was working with an environmental firm when she learned that five million farmers, most of whom make less than $2 a day, produce 90 percent of the world's cacao for the $100 billion-dollar chocolate industry.

That made no sense to Emily. She's an amazing woman who likes chocolate. But she loves justice. She wondered why global commodities pricing was the only guide to pay smallholder farmers, and made a conscious decision to ignore it. After all, retailers ignore how much the farmers earn when they charge $10 for a premium chocolate bar, right?

So she used her moral imagination, understanding the realities of farmers, and dreaming of what could be in a flawed but important industry.

Her company, Uncommon Cacao, works to understand farmers' production costs and then adds an ample margin, sometimes paying two to three times the global price. The business model is based on trust and transparency for all stakeholders. Farmers can see how much their chocolate is selling at every level of the supply chain. It isn't always comfortable but it works.

Emily now sells to more than 100 chocolate companies. The farmers with whom she partners are moving out of poverty – with agency. In a world where there is so little trust, building such networks is more valuable than gold.

Third, moral leadership requires the skills of building partnerships. Manik Bhat is a young entrepreneur working to solve some of America's toughest issues. On his way to becoming a doctor, he dropped out of medical school and founded Healthify, a company to help health care providers and government organizations coordinate with social services workers to keep low-income people healthy. Manik's work starts with seeing every patient as a whole person who requires social support. To make his company work, Manik must understand and use the language of medicine, of markets, and of policy. Yet he's driven by supporting the underserved.

We need more models in this country that get the best of business and government, the Right and the Left. It requires rallying different stakeholders around a common end, holding the values of including the poor, learning to partner sometimes across uncomfortable lines. This requires holding out for a hard-edged hope.

Finally, moral leadership requires learning to hold two contradictory ideas and reject neither. This is a massive challenge of our generation, especially in this age of rapid-fire response on social media where nuance is rarely rewarded. We move too quickly to outrage and blame. It is as if I cannot be right unless I prove you wrong. Or at least say you are wrong.

But a winner-takes-all society strips us of our individual humanity. It diminishes us, enabling a vulgar laziness with language that divides and shames and too often humiliates. The real winners are cynicism and fear, and there are no greater allies of the status quo than those two.

At Acumen, in addition to investing in companies, we support young leaders through a fellowship focused on leading in uncertain times. Last year, a group of Indian and Pakistani Acumen Fellows decided they'd had enough talking with just their fellow countrymen and women about Kashmir, a topic that provokes heated conversation in each country. They courageously organized a series of discussions across national lines via videoconference. Though most were nervous and the conversations uncomfortable, the fellows were rightly proud for creating a platform for discussion.

One of the Indians posted a screenshot of the conversation on Facebook. For this, he was immediately bombarded with hateful comments.

Even his parents shared their disapproval. "It is bad enough that you decided to be a social entrepreneur," they said. "But now you are consorting with the enemy. You have to decide if you are a patriot, if you are with this family or with the enemy."

Later, he asked: "Can I be a patriot and a global citizen?"

Of course you can. In fact, you must. We can love our countries and, at the same time, be curious about other people and other nations. Most important, we can learn from them. We can hold onto a strong sense of identity without presuming that the wounds of our own past are more legitimate than another person's or group's.

Being a patriot and a global citizen should be mutually reinforcing. But don't be tricked by language. The Indian fellows' parents weren't speaking about patriotism. They were speaking about nationalism. That is an entirely different kettle of fish.

Nationalism is an arrogant love of country based on notions of us vs them, blaming others to justify one's own superiority. Patriots love their country with a sense of duty to seek the nation's betterment, to renew its values and confront the difficult because it will lead to a better place. Patriots see themselves as part of a greater whole.

An either – or world limits our chances for shared humanity. In our interdependent world, we all must reject false polarities. There is a space that connects love of country and love for the world, that bridges left and right, that goes beyond shallow judgments of right and wrong. The opportunity, indeed, imperative of moral leadership, is to create a set of values and possibilities in which we can all see ourselves. So, learn to navigate the contradictions.

Your generation also has the chance to drop the excess baggage carried by mine. But don't jettison everything, for there is wisdom in history. Seek it out. It is up to you to learn to hold those values from the past, whose beauty must be carried forward, while having the courage to let go of what no longer serves.

The work of change is not easy. But you know that already. If you are here, you didn't sign up for easy.

I promise you, if you focus on developing your character and not only your career, if you practice the principles of a leadership focused on the world and not simply yourselves, you will find richness and joy in the privilege of being a part of the great questions of our times.

Thirty years after starting this work, I have discovered in myself a soulful connection to my own and others' humanity. It has opened me to the deepest love. It has taught me to see beauty in, well, everything.

If there is one thing to leave with it is this: the world needs you to be the leaders and foot soldiers of a moral revolution. Go out in the world with a sense of confidence in what you have learned and what you know. And with responsibility, too.

If we dare to act with moral leadership, this can be the most hopeful time in history. You are the first generation with the ability to imagine and build new frameworks and institutions for a world that is more inclusive, less wasteful, and more sustainable. Our promise is nothing less than the flourishing of every human being on the planet, of human dignity.

Good luck and warm wishes!

Jacqueline

Letters from tomorrow's social impact leaders

Curated by Amirah Jiwa

Social Impact Strategist

I'm honored to be responding to Jacqueline Novogratz's call for moral leadership. Because of Jacqueline and her work at Acumen, many of us who are still in the earlier stages of our careers (and lives!) in impact had an additional model – that of the for-profit – nonprofit hybrid – to consider as we explored the various ways we could change the world.

Fortunately for us, opportunities today to make an impact can be found everywhere. How to do some good (or at the very least, do less harm) is no longer solely the domain of aid workers or policymakers, but a challenge that organizations of all kinds, from investment banks and multinational conglomerates to hot new tech start-ups are forced to wrestle with – even if only to attract the best talent as those entering the workforce increasingly demand a commitment to sustainability or giving back.

Jacqueline points out in her letter that my generation is the first "with the ability to imagine and build new frameworks and institutions for a world that is more inclusive, less wasteful, and more sustainable." This is true, and very exciting, but means that now the question for us becomes not whether we should dare to work for the world rather than for ourselves – that feels like a forgone conclusion – but rather, how best to work for the world.

This is a question I've been working to answer for myself since childhood. A third-culture kid raised between the United Kingdom and the Netherlands with extended family across Asia and Africa, I grew up very aware of the size of the world and the innumerable issues that needed solving. There was never any doubt that I would pursue making some positive difference, but what continually evolved was my vision for how I could best effect change. I started out keen to pursue a career in human rights law and equipped myself with experience interning at criminal law firms and nonprofits legally advocating against torture. However, the slow and tireless nature of advocating for changes in international law frustrated me, so in college I turned my eye to the power of research and policymaking instead, thinking that I might end up at a think tank or in government. However, when a nonprofit internship opportunity fell through the summer after my sophomore year of college, I found myself, somewhat surprisingly, at start-up darling Warby Parker – a direct-to-consumer brand I was a fan of that built giving back into its profit model. That experience opened my eyes to the potential that business had to inspire and drive change and set me on the path to my current role as a Social Impact Strategist who helps brands explore ways to use their platforms and resources for good.

While some might view the path I've taken as less noble or self-sacrificing than my original goal of prosecuting war criminals at the International Criminal Court, I see things differently. I've found a way to put my skills to use at an intersection that combines my long-standing interest in consumer brand innovation (even as I interned at law firms, I keenly kept up with lifestyle, food, and fashion trends!) with my passion for change-making.

All sectors and industries have the power to make a difference and need people working to unlock their potential for impact. In the notes that follow, you will hear from young leaders driving improvement in very varied contexts – working within a multinational corporation, building a social enterprise from the ground up, or steering the direction of a multi-million-dollar nonprofit are just a few. And, because real impact always stems from a close and open-minded examination of the problem at hand, with understanding usually gained from those who face the problem rather than time-worn assumptions, the following perspectives all also emphasize curiosity and humility as key tools of the trade.

These examples of moral leadership are bold and audacious in their vision of what is possible, yet very thoughtful about the approach taken. I hope that the breadth of roles and industries represented will serve both as a reminder that there are opportunities to positively change the world in almost any context, and as inspiration to deeply interrogate how best to make that change a reality.

Griffin Gaffney, CEO and Founder, Possible

I first met Jay one Friday morning at 5:45 am on a San Francisco street corner. We'd both showed up there for an organization that addresses homelessness through running.

Jay's a 68-year-old African-American man from Georgia who moved to the Bay Area after completing a multi-decade sentence in federal prison for shooting a police officer in the face. Jay works odd jobs to make ends meet and over the past few years has struggled to keep a roof over his head.

After greeting everyone else in the group that morning, I introduced myself to Jay. We immediately hit it off after he laughed at my best attempt of a Georgian accent. As the group darted into the city's sunrise, I noticed that Jay held to the back of the group.

Not long after, Jay told me that he was looking for a new job. At the time, I worked in marketing for a large technology company in San Francisco. The company served breakfast, lunch, and dinner to employees, so I made the natural connection that Jay could work in our company's kitchen. It only paid minimum wage, but I thought working at a tech company, with all its other perks and benefits, would be the dream for someone like him. I was certain that he, like me and my other 'techy' colleagues, would leverage the company's money and resources as an opportunity to launch a new career and find financial freedom.

A week later I prepared a batch of brownies for Jay's first day of work. I excitedly got to the office in time for the 6:00 am kitchen shift to welcome Jay to his new home. I introduced him to everyone else in the kitchen I knew and I checked in on him throughout the day to make sure everything was going smoothly. He seemed happy to be there and his boss said he'd had a good start to the day. I thought my work was done.

Two days later Jay was fired.

There were numerous signs that the job wasn't right for Jay. He told me that his commute would be unreasonably long. He told me that the job didn't pay enough for him to live. He had a hard time physically keeping pace on our walks. Yet I chose not to listen. I assumed that what worked for me would work for him, and that if I could make it at a tech company he could, and would want to, too.

In all the time I've lived in San Francisco I've felt that my presence inescapably strengthens inequality's tightening grip over the city and its people. It was that growing sense of guilt that led me to meet Jay in the first place – I wanted to find a way to give back which felt meaningful to me.

But that was the problem – I made helping Jay about me. My guilt. My definition of success. My view of Jay. I was so wrapped up in my own world view that I never took the time to stop and listen.

After Jay left the company I helped four more people experiencing homelessness find work at the same company. With each new arrival I started from a place of observation and curiosity, not one of ivory-tower assumptions and pontificating. How did each new hire integrate into the company's working culture? Were they able to make ends meet on their hourly income? How long was their commute?

That's how I arrived at what I'm working on today; a fully subsidized, living-wage employment program for people who are experiencing homelessness, housing insecurity, or poverty.

The goal is to permanently break cycles of homelessness and poverty. The plan is to employ people who are experiencing homelessness at Bay Area tech companies while offering financial subsidies that adjust incomes to be a full living wage. Throughout, full-time social workers bridge the gap between employment partners and each program member to ensure each member has a path to independence.

My experience with Jay taught me to approach this work with genuine curiosity. That, I think, is the best I can do.

Eliana Piper, Director, Strategy and Innovation, American Civil Liberties Union

While studying Arabic in Oman during the summer of 2011, a bedouin man told me that in ancient times, bedouins in the desert would wrap cloth around a tall stick, plunge it into the ground and set it on fire as a beacon for members of their tribe to find their way home. From this practice emerged the saying, 'more famous than a pole in the desert' since a lighted pole at night could be seen for miles.

I love this image: a beacon guiding you through an environment that feels hopeless. To me, this pole in the desert represents the work of social impact and innovation: to cast light upon seemingly impossible solutions to society's problems, serving as a reminder of what could be and a radical recognition of the journey to reach that ideal. To be truly radical, a professor of mine once told me, a solution must illuminate the root of something, whether that thing is a problem, a habit, or a system.

Much of my professional journey has been that process: of imagining and building solutions to seemingly inextricable problems – of building poles in the desert.

When I started my career, I was lucky to land at Google, which proved an important training ground for thinking audaciously about complex problems. I left Google to take a job with the Hillary Clinton campaign in Iowa with the hope of promoting civic engagement among Americans. I now work at the International Rescue Committee on a team creating a new educational initiative for Syrian refugee children and their host communities.

My work in technology, civic engagement, and now humanitarian intervention, were all guided by the search for one key 'root': simplifying access to information and resources in new ways. At Google, we were tasked with the deceptively simple task of making a platform that would universalize Google's people practices for any workplace and inspire a movement of increased equity at work. The solution was a platform, called re:Work, that took traditional HR practices and infused them with Google's tested research, making fair practices open to all entrepreneurs and HR managers.

As a Regional Director for Hillary Clinton's campaign in Iowa leading voter turnout efforts, each moment felt momentous. We thought of the millions of Americans who would be impacted if we lost and tried innovative approaches to reach voters and minds in the wake of the despair experienced by many Americans. Even when we lost, it became a question of 'what now?', of trying new ways of making information accessible across different cross-sections of the population.

In my current job on the start-up team of the IRC and Sesame Workshop's joint educational initiative, my team aims to innovate within a crisis that feels hopeless. It's easy to feel the weight of the situation at hand, and equally easy to numb ourselves to the pain of our target beneficiaries. It's harder to keep trying new means of reaching the most vulnerable populations with our content.

In a world increasingly seeking simplicity, I have found that the exercise of building solutions often leads into a simplification of problems rather than a simplification of solutions. Human problems are messy, complicated, and intractable. The act of simplification in and of itself can easily become a distortion of the very things that keep us human and connected and produce the desire to build something new in the first place. My hope for young people in social impact is that we not conflate mess with problem, but take ownership as beacons for a better world.

Mark Muriithi Laichena, Country Director for Kenya, GiveDirectly

Many of us have wondered about how to end global poverty. What interventions can we support? What expertise can we apply? What can *we* do? I've certainly asked those questions. And in the last two years, I've arrived at a surprising answer: we can step out of the way. What does that mean in practice? I run the Kenya office of an organization called GiveDirectly. We don't deliver cows, we don't build schools, we don't offer job training. We identify very poor households across East Africa, transfer digital currency to their phones, and then we step out of the way; which is to say we let recipients spend the money as they see fit.

How does this depart from the traditional aid model (and why did some call this approach 'crazy' in the beginning)? Historically, aid agencies have owned decision-making power around allocating resources and setting priorities. Put simply: expertise held in Washington and Geneva trumped expertise held by the poor themselves. GiveDirectly flips that paradigm by eliminating guesswork and intermediaries, and allowing recipients to decide what they need most.

Despite perceptions that poverty prevents people from spending money responsibly, rigorous research indicates otherwise. With a body of literature informed by 200+ studies, the takeaway is clear: on average poor people put money to good use, and whether manifest as improved savings, assets, child health, or education spending, the benefits of cash are material.

I see evidence of this every day – I've been lucky enough to oversee the enrollment of over 17,000 households during my tenure as Country Director. One of the things I've been most struck by when visiting recipients is the dignity afforded by cash. If a head of household doesn't have a chair, visits can be an embarrassment. If a husband can't afford to pay a dowry, he may be shunned for years. If a mother must seek piecework from her neighbors every day, humiliation often follows. Cash offers a unique measure of flexibility to change those things.

That said, this approach was hardly uppermost in my mind before I joined GiveDirectly. I moved to Nairobi three years ago, the product of a Kenyan father, an English mother, and an American education. GiveDirectly's hiring philosophy, similar to our model, is not conventional. We typically preference entrepreneurial thinking over years of experience and often hire from the private sector. Prior to joining, I consulted for McKinsey and advised leaders in Kenya's Ministry of Health. I was not building a traditional nonprofit career, but GiveDirectly's appeal lay in the boldness of its vision to change the sector, and in its commitment to operational excellence and rigor.

Our bottom line as a company is simple: how many dollars did we deliver to poor families? The execution is far from simple. We invest heavily in systems to prevent fraud, deliver quality customer service to our recipients, and source top-tier talent. Managing a $36 million operation has been humbling. We are, on average, a young team and I'm a young leader. I've had to learn, often the hard way, how to navigate the good and the bad: staff layoffs and mass hiring; political pressure and praise; welcoming community receptions and (understandably) suspicious ones.

Ultimately, I have big hopes for the social impact sector. I want us to keep throwing our best ideas and creativity at the problem of extreme poverty. But I now recognize that what might be required is something less obvious: *giving* more and *doing* less. At GiveDirectly we're excited about building a new status quo: one in which those living in poverty – and not us – choose how to tackle it.

Sheeza Shah, Co-Founder, UpEffect

For five years I volunteered for disaster relief, children protection and refugee aid charities alongside my studies and full-time employment. After raising thousands of pounds in donations wearing assorted hats in fundraising, project management and events, however, I failed to see my work yielding meaningful change. My questions on fund allocation or KPI performance were often squashed or ignored and I soon realized that similar issues could be common in nonprofits.

People often give to charities with the hope their contribution will aid the poor, but much of this capital can be lost in unsustainable programs, administration or tick-box reporting; ultimately failing communities and trapping many in an endless cycle of poverty. Tackling global societal and environmental problems is no small undertaking and for solutions to be successful, they need to leverage the same infrastructure conventional businesses are built on: profitability.

As I began to explore the social enterprise world, however, I encountered a new problem. Social entrepreneurs were often bypassed by traditional investors who were typically interested in funding solely profit-driven companies led by founders with the same profile: white and male. This trend partially explains why more than 82 percent of wealth created in 2017 went to 1 percent of the world's population. Frustrated by the limited options available for those founders – often women or people of color – who wanted to start businesses that were impact-driven, I co-founded UpEffect, a crowdfunding platform built on the premise that any entrepreneur with the potential to have a profound impact on the world should have the opportunity to turn their idea into a venture.

As Muslim founders, we took inspiration from the Prophet Muhammad (PBUH), whose personal examples in business dealings always espoused honesty, integrity, as well as from the Islamic financial system which is designed to spread wealth fairly by providing business and employment opportunities, education, and skills.

UpEffect equips entrepreneurs with the capital and skills to start their own impactful businesses. We connect social entrepreneurs directly to ethical customers, enabling sustainable enterprise growth, and we bet on our founders, by taking no upfront fees and instead investing time and resources in helping social entrepreneurs get market-ready. If entrepreneurs succeed at securing seed capital through crowdfunding, UpEffect applies a success fee. If the campaign fails, we share in the losses.

The world has been quick to champion businesses that have the potential to increase wealth but we have been slower to provide a dedicated space for ventures that promote impact to flourish. UpEffect addresses this issue by allowing smaller players that may be neglected on larger crowdfunding platforms or overlooked by traditional investors to convert their powerful ideas into successful campaigns, not only to meet a funding target but also to successfully launch a product to a loyal customer base. This is especially important for social entrepreneurs who have powerful ideas but don't know where to begin.

For example, Pakistani entrepreneur Khizr Imran used UpEffect to successfully raise seed funding for Jaan Pakistan, his renewable energy cookstove venture. Imran developed the first commercially available cookstove for rural Pakistan and the stoves have been proven to eliminate energy poverty and increase income-generation opportunities for local people, all while improving their health.

We believe UpEffect is the go-to platform for entrepreneurs who are driven not by how much money they can make, but how many lives they can impact. Fortunately, a new wave of founders and consumers is on the rise. 89 percent of Millennials are likely to switch between brands and support ones that promote conscious spending – equal pay, human trafficking and environmentallyconscious manufacturing processes are common issues at the forefront of their minds when making these buying decisions.

The poorest in society should be able to trust that the system will not forget them and I believe both entrepreneurs and consumers have the power to build a world of financial equality and economic prosperity for all.

William Smith, Executive Director, LEAD Africa

I have had many opportunities to lead in my life, but none captures the complexity of empathetic and entrepreneurial leadership like my time in Liberia.

I first visited the coastal West African nation in 2013. During my three-month stay, I conducted honors thesis research, completed an internship in the U.S. Embassy Monrovia, and prepared for my final season of college soccer. The experience I had – and the friendships I made – set me on a lifelong journey.

I left Liberia captivated. It was a country of incredible warmth and dynamism, yet its potential was undercut by the effects of a protracted civil conflict on education, health, gender disparities, and the like. Upon returning to the United States for my final year of university, I committed to enhance my understanding of Liberian history. I read everything in sight. My curiosity and conversations with Liberian friends led to a vital realization – at the core of Liberia's social challenges was one defining problem: leadership.

In 2015, upon completing my graduate studies, I joined forces with a former Liberian national football team player, Sekou Dgeorges Manubah, to address Liberia's leadership gap. Together, Sekou and I had experienced the power of football in Liberia, and we committed to use it as a tool for impact.

Today, Monrovia Football Academy is the first school in Liberia to combine high-quality education with professional sport training. We use football as a positive-incentive mechanism to improve academic performance, break down gender barriers, and prepare our student-athletes to lead positive change. Our boys and girls receive high-quality education, professional football training, good nutrition, health care, and life skills. It is a holistic approach to the total development of Liberia's future leaders.

The Academy's model and evidence-based impact has captured the attention of several philanthropists and institutions: the 2011 Nobel laureate, Leymah Gbowee; the Chair of the African Philanthropy Forum, Tsitsi Masiyiwa; FC Barcelona; Oxford

University; and many more. In 2018, I am working with them to replicate this leadership training model across the African continent. Our new pan-African initiative, LEAD Africa, will be a network of African sport academies, all of which are founded by local champions and based on Monrovia Football Academy's model. The goal? To empower Africa's future leaders through quality education and sport.

In her introduction to this chapter, the indomitable Jacqueline Novogratz writes that we need leaders who care about the world and can navigate the complexity of our times. In short, we need skilled, ethical, and entrepreneurial people with solutions to the world's most pressing problems.

But to truly understand and confront today's social challenges, we must unpack our preconceived notions of the world. What is impact? What is development? What is progress? The answers to these questions are case-specific. They depend on history, culture and tradition, and ways of life.

I have learned that effective leadership thus requires empathy. Social entrepreneurs across the world must stand in the shoes of those with whom we work. Listen. Collaborate. Empower. Only then can we develop effective strategies that yield systemic change.

Graham Palmer, Federal Strategy Consultant and D2i Lead, Deloitte

Growing up, I devoured stories about the grand trends that shaped history, and was desperately worried that I had missed my chance to join them. This early fascination nurtured an interest in foreign policy and a desire to find and shape the next trend that would change the world. I am now convinced that social intrapreneurship is such a trend. But until I left college, I had never heard the term.

The seeds were planted the summer before my senior year, when I interned for Tugende, a lease-to-own asset financing company for motorcycle taxi drivers in Uganda. I saw firsthand how a for-profit company could change lives permanently by offering drivers a path to doubling their take-home income by owning their own bikes. Tugende's explosive growth and financial success were evidence of a new approach to solving development problems, one that didn't rely on endless grant funding and replicated itself.

But Tugende was just a taste. Months later, I took a job with Deloitte's federal consulting practice. In my first year, I was accepted into the D2i Fellowship, through which 30 Fellows a year conduct a pro bono consulting project for a partner nonprofit or social enterprise.

D2i creates change by empowering our partner organizations but also by using Deloitte's resources to mold practitioners who care about social impact and will either rise into firm leadership or go on to lead elsewhere. It didn't hit me until after the Fellowship, but I had found the force shaping our time that I wanted to be a part of. Deloitte's prodigious resources powered the Fellowship – I got to learn from experts in just about every relevant field. The Fellowship gave me the tools to contribute to social impact by teaching me the basics of strategic choice framing, human-centered design, logic modeling, impact evaluation, wicked problems analysis, and more. We Fellows were able to hone these skills learned in the curriculum through our consulting work with our partner organization, Days for Girls, which worked to provide menstrual hygiene pads to girls throughout the world. My team, for example, built a market evaluation tool and provided analysis on five potential markets into which they could expand.

By the end, the Fellowship had given me and 29 others the tools to help socially impactful organizations and a burning desire to continue doing so. I have been leading similar projects ever since, hoping to create similar change in other practitioners. The next year, I led a team for the D2i Fellowship, and I'm now using the leadership skills I gained from that experience to lead 12 other practitioners in consulting for an accelerator for social franchising companies. Other D2i alumni have gone on to work in Turkey using technology to address the refugee crisis and as an advisor to the president of Liberia. The Fellowship has created a community of changemakers that extends far beyond Deloitte.

My story demonstrates the power of social intrapreneurship, the act of working within a large organization to increase its emphasis on creating positive change. The power and reach of multinational corporations are extraordinary, and orienting them towards social impact is powerful. It's like nudging an elephant – you may only slightly change its direction, but the organization is so powerful that even small change can matter immensely.

Natasha Sumant, Founder, Gundi Studios

I am the founder of Gundi, a slow fashion brand that aims to empower South Asian women, at home and in the diaspora. I grew up in an upper middle-class family in Bangalore, continually exposed to media and advertising selling and reinforcing the idea that a woman's place is in the home.

While my mother never needed to work to support our family, her lack of financial independence led her to feel somewhat trapped in her marriage and role as a housewife. Indian culture has historically prioritized marriage above everything else for women, and though my mother placed great value on my education and raised me to be financially independent, getting married will still be seen as the ultimate mark of my success.

On the other end of the economic spectrum, however, a huge swathe of working-class women support the Indian economy, though their labor is rarely acknowledged, let alone rewarded by society. My family's maid, for example, was the primary breadwinner in her family, and my relationship with her gave me my first glimpse into the issues – low pay, long hours, little government support – that lower-income working women across South Asia face.

As I started to understand the extent to which patriarchal capitalism shapes and controls female lives in India, I was inspired to build a brand that empowered women across class divisions. Gundi works to tackle the fact that women are often the biggest victims of modern-day consumerism on both the demand and supply side – advertising often plays off female insecurities to generate demand for products, and the fashion industry is reliant on low-paid (and most often female) garment workers for manufacturing. While these issues face women universally, they are felt even more deeply in South Asia given that the region is a hub for garment production and most of the workers are women.

My goal is to build a profitable brand that serves both the consumer and the production worker and highlights the connection and relationship between them. To that end, I have worked to build in impact at each stage of the business: from design, to manufacturing, and to promotion.

Gundi's design addresses the fact that traditional crafts in the Global South are at risk of being wiped out as global fast fashion brands open factories that provide more business for those willing to make lower-quality clothing. Our streetwear-inspired jackets, dresses, and sweatshirts are embroidered using techniques (Aari, Zari, and Cut Dana) traditionally used on Sarees and Burkas, providing an opportunity for a modern brand to help keep an ancient craft and the community surrounding it alive. Key to our production philosophy is the belief that everyone that works on a Gundi product should be paid fair wages and labor in safe conditions; however, our ultimate aim is to create new income-generating opportunities for rural women by training those who may not already have the skills needed to work on our products and then offer them a reliable source of income via employment in our supply chain. Finally, our consumer-facing content and messaging goes well beyond product promotion and aims to inspire and educate our audience on issues related to feminism and navigating the world as a South Asian woman.

Young people are increasingly becoming conscious consumers, and I believe that they will be a driving force for impact in the coming decades as questions about social and environmental impacts of sourcing, manufacturing, and selling force small brands and multinationals alike to evolve their business practices so that they are truly adding value for people rather than generating value off the backs of people. I hope Gundi can serve not only as a model for what future business will look like, but by putting women's issues front and center of our brand, that we will also encourage consumers to think about what they sold and how they are sold to so they start demanding more from brands immediately. The ultimate goal is for Indian women growing up to be surrounded by messaging that values the work they do and not just their potential for marriage.

Notes

Introduction

1 This introduction benefited greatly from Professor Pramit Chaudhuri's incisive feedback and development. I'm also grateful for early and ongoing conversations with Jane Nelson, Cynthia Warner, Griffin Gaffney, Amirah Jiwah, and Caela Murphy on how best to introduce this collection.

2 A quick Amazon search for 'impact' yields over 50,000 book results; clearly, putting a word like this in our title doesn't give someone browsing a bookstore (or Amazon) a clear sense of what to expect. For the purposes of this book, impact is defined rather broadly as an intended outcome. By *intended*, the focus is on the deliberate attempt to influence a particular consequence; by *outcome*, emphasis is placed on the results of an action – the net effect, or change – rather than the action itself. Some contributors offer their own, nuanced definitions.

3 This conceptualization is borrowed from D. Meadows, *Thinking in Systems: A Primer* (White River Junction, VT: Chelsea Green Publishing, 2008), 11. She defines the system as, "an interconnected set of elements that is coherently organized in a way that achieves something." (*ibid.*, 11)

4 The categorization and characterization of systems' elements varies widely. But we follow here a description of elements from Oxfam's excellent introduction to systems thinking: K. Bowman, J. Chettleborough, H. Jeans, J. Whitehead, and J. Rowlands, *Systems Thinking: An Introduction for Oxfam Programme Staff* (Oxford: Oxfam, 2015).

5 Among the most influential voices on this topic are John Kania and Mark Kramer. Of their growing body of work, a great overview of the mismatch between dominant approaches to impact and the nature of the problems we face can be found in their article with Patty Russell, 'Strategic Philanthropy for a Complex World,' *Stanford Social Innovation Review*, Summer 2014, https://ssir.org/up_for_debate/strategic_philanthropy/kania_kramer_russell#.

6 M. R. Kramer, 'Systems Change in a Polarized Country,' *Stanford Social Innovation Review*, 11 April, 2017, https://ssir.org/articles/entry/systems_change_in_a_polarized_country.

Chapter 1

1 This chapter draws from D. Green, *How Change Happens* (Oxford: OUP, 2016).

2 R. Krznaric, 'How Change Happens: Interdisciplinary perspectives for human development,' *Oxfam Research Report* (Oxford: Oxfam GB, 2007) http://policypractice. oxfam.org.uk/publications/how-change-happens-interdisciplinary-perspectivesfor-human-development-112539.

3 D. Green, *From Poverty to Power: How Active Citizens and Effective States Can Change the World* (Rugby: Practical Action Publishing, 2012).

4 A. Sweetman and J. Zhang, *Economic Transitions with Chinese Characteristics* (Montreal: McGill-Queen's UP, 2009), 1.

5 J. Boulton, P. Allen, and C. Bowman, *Embracing Complexity: Strategic Perspectives for an Age of Turbulence* (Oxford: OUP, 2015).

6 D. Acemoglu and J. Robinson, *Why Nations Fail* (New York: Crown Publishers, 2012).

7 M. Friedman, *Capitalism and Freedom* (Chicago: The University of Chicago Press, 1982), ix.

8 N. Klein, *The Shock Doctrine: The Rise of Disaster Capitalism* (New York: Metropolitan Books Henry Holt and Company, 2007).

9 *Ibid.*, 6.

10 D. Green, 'Will Horror and Over a Thousand Dead Be a Watershed Moment for Bangladesh?' From Poverty to Power blog, May 17, 2013, https://oxfamblogs.org/fp2p/will-horror-and-over-a-thousand-dead-be-a-watershed-moment-for-bangladesh/.

11 B. Ramalingam, *Aid on the Edge of Chaos* (New York: OUP, 2013), 257.

12 D. Meadows and D. Wright, *Thinking in Systems: A Primer* (Abingdon: Routledge, 2009).

13 Lecture, University of Lille (December 7, 1854).

14 S. Blank, 'Why the Lean Start-Up Changes Everything,' *Harvard Business Review* (May 2013), 63–72.

15 Tim Harford proposes a "three step recipe for successful adapting: try new things, in the expectation that some will fail; make failure survivable, because it will be common; and make sure that you know when you have failed . . . distinguishing success from failure, oddly, can be the hardest task of all." T. Harford, *Adapt: Why Success Always Starts with Failure* (London: Little, Brown, 2011), 38–39.

Chapter 2

1 This tendency – to develop theories of change that lack a core theory of *how* the world will be altered – runs counter to the original intent behind the theory of change approach. Theories of change were initially designed to encourage strategic thinking and learning in the complex environment of social change. The idea was that funders and nonprofits, by stating clearly the implicit assumptions behind their strategy, could better evaluate progress and evolve their approach over time. See P. Patrizi, E. H. Thompson, J. Coffman, and T. Beer, 'Eyes Wide Open: Learning as Strategy Under Conditions of Complexity and Uncertainty,' *The Foundation Review* 5, no. 3 (2013), 7.

2 Bureau of Labor Statistics, 'The Employment Situation – June 2015,' July 2, 2015, www.bls.gov/news.release/archives/empsit_07022015.pdf.

3 The imperative was clear and urgent. Young people who can't find stable jobs by their early 20s are at risk of more frequent and prolonged spells of joblessness, permanently lower earnings over their lifetime, and greater difficulty building a secure financial future for themselves and their families.

4 Year Up is an intensive one-year program that combines hands-on, job-specific training with high-quality, six-month job placements.

5 G. A. Moore, *Crossing the Chasm: Marketing and Selling Disruptive Products to Mainstream Customers* (New York: HarperCollins, 2002).

6 This goal was in fact achieved two years earlier than originally expected (in August 2016), and the Coalition raised its sights to the goal of one million hires by 2021. See '100,000 Opportunities Initiative Exceeds Goal and Hires 100,000 Opportunity Youth in First Year,' *100,000 Opportunities Coalition,* August 31, 2016, www.100kopportunities.org/2016/08/31/100000-opportunities-initiative-exceeds-goal-and-hires-100000-opportunity-youth-in-first-year/.

7 'This Manicure Might Just Save Her Life,' *IDEO.org,* www.ideo.org/project/diva-centres.

8 *Ibid.*

9 In addition to Diva Centres, there has been a range of efforts to apply HCD to adolescent and sexual reproductive health. They include Adolescents 360 (A360), a four-year project begun in January 2016 to increase voluntary, modern contraceptive use among adolescent girls in Tanzania, Ethiopia, and Nigeria; Future Fab, an adolescent lifestyle brand targeted in five regions across Kenya, that provides a new way to talk with teens, their communities, and their health care providers about the value of contraception; and Beyond Bias, which brings together providers and the young people they serve to increase contraceptive access and method choice for youth in Burkina Faso, Tanzania, and Pakistan. For more on HCD-ASRH projects or HCD in global health, see *Design for Health,* www.designforhealth.org/project-library/.

Chapter 3

1 This framework builds on the three levels of leadership outlined by the author in: J. Nelson, *Corporate Sustainability Leadership at the Edge* (Cambridge: University of Cambridge, Programme for Sustainability Leadership, 2011).

2 This framework for system leadership was developed in: J. Nelson and B. Jenkins, *Tackling Global Challenges: Lessons in System Leadership from the World Economic Forum's New Vision for Agriculture Initiative.* (Cambridge, MA: Corporate Responsibility Initiative, Harvard Kennedy School, 2016).

Other frameworks focused on defining and describing system leadership include:

L. Dreier, D. Nabarro, and J. Nelson, *System Leadership for Sustainable Development: Taking Action on Complex Challenges through the Power of Networks.* (Cambridge, MA: Corporate Responsibility Initiative, Harvard Kennedy School, 2019).

P. Senge, H. Hamilton, and J. Kania, The Dawn of System Leadership, *Stanford Social Innovation Review*, Winter 2015.

For other sources on research focused on system leadership, bibliographies are included in several of the above reports.

3 Drawn from a speech made by Jane Nelson at the 2016 IFC Sustainability Exchange entitled 'Reflecting on a Decade of Bridging Communities, Companies and Governments: Trends and Tensions.'

4 www.globalethicsnetwork.org/profiles/blogs/what-do-you-mean-by-moral-leadership (accessed August 25, 2018).

5 J. Novogratz, Beyond Success: Four Lessons in Building Character (in this volume).
6 See http://mbaoath.org/.
7 www.globalcitizen.org/en/content/ethiopia-cabinet-ministers-women-abiy-ahmed/.
8 Z. Mejia, 'Just 24 female CEOs Lead the Companies on the 2018 Fortune 500 – Fewer Than Last Year,' *CNBC*, May 21, 2018, www.cnbc.com/2018/05/21/2018s-fortune-500-companies-have-just-24-female-ceos.html.
9 Information on the Prince's Seeing is Believing program is available at: www.bitc.org.uk/campaigns-programmes/Leadership/seeingisbelieving.
10 Speech made by J. K. Rowling on receiving an honorary degree from Harvard University, June 5, 2008. The speech is entitled 'The Fringe Benefits of Failure, and the Importance of Imagination,' https://news.harvard.edu/gazette/story/2008/06/text-of-j-k-rowling-speech/.
11 Emergent Design: What Does This Mean? December 18, 2016, https://thevalueweb.org/emergent-design-meaning/.
12 2018 Edelman Trust Barometer.
13 This framework draws on other work by the author, including:

- J. Nelson, *Partnerships for Sustainable Development: Collective Action by Business, Governments and Civil Society to Achieve Scale and Transform Markets*. Report commissioned by the Business and Sustainable Development Commission (2017).
- J. Nelson, 'Scaling Up Impact through Public – Private Partnerships,' in L. Chandy, A. Hosono, H. Kharas, and J. Linn (eds), *Getting to Scale: How to Bring Development Solutions to Millions of Poor People* (Washington, DC: The Brookings Institution Press, 2013).

14 R. Gilbert and J. Nelson, *Advocating Together for the SDGs: How Civil Society and Business Are Joining Voices to Change Policy, Attitudes and Practices* (Cambridge, MA: Corporate Responsibility Initiative, Harvard Kennedy School and Business Fights Poverty, 2018).

Chapter 4

1 Ideas in this piece were previously published in the Winter 2019 issue of *Stanford Social Innovation Review*.
2 B. Sapp, 'YouthTruth: Shifting Culture Through Student Feedback,' *YouTube*, January 6, 2014, www.youtube.com/watch?v=mUkeAuqReho.
3 I use the term 'nonprofit' as shorthand but really the concepts also hold for government direct service providers – like welfare programs or even the post office as these are social sector entities that provide a direct service or product to individual customers.
4 In fact, Sam Schaefer, the CEO of the Center for Employment Opportunities, was the first person to reference feedback as the third leg of a three-legged measurement stool.

Chapter 5

1 This chapter was adapted from my 2018 doctoral dissertation, 'The Practice of Change,' at Keio University Graduate School of Media and Governance. The full text can be found here: https://joi.ito.com/the-practice-of-change.html.

2 Portions of this section were adapted from J. Ito, 'Design and Science,' *Journal of Design and Science* (2017), https://doi.org/10.21428/f4c68887/406cdc95.

3 S. Papert, 'Constructionism: A New Opportunity for Elementary Science Education' (1986).

4 G. Kolata, 'M.I.T. Deal with Japan Stirs Fear on Competition,' *New York Times*, December 19, 1990, www.nytimes.com/1990/12/19/us/mit-deal-with-japan-stirs-fear-on-competition.html.

5 J. Ito and J. Howe, *Whiplash: How to Survive Our Faster Future* (New York: Grand Central Publishing, 2016).

6 R. Ryan and E. Deci, 'Self-Determination Theory and the Facilitation of Intrinsic Motivation, Social Development, and Well-Being,' *American Psychologist* 55, no. 1 (January 2000), 68–78.

7 I am certainly not the first to ask this question. As far back as the 1990s, Andrew Lippman (then associate director of the Lab) similarly stated: "Right now, it's unfortunate that the [Media Lab] is unique in the breadth and scope of what it's doing. More [Media Labs] can only be better." (Kolata, 'M.I.T. Deal with Japan Stirs Fear on Competition,' 1990).

Chapter 6

1 A. Peters, 'At These Camps, Refugees Can Give Real-Time Customer Feedback,' *Fast Company*, May 22, 2018, www.fastcompany.com/40575160/at-these-camps-refugees-can-give-real-time-customer-feedback.

2 'Sparking a Human-Centered Revolution,' *PSI* blog, April 24, 2018, www.psi.org/2018/04/a360-hcd-aysrh-revolution/.

3 A. Peters, 'At These Camps, Refugees Can Give Real-Time Customer Feedback.'

4 M. Amatullo, B. Boyer, L. Danzico, and A. Shea, *LEAP Dialogues: Career Pathways in Design for Social Innovation* (Pasadena, CA: Design Matters at ArtCenter College of Design, 2016).

5 T. Brown and J. Wyatt, 'Design thinking for social innovation,' *SSIR* (Winter 2010), 31–35.

6 For more on design attitudes, see: K. Michlewski, 'Uncovering Design Attitude: Inside the Culture of Designers,' *Organization Studies* 29, no. 3 (2016), 373–392; M. Amatullo, 'Explaining the Effects of Design Attitude on Team Learning, Process Satisfaction and Social Innovation Outcomes,' Thesis submission for Doctor of Management Program at the Weatherhead School of Management (2014).

7 B. Boyer, J. W. Cook, M. Steinberg, and Helsinki Design Lab, *In Studio: Recipes for Systemic Change* (Helskini: Sitra, 2011).

8 M. Amatullo, 'Explaining the Effects of Design Attitude,' 106.

9 For the independent process evaluation, see: 'Evaluation of The Hewlett Foundation Strategy to Apply Human-Centered Design to Improve Family Planning and Reproductive Health Services in Sub-Saharan Africa,' *Itad*, November 10, 2017, https://hewlett.org/wp-content/uploads/2018/07/Itad-HCD-Evaluation_Final-Report_Nov-10-2017.pdf.

10 S. J. Staats, 'Q&A with Margot Fahnestock: A Teen-Centered Approach to Contraception in Zambia and Kenya,' *Hewlett Foundation*, July 25, 2018, https://hewlett.org/qa-with-margot-fahnestock-a-teen-centered-approach-to-contraception-in-zambia-and-kenya/.

11 K. Michlewski, *Design Attitude* (Surrey: Routledge, 2015).
12 E. Beck, 'Human Centered Design Inspires Innovation . . . and Trust,' *Adolescent 360 Learning Hub*, www.a360learninghub.org/learning-blog/2018/4/4/human-centered-design-inspires-innovation-and-trust.
13 M. Dotson, 'Four Big Insights from HCD Exchange,' *Adolescent 360 Learning Hub*, www.a360learninghub.org/learning-blog/fourinsightshcdexchange.
14 C. W. Churchman, 'Wicked Problems,' *Management Science* 14 (1967), 4.
15 T. Both, 'Human-Centered, Systems-Minded Design.' *SSIR*, March 9, 2018, https://ssir.org/articles/entry/human_centered_systems_minded_design.
16 S. Wright, *Toward a Lexicon of Usership* (Eindhoven: Van Abbemuseum, 2013).
17 N. Cross, 'Design Research: A Disciplined Conversation,' *Design Issues* 15, no. 2 (1999), 7.
18 J. Kolko, 'The Divisiveness of Design Thinking,' *Interactions* 25, no. 3 (May – June 2018), http://interactions.acm.org/archive/view/may-june-2018/the-divisiveness-of-design-thinking.
19 For this thought and others, see Di Russo's blog, I Think I Design, *ithinkidesign.com*.
20 'HCD in Global Health & Development: Guidance to Maximize Impact and Mitigate Risk,' AVAC report for the Bill & Melinda Gates Foundation (March 2017).
21 For more on this community, see *Design for Health*, www.designforhealth.org/.

Chapter 7

1   'Haiti Quake Death Toll Rises to 230,000,' *BBC News*, February 11, 2010, http://news.bbc.co.uk/2/hi/americas/8507531.stm.
2   Google's '20 percent time' gives engineers one day a week to work on innovative side projects.
3   'New Imagery of Port-au-Prince,' *Google Maps Blog*, January 19, 2010, maps.googleblog.com/2010/01/new-imagery-of-port-au-prince.html.
4   For more information, see nethope.org.
5   'Ideas for Haiti's Internet Reconstruction,' *Google.org*, October 2010, www.google.org/docs/Haiti.pdf.
6   For more on Person Finder, see support.google.com/personfinder/?hl=en.
7   E. Woyke, 'What the Red Cross Learned from Its Haiti Mobile Campaign,' *Forbes*, August 16, 2010, www.forbes.com/sites/elizabethwoyke/2010/08/26/what-the-red-cross-learned-from-its-haiti-mobile-campaign/#305839293462.
8   'Helping Haiti Respond to the Earthquake,' *Google.org Blog*, January 14, 2010, http://blog.google.org/2010/01/helping-haiti-respond-to-earthquake.html.
9   'Medical Need in Haiti Remains High as MSF Moves into Next Crucial Phase,' *Medecins Sans Frontieres*, March 26, 2010, www.msf.org/medical-needs-haiti-remain-high-msf-moves-next-crucial-phase.
10 Certain 'disasters' like Amazon Prime Day may result in servers crashing due to load, but the Internet itself is comprised of more than one site!
11 'Mobile is eating the world' is a famous phrase by Benedict Evans.
12 R. Molla, 'Mary Meeker's 2018 Internet Trends Report: All the slides, plus analysis,' *Recode*, May 20, 2018, www.recode.net/2018/5/30/17385116/mary-meeker-slides-internet-trends-code-conference-2018.
13 C. Riley and M. Arora, 'India's Richest Man Offers Free 4G to One Billion People,' *CNN Business*, September 6, 2016, https://money.cnn.com/2016/09/06/technology/india-reliance-jio-4g-Internet/index.html.

14 Usually someone skilled in areas ranging from ethnography, anthropology, human computer interaction, or user interface design.

15 P. Vlaskovits, 'Henry Ford, Innovation and That 'Faster Horse' Quote,' August 29, 2011, https://hbr.org/2011/08/henry-ford-never-said-the-fast.

16 C. Christensen, *The Innovator's Dilemma: The Revolutionary Book that Will Change the Way You Do Business* (New York: HarperBusiness Essentials, 2011).

17 For more information on user needs validation, read E. Ries, *The Lean Startup: How Today's Entrepreneurs Use Continuous Innovation to Create Radically Successful Businesses* (New York: Crown Business, 2011).

18 G. A. Moore, *Crossing the Chasm: Marketing and Selling Disruptive Products to Mainstream Customers* (New York: HarperCollins, 2002).

19 Of course, opportunity costs still exist.

20 But whose nemesis is soap.

21 A. Kaplan, *The Conduct of Inquiry: Methodology for Behavioral Science* (New Brunswick, NJ: Transaction Publishers, 1964).

22 C. Christensen, *The Innovator's Dilemma* (2011).

23 For the launch of our Symptom Search feature, see V. Pinchin, 'I'm Feeling Yucky : (Searching for Symptoms on Google,' *Google Blog*, June 20, 2016, www.blog.google/products/search/im-feeling-yucky-searching-for-symptoms/.

24 O. Khazan, 'A Shocking Decline in American Life Expectancy,' *The Atlantic*, December 21, 2017, www.theatlantic.com/health/archive/2017/12/life-expectancy/548981/.

25 A. D. I. Kramer, J. E. Guillory, and J. T. Hancock, 'Experimental Evidence of Massive-Scale Emotional Contagion through Social Networks,' *PNAS*, March 25, 2014, www.pnas.org/content/pnas/111/24/8788.full.pdf.

26 S. Kotsis and K. Chung, 'Institutional Review Boards: What's Old, What's New, What Needs to Change?' *US National Library of Medicine National Institutes of Health* (2014), www.ncbi.nlm.nih.gov/pmc/articles/PMC3905624/.

27 2004 Founder's IPO Letter, 'An Owner's Manual for Google Shareholders,' *Alphabet: Investor Relationship*, https://abc.xyz/investor/founders-letters/2004/ipo-letter.html.

28 This is the central question explored in the sister volume to this book, *Perspectives on Purpose: Leading Voices on Building Brands and Businesses for the Twenty-First Century*.

29 Tesla's market capitalization is over $50 billion as of 2018.

30 These include Apple, Amazon, Microsoft, Alphabet, Berkshire Hathaway, Facebook, Alibaba, Tencent, as of Q3 2018.

31 T. Shamma, 'Is Computer Science a Foreign Language? Ga. Says Yes, Sees Boost in Enrollment,' *Wabe*, November 13, 2017, www.wabe.org/computer-science-foreign-language-state-sees-boost-enrollment/.

32 K. Kokalitcheva, 'Meet the "Tech for Good" Startups at Y Combinator's Demo Day,' *Venture Beat*, March 25, 2014, https://venturebeat.com/2014/03/25/meet-the-tech-for-good-startups-at-y-combinators-demo-day/.

33 A. Vance, 'This Tech Bubble is Different,' *Bloomberg Businessweek*, April 14, 2011, www.bloomberg.com/news/articles/2011-04-14/this-tech-bubble-is-different.

34 'A View from the Valley,' *The Atlantic*, November 2014, www.theatlantic.com/magazine/archive/2014/11/the-view-from-the-valley/380802/.

Chapter 8

1 This piece has been slightly modified from an original version, published in *Stanford Social Innovation Review* 15, no.2 (Spring 2017) on February 15, 2017.

2 For shorter deadlines leading to greater responsiveness, see: A. Tversky and E. Shafir, 'Choice Under Conflict: The Dynamics of Deferred Decision,' *Psychological Science* 3, no. 6 (1992). For too much choice leading people to choose nothing, see: S. Iyengar and M. Lepper, 'When Choice Is Demotivating: Can One Desire Too Much of a Good Thing?' *Journal of Personality and Social Psychology* 79, no. 6 (2000).

3 For several examples, see ideas42's June 2016 report *Nudging for Success: Using Behavioral Science to Improve the Postsecondary Student Journey*, www.ideas42.org.

4 D. Baals and W. Corliss, *Wind Tunnels of NASA* (Washington D.C.: Scientific and Technical Information Branch, National Aeronautics and Space Administration, 1981).

5 K. Ashton, *How to Fly a Horse: The Secret History of Creation, Invention, and Discovery* (New York: Anchor, 2015).

6 U. Gneezy and A. Rustichini, 'A Fine Is a Price,' *Journal of Legal Studies* 29, no. 1 (2000).

7 E. Pronin, T. Gilovich, and L. Ross, 'Objectivity in the Eye of the Beholder: Divergent Perceptions of Bias in Self Versus Others,' *Psychological Review* 111, no. 3 (2004).

8 This process was previously described briefly by ideas42 Managing Director Saugato Datta and Co-Founder Sendhil Mullainathan in their paper 'Behavioral Design: A New Approach to Development Policy,' *Review of Income and Wealth* 60, no. 1 (2014).

9 For good examples of quick tests, see D. Asch and R. Rosin, 'Innovation as Discipline, Not Fad,' *New England Journal of Medicine* 373, no. 7 (2015).

10 D. Kahneman and A. Tversky, 'Prospect Theory: An Analysis of Decision under Risk,' *Econometrica* 47, no. 2 (1979).

Chapter 9

1 H. Chesbrough and W. Vanhaverbeke, *New Frontiers in Open Innovation* (Oxford: OUP, 2014).

2 D. Hull, 'The PayPal Mafia of Self-Driving Cars Has Been at It a Decade,' *Bloomberg*, October 30, 2017, www.bloomberg.com/news/features/2017-10-30/it-s-been-10-years-since-robots-proved-they-could-drive.

3 D. White, 'FDA's First Food Safety Challenge Targets Salmonella Detection,' *U.S. Food and Drug Administration*, September 23, 2014, https://web.archive.org/web/20180104231016/https://blogs.fda.gov/fdavoice/index.php/2014/09/fdas-first-food-safety-challenge-targets-salmonella-detection.

4 'Gartner Says Worldwide Video Game Market to Total $93 Billion in 2013,' *Gartner*, October 29, 2013, www.gartner.com/newsroom/id/2614915.

5 K. Olmstead, 'Nearly Half of Americans Use Digital Voice Assistants, Mostly on Their Smartphones,' *FactTank*, December 12, 2017, www.pewresearch.org/fact-tank/2017/12/12/nearly-half-of-americans-use-digital-voice-assistants-mostly-on-their-smartphones/.

6 'Open Innovation Outcomes, By the Numbers,' *Luminary Labs*, www.luminary-labs.com/insight/open-innovation-outcomes-prize-recipient-survey/.

7 L. Grush, 'It's Official: No One Is Going to Win the Google Lunar X Prize Competition,' *The Verge*, January 23, 2018, www.theverge.com/2018/1/23/16924020/google-lunar-x-prize-competition-moon-no-winner.

8 C. Fink, 'Osso VR Surgical Training Makes Push Into Med Schools,' *Forbes*, June 26, 2018, www.forbes.com/sites/charliefink/2018/06/26/osso-vr-surgical-training-makes-push-into-med-schools/#4489b6e94f6e.

Chapter 10

1 Barack Obama, 'A New Beginning' (speech, Cairo, June 4, 2009), *The White House*, https://obamawhitehouse.archives.gov/issues/foreign-policy/presidents-speech-cairo-a-new-beginning.

2 '"Impossible Foods" 2018 Impact Report Details the Food Tech Startup's Strategic Roadmap,' *Business Wire*, August 8, 2018, www.businesswire.com/news/home/20180808005236/en/Impossible-Foods%E2%80%99-2018-Impact-Report-Details-Food.

3 *Ibid.*

4 *Ibid.*, for all following statistics.

5 R. Kurzweil, *The Age of Spiritual Machines* (New York: Penguin, 2000).

6 R. Kurzweil, 'The Law of Accelerating Returns,' *Kurzweil: Accelerating Intelligence*, March 7, 2001, www.kurzweilai.net/the-law-of-accelerating-returns.

7 *Ibid.*

8 *Ibid.*

9 R. Molla, 'Mary Meeker's 2018 Internet Trends Report: All the slides, plus analysis,' *Recode*, May 20, 2018, www.recode.net/2018/5/30/17385116/mary-meeker-slides-internet-trends-code-conference-2018.

10 For more on the Fourth Industrial Revolution and how information and communication technologies are shaping people and society, see: L. Floridi, *The Fourth Industrial Revolution: How the Infosphere is Reshaping Human Reality* (Oxford: Oxford University Press, 2014).

11 Y. N. Harari, 'Why Technology Favors Tyranny,' *The Atlantic*, October 2018, www.theatlantic.com/magazine/archive/2018/10/yuval-noah-harari-technology-tyranny/568330/.

12 S. Pichai, 'AI at Google: our principles,' *Google*, June 7, 2018, www.google.com/search?q=googl+ai+principles&rlz=1C5CHFA_enUS766US766&oq=googl+ai+princ iples&aqs=chrome..69i57j69i60l4j69i64.2105j0j7&sourceid=chrome&ie=UTF-8.

13 The Institute of the Future and Omidyar Network's Tech and Society Solutions Lab, 'Ethical OS: A Guide to Anticipating the Future Impact of Today's Technology,' 2018, https://ethicalos.org/wp-content/uploads/2018/08/Ethical-OS-Toolkit-2.pdf.

Chapter 11

1 This chapter was edited by Caela Murphy.

2 For more on the H.E.R.S. Framework, see 'Our Mission,' *Women's March Global*, www.womensmarchglobal.com/mission/.

3 N. Mandela, 'Inaugural Speech' (speech, Pretoria, May 10, 1994).

Chapter 13

1 J. G. Cooney, 'The Potential Uses of Television in Preschool Education' (1967).

2 M. Mares and Z. Pan, 'Effects of *Sesame Street*: A Meta-Analysis of Children's Learning in 15 Countries,' *Journal of Applied Developmental Psychology* 34, no. 3 (May – June 2013), 140–151.

3 Glevum Associates, 'An impact assessment of *Baghch-e-Simsim*: A report on findings from a pilot experimental study' (Gloucester, MA: Glevum Associates, 2013).

4 'The Impact of Baghch-e-Simsim TV on Views of Gender Equality in Afghanistan,' *Sesame Workshop* (2017).

5 Sesame Street Nigeria Team, 'Sesame Street Nigeria pilot child study: Findings from an informal assessment of children' (Report prepared for Sesame Workshop) (Abuja, Nigeria: Sesame Street Nigeria, 2009).

6 Fluent Public Opinion & Market Research, 'Assessment of Educational Impact of *Rruga Sesam* and *Ulica Sezam* in Kosovo: Report of Findings' (New York, NY: Fluent, 2008).

Chapter 14

1 This chapter was edited by Deirdre Dlugoleski.

Chapter 15

1 For more on these models and public policy generally, see the suggested bibliography in the 'Further reading' section of this book.

2 J. Amrhein, 'Quote . . . Misquote,' *The New York Times Magazine*, July 21, 2008, www.nytimes.com/2008/07/21/magazine/27wwwl-guestsafire-t.html.

3 These statistics reflect research conducted by the Government of Liberia, the World Bank, and other educational sector stakeholders in Liberia captured in the November 2016 'Liberia Education Sector Analysis,' 21.

4 *Ibid.*, 130, cf. 91.

5 *Ibid.*, 138.

6 *Ibid.*, 91.

7 M. Romero, J. Sandefur, and W. A. Sandholtz, 'Can a Public-Private Partnership Improve Liberia's Schools?' *Center for Global Development*, September 7, 2017, www.cgdev.org/publication/can-public-private-partnership-improve-liberias-schools; 'Independent Report Proves Liberia's Bold Education innovation is Working,' *Bridge*, September 7, 2017, www.bridgeinternationalacademies.com.

8 M. Romero et al., 'Can a Public – Private Partnership Improve Liberia's Schools?'; 'Independent Report Proves Liberia's Bold Education innovation is Working.'

Chapter 16

1 United Nations Framework Convention on Climate Change, 'Report of the Conference of the Parties on its Fifteenth Session, held in Copenhagen from 7 to 19 December 2009,' *United Nations*, March 30, 2010, https://unfccc.int/resource/docs/2009/cop15/eng/11a01.pdf.

2 The definition of 'risk' varies across asset classes and, in many cases, among investors in the same asset class. While some asset classes define risk as 'variability from the expected value,' we will stick with the more common conception of risk, also known as downside risk: 'Risk is the probability that an asset delivers lower-than-expected

returns.' 'Return' is the money that is returned to the investor in addition to the return of the original amount invested. If you 'invest' $100 and you get $20 back, your returns are not '$20' or '20 percent.' Your returns are – 80 percent, and goodness me, you've been fired and will need to get a new job, perhaps on the Theranos investor relations team.

3 R. Eccles, I. Ioannou, and G. Serafeim, 'The Impact of Corporate Sustainability on Organizational Processes and Performance,' *Management Science* 60, no. 11 (November 2014), 2835–2857.

4 'Allocating Capital for Long-Term Returns: The Strengthened Case for Sustainable Capitalism,' *The Generation Foundation*, May 2015, www.generationim.com/media/1131/advocacy-1-allocating-capital-for-long-term-returns.pdf; J. Vincent, 'Tracking Al Gore's Generation Investment Management Portfolio – Q2 2017 Update,' *Seeking Alpha*, August 28, 2017, https://seekingalpha.com/article/4102202-tracking-al-gores-generation-investment-management-portfolio-q2-2017-update.

5 C. Asness, 'Virtue is its Own Reward: Or, One Man's Ceiling is Another Man's Floor,' *AQR*, May 18, 2017, www.aqr.com/Insights/Perspectives/Virtue-is-its-Own-Reward-Or-One-Mans-Ceiling-is-Another-Mans-Floor.

6 Hays, C. 'Ben & Jerry's To Unilever, With Attitude,' *New York Times*, April 14, 2000, www.nytimes.com/2000/04/13/business/ben-jerry-s-to-unilever-with-attitude.html.

7 'About Impact investing,' *Global Impact Investing Network (GIIN)*, https://thegiin.org/impact-investing/.

8 L. Fink, 'Larry Fink's Annual Letter to CEOs: A Sense of Purpose,' *BlackRock*, 2018, www.blackrock.com/corporate/investor-relations/larry-fink-ceo-letter.

Chapter 17

1 Parts of this chapter have been adapted from L. Janah, *Give Work: Reversing Poverty One Job at a Time* (New York: Portfolio, 2017).

2 For more on Yunus' work, see: M. Yunus, *Building Social Business: The New Kind of Capitalism That Serves Humanity's Most Pressing Needs* (New York: PublicAffairs, 2011).

Conclusion

1 This letter is an abbreviation of a speech delivered to the graduating class of New York University's Wagner School of Public Service in 2018 – an effort to illustrate the need for moral leadership in our ever-evolving, interdependent world.

Further reading

On twenty-first century dynamics

Christian, David. *Origin Story: A Big History of Everything*. New York: Little, Brown and Company, 2018.

'Global Phase Shift with Daniel Schmachtenberger,' *Future Thinkers Podcast*, Episode 36, February 11, 2017, https://futurethinkers.org/daniel-schmachtenberger-phase-shift/.

Harari, Yuval Noah. *Homo Deus: A Brief History of Tomorrow*. New York: Harper, 2017.

Heimans, Jeremy, and Henry Timms. *New Power: How Power Works in Our Hyperconnected World – and How to Make It Work for You*. New York: Doubleday, 2018.

Ito, Joi, and Jeff Howe. *Whiplash: How to Survive Our Faster Future*. New York, NY: Grand Central Publishing, 2016.

Menand, Louis. 'Francis Fukuyama Postpones the End of History,' *The New Yorker*, August 27, 2018, www.newyorker.com/magazine/2018/09/03/francis-fukuyama-postpones-the-end-of-history.

Raworth, Kate. *Doughnut Economics: Seven Ways to Think Like a 21st-Century Economist*. White River Junction: Chelsea Green Publishing, 2017.

Fields, Joshua. 'Is Civilization on the Verge of Collapse?' *Medium Blog*, July 10, 2018, https://medium.com/@joshfields/is-civilisation-on-the-verge-of-collapse-14ffa9cac6e4.

On systems thinking

Acemoglu, Daron, and James A. Robinson. *Why Nations Fail: The Origins of Power, Prosperity, and Poverty*. Reprint edition. New York, NY: Currency, 2013.

Bowman, Kimberly, John Chettleborough, Helen Jeans, James Whitehead, and Jo Rowlands. *Systems Thinking: An introduction for Oxfam Programme Staff*. Oxford: Oxfam GB, 2015.

Green, Duncan. *How Change Happens*. Oxford: Oxford University Press, 2016.

Green, Duncan, and Amartya Sen. *From Poverty to Power: How Active Citizens and Effective States Can Change the World*. Bourton on Dunsmore, Rugby, Warwickshire, UK: Practical Action, 2012.

Harford, Tim. *Adapt: Why Success Always Starts with Failure*. First Picador Edition edition. New York: Picador, 2012.

Kay, John. *Obliquity: Why Our Goals Are Best Achieved Indirectly*. Reprint edition. New York: Penguin Books, 2012.
Klein, Naomi. *The Shock Doctrine: The Rise of Disaster Capitalism*. New York: Picador, 2008.
Krznaric, Roman. *How Change Happens: Interdisciplinary Perspectives for Human Development*. 1st edition. Oxford: Oxfam Publishing, 2007.
Meadows, Donella H. *Thinking in Systems: A Primer*. Edited by Diana Wright. White River Junction, VT: Chelsea Green Publishing, 2008.
Stroh, David Peter. *Systems Thinking for Social Change: A Practical Guide to Solving Complex Problem, Avoiding Unintended Consequences, and Achieving Lasting Results*. White River Junction: Chelsea Green Publishing, 2015.
The Systems Thinker, www.thesystemsthinker.com.

On systems change

Banerjee, Banny. 'Systems Leadership: Tackling Complexity and Scale,' *The Aspen Institute*, July 1, 2017, www.youtube.com/watch?v=HMBT3wkY6KE&t=1333s.
Boulton, Jean G., Peter M. Allen, and Cliff Bowman. *Embracing Complexity: Strategic Perspectives for an Age of Turbulence*. 1st edition. Oxford: Oxford University Press, 2015.
Forrester, Jay. *Urban Dynamics*. Waltham, MA: Pegasus Communications, 1969.
Gaddis, John Lewis. *On Grand Strategy*. New York, New York: Penguin Press, 2018.
Patrizi, Patricia, Elizabeth Heid Thompson, Julia Coffman, and Tanya Beer. 'Eyes Wide Open: Learning as Strategy Under Conditions of Complexity and Uncertainty,' *The Foundation Review* 5, no. 3 (January 1, 2013), https://doi.org/10.9707/1944-5660.1170.
Ramalingam, Ben. *Aid on the Edge of Chaos: Rethinking International Cooperation in a Complex World*. Reprint edition. Oxford: Oxford University Press, 2015.
Rumelt, Richard. *Good Strategy/Bad Strategy: The Difference and Why It Matters*. London: Profile Books, 2017.
Senge, Peter, Bryan Smith, Nina Kruschwitz, Joe Laur, and Sara Schley. *The Necessary Revolution*. New York: Broadway Books, 2008.

On collective impact

Boyer, Bryan, Justin W. Cook, Marco Steinberg, and Helsinki Design Lab. *Legible Practises: Six Stories About the Craft of Stewardship*. Helsinki: Sitra, 2013.
Holman, Peggy, Tom Devane, Steven Cady, and William A. Adams. *The Change Handbook: Group Methods for Shaping the Future*. 2nd edition. San Francisco, CA: Berrett-Koehler Publishers, 2007.
Fullan, Michael, and Peter Senge. *All Systems Go: The Change Imperative for Whole System Reform*. 1st edition. Thousand Oaks, CA; Toronto: Corwin, 2010.
Kania, John, Mark Kramer, and Patty Russell. 'Up For Debate: Strategic Philanthropy for a Complex World,' *Stanford Social Innovation Review*, Summer 2014: 26–37.
Senge, Peter, Hal Hamilton, and John Kania. 'The Dawn of System Leadership,' *Stanford Social Innovation Review*, Winter 2015: 27–33.
Walzer, Norman, and Liz Weaver, eds. *Using Collective Impact to Bring Community Change*. 1st edition. New York, NY: Routledge, 2018.

Index